The Rhetoric of Exile
Duress and the Imagining of Force

LEGENDA

LEGENDA is the Modern Humanities Research Association's book imprint for new research in the Humanities. Founded in 1995 by Malcolm Bowie and others within the University of Oxford, Legenda has always been a collaborative publishing enterprise, directly governed by scholars. The Modern Humanities Research Association (MHRA) joined this collaboration in 1998, became half-owner in 2004, in partnership with Maney Publishing and then Routledge, and has since 2016 been sole owner. Titles range from medieval texts to contemporary cinema and form a widely comparative view of the modern humanities, including works on Arabic, Catalan, English, French, German, Greek, Italian, Portuguese, Russian, Spanish, and Yiddish literature. Editorial boards and committees of more than 60 leading academic specialists work in collaboration with bodies such as the Society for French Studies, the British Comparative Literature Association and the Association of Hispanists of Great Britain & Ireland.

The MHRA encourages and promotes advanced study and research in the field of the modern humanities, especially modern European languages and literature, including English, and also cinema. It aims to break down the barriers between scholars working in different disciplines and to maintain the unity of humanistic scholarship. The Association fulfils this purpose through the publication of journals, bibliographies, monographs, critical editions, and the MHRA Style Guide, and by making grants in support of research. Membership is open to all who work in the Humanities, whether independent or in a University post, and the participation of younger colleagues entering the field is especially welcomed.

ALSO PUBLISHED BY THE ASSOCIATION

Critical Texts
Tudor and Stuart Translations • *New Translations* • *European Translations*
MHRA Library of Medieval Welsh Literature

MHRA Bibliographies
Publications of the Modern Humanities Research Association

The Annual Bibliography of English Language & Literature
Austrian Studies
Modern Language Review
Portuguese Studies
The Slavonic and East European Review
Working Papers in the Humanities
The Yearbook of English Studies

www.mhra.org.uk
www.legendabooks.com

The Rhetoric of Exile

Duress and the Imagining of Force

Vladimir Zorić

LEGENDA

Studies in Comparative Literature 39
Modern Humanities Research Association
2016

Published by Legenda
an imprint of the Modern Humanities Research Association
Salisbury House, Station Road, Cambridge CB1 2LA

ISBN 978-1-910887-05-9 (HB)
ISBN 978-1-78188-348-8 (PB)

First published 2016

Copy-Editor: Richard Correll

CONTENTS

ACKNOWLEDGEMENTS

Writing about exile in an ostensibly non-exilic age proved to be more challenging than I ever expected it to be. When I first embarked on this subject, at the beginning of my doctoral research in the early 2000s, I expected to explore a well-defined structure in a clearly delineated context. Instead, I found a forest of metaphors, in which everything seemed to be related to everything else. It took me some time to decide that it was exactly that metaphoricity of exile that I should be exploring.

Over the course of years, many people have helped me through that forest. In particular, I would like to recognize the invaluable support I received from Dr Aleksandar Pavlović (University of Belgrade), a friend and a true pivot of common sense, who patiently read different parts of this manuscript at their different stages, providing encouragement as well as competent advice. I am also indebted to my colleagues and friends, Dr David Norris and Dr Vladislava Ribnikar (University of Nottingham), whose sound judgment and critical verve helped me to get out of many blind alleys and to tap the most productive strands. At the early stage of the project, Professor Stephen Wheatcroft (University of Melbourne) encouraged me to draw a clear distinction between external emigration and internal exile, which in the long run helped me to lay the theoretical foundation and define the analytic sample for my research. Dr Ivan Dodovski (American University of Skopje) taught me to think of my research with a healthy mixture of humility and optimism. My colleagues Dr Polly McMichael (University of Nottingham), Professor Zoran Milutinović (School of Slavonic and East European Studies, UCL), Dr Stijn Vervaet (University of Oslo) and Dr Adrijana Marčetić (University of Belgrade) also read parts of the manuscript and gave me some very useful suggestions. It goes without saying that such mistakes as may remain after these revisions are entirely mine.

Several parts of this study first appeared in comparatist journals. Chapter 1 was initially published under the title 'Banished with No Force: Exile and Metonymy in Cicero's *Pro Caecina Oratio*', in *Diacritics*, 40.4 (2012), 72–103. The article 'The Furies of Orestes: Constructing Persecutory Agency in the Narratives of Exile', published in *Comparative Critical Studies* 5.3 (2008), 179–92, is incorporated into Chapter 3. Chapter 5 appeared under the title 'Radiating Nests: Metalingual Tropes in Poetry of Exile' in *Comparative Literature*, 62.3 (2010), 201–27. The editorial boards and peer reviewers of these journals suggested important improvements which I would like to acknowledge.

v.z., Nottingham, July 2016

INTRODUCTION

The Death of the Exile and other Riddles

In the political conflicts and artistic bedlams of the twentieth century, exile acquired a self-perpetuating aura of primordial and iconic simplicity. Everybody was attracted to the authoritative discourse on exile and almost everyone claimed to have, and to live through, their own exile. In the twenty-first century, now that this fashion has somewhat subsided, it appears that the ubiquity of exile was deceptive. Upon a closer examination, the phenomenon resists a direct heuristic access. Even a basic working definition of exile would necessitate an arbitrary discrimination between its many accrued connotations: Is it spatial or spiritual? Enforced or voluntary? Individual or collective? A practice or a condition? These questions are bound to remain unanswered. For better or for worse, there can never be a theory of exile forceful enough to match those of the state and of man: the phenomenon has purveyed paradoxes rather than comfortable truths. Yet, by its slightly antique title, this book may provoke fears that it wants to do precisely that, i.e. to theorize exile and compress its diversity into a few coherent patterns. In order to alleviate those fears I will start by spelling out some of the historical paradoxes of exile and its intrinsic ethical and legal pitfalls, before introducing the scholarly perspectives on these antinomies and sketching out the argument proposed in this book.

The Paradoxes of Exile

For many observers, the puzzling question about exile is not what it is but where it has disappeared. As early as the second half of the nineteenth century, in a study on Sophocles' *Oedipus Coloneus*, the Prussian conservative philosopher Paul Yorck von Wartenburg pronounced exile dead in modern times: 'Our cosmopolitan age cannot empathize [nachzuempfinden] with this ancient pain of homelessness. Man himself has turned from immobility to mobility. We know, however, that in antiquity death was frequently preferred to exile and therefore we can fathom the immensity of the pain which the Greeks, who knew of no celestial homeland, felt when they were separated from their fatherland.'[1] Was this emotional *post mortem* not slightly premature? History sometimes plays tricks on those who look too far back into the past: more of the same was to come. Von Wartenburg's nostalgic pronouncement preceded by some two decades the mass expulsion of Poles from Prussia under Bismarck (1885–90), which he was to witness, and the century of expulsions, unleashed by the First World War and ended by the wars in former Yugoslavia, not to mention the cataclysmic events outside Europe, such as the recent exodus of Syrian refugees.

Yet, von Wartenburg's claim was not entirely out of place. He did not propose that exile had ceased as a practice; he merely suggested that it had ceased to be forceful. Bereft of its tragic overtones, which resonated in Oedipus's plea to the Colonians, 'Strangers, I am an exile [ἀπόπολις]',[2] exile is said to have morphed into a dubious cosmopolitanism, a painless drifting over porous political borders and through fleeting realms of identity. At the very least, the emphasis has shifted from the opposition between home (settlement) and exile (movement) to that between different types of movement and their orbits: within home, profession or abroad (travel, tourism).[3] More than a century after von Wartenburg, Joseph Brodsky too would ironically refer to the 'good old exile', a characteristic invocation of cherished but defunct things.[4]

Furthermore, this change of cultural paradigm has been compounded by legal and political processes essentially adverse to exile. On the one hand, the historical agency which exiled people, from the Apostle Paul to Einstein, had in the creation of political cultures of the modern world has been firmly established. On the other hand, the political bodies arising from this illustrious succession have done their best to put an end to this practice, through legal stipulations in national constitutions and supranational charters of human rights.[5] Political changes did not help, either. Empires of the late nineteenth century still coveted the institution of individual exile and, when needed, resorted to mass expulsions until the point came, at the end of the First World War, when emperors themselves had to depart into exile. With the merger of the nation-states and the rise of the European super-state in the second half of the twentieth century, exile has become impracticable or at least much more difficult to execute than its ancient archetypes. Most of the iconic loci of the European exile — from Ovid's Constance at the Black Sea to Benjamin's Paris and Brecht's Svendborg — are now within the European Union.

At about the same time as the lofty discourse on exile was to reveal its Eurocentric slant, the myth was threatened from a different corner. The Union's borders on land and sea started to be negotiated by throngs of refugees, economic migrants and victims of human trafficking from the neighbouring regions and other parts of the world. Their civic identities — as well as their freedom of movement and economic prospects — are not determined by any lofty archetypes but rather emerge as a by-product of the changing bureaucratic regulations of the host countries. Europe has grown increasingly suspicious of exiles' credentials and even those few who could still qualify as exiles are reluctant to use that tag as it does not bring any comparative advantages. Cases of persecution are no longer evidenced by the display of symbolic stigmata but proven by fingerprints, stored in shared databases, and followed up in convoluted procedures which dissolve any vestiges of personal identity in a net of regulations and precedent case histories. Non-qualifying applicants are routinely removed from the territory of the signatories of the Schengen Protocol as part of their coordinated immigration policies. For those who have managed to spend some years in the reception countries this amounts to expulsion but in legal terms it is referred to as readmission. Curiously, thus, these latter-day expellees move in the opposite direction to conventional exiles: to, rather than from, their country of origin. At this point it is apposite to paraphrase Barthes's essay 'The Death of the Author': it is precisely in the context of migrancy that the (inter-)text has taken a decisive practical victory over the Author. The birth of the asylum seeker must be at the cost of the death of the Exile.[6]

This political antinomy is compounded by the fact that exile has been a coveted subject of artistic mimesis. In the literary field, in particular, political exile received a metaphoric spin with weak reference which entered and pollinated the broader semiotic circuit. Authors and their heroes adopted the fashion of emulating mythic expellees and readers have, consequently, aligned their interpretation to accommodate this loose metaphor rather than the actual practices of political exile. It is sufficient to quote the pathetic words of farewell by Rodolphe Boulanger, the petty seducer of Flaubert's *Madame Bovary*: 'Car je me punis par l'exil de tout le mal que je vous ai fait' [For I am going to punish myself by exile for all the ill I have done you].[7] One could argue that this is frivolous. Probably it is: Boulanger's penchant for pulp-fiction sentimentality indicates that in declaring himself an exile he might well be repeating a line from a sentimental novel. However, that does not make it unworthy of serious attention. Just like Flaubert's hero, most readers have received a continuous training in various metaphoric understandings of exile. They have become aware of another major paradox of exile: the word which semantically denotes boundaries and the deprivation of land creates a metaphoric universe of virtually boundless latitude.

This, however, is not the end of the metaphorical process. In addition to literature and religion, exile has also been integrated into various discourses of the humanities, but on entirely different terms of service, as a unilateral heuristic metaphor aimed at pinning down other, heterogeneous phenomena. Exile and its derivatives are now comfortably lodged in many disciplines: literary theory and criticism (Shklovsky's остранение, Bakhtin's вненаходимость, Lukacs's transzendentale Obdachlosigkeit), theatre (Brecht's Verfremdungseffekt), psychoanalysis (Freud's Verdrängung), psychiatry (Lacan's forclusion), legal studies (denaturalization) and political philosophy (Marx's Entfremdung). Not only are there many metaphors relying on exile; even metaphoric transference itself could be described in terms of enforced displacement, as Paul Ricoeur did, with remarkable success, in his *The Rule of Metaphor*. Metaphor is said to create 'the form of a movement in a portion of the trajectory of meaning that goes beyond the familiar referential field where the meaning is already constituted. [...] This ontological vehemence cuts meaning from its initial anchor, frees it as the form of a movement and transposes it to a new field.'[8] In other words, metaphor is not an abstract analogical relation but an ontological event of a violent nature: a meaning is torn from its initial haven and cast into a terra incognita.

Exile and the Force of Law: Between Convict and *Hostis*

So, exile had a troubled, paradoxical evolution. In Europe's political subconscious, it was converted from the banishment of citizens to the repatriation of asylum seekers. In the history of its semiosis, it has been pushed beyond all conceptual and disciplinary boundaries and precisely boundaries are its condition of possibility in the geopolitical arena. Yet, these historical paradoxes are dwarfed by an intrinsic dilemma which affects the very foundations of exile as a legal and political practice: why use it in the first place? Broadly speaking, one could propose two possible rationales for applying this measure. On the one hand, it could be argued that exile is advantageous as a regular dispensation of the law, especially when meted out as punishment. On the other hand, one could also claim that exile only makes sense as a nonstandard measure of the law and, what is more, that it works best when it boosts 'states of exception', during which the law is suspended for pragmatic reasons. I will briefly examine both models and try to show that neither of them applies entirely and that they need to be supplemented by imaginative resources.

The argument about the punitive nature of exile is ancient and famous enough. From the most painful memory of Judeo-Christianity, the Expulsion from the Garden of Eden, to Boulanger's frolicsome atonement for *crimen amoris*, banishment has been associated with punishment, legally and etymologically. Shakespeare's *Coriolanus* encapsulates the dread of the sentence and its performative drama:

> [...] in the name o'the people,
> And in the power of us the tribunes, we,
> E'en from this instant, banish him our city,
> In peril of precipitation
> From off the rock Tarpeian, never more
> To enter our Rome gates. I'th' people's name,
> I say it shall be so.[9]

The method was routinely recommended by political philosophers as different as Plato (for murder), Montesquieu (for felony) and Rousseau (again for felony).[10] Not only was it advised, it was also applied: in Ancient Greece as ostracism, in the Roman Empire as relegation, in the Middle Ages as banishment from the court, in Renaissance Italy as summary expulsion from the city, in the twentieth century as ethnic cleansing. The apparent analogies between these speculative regulations should not obscure significant differences between underlying political theologies. Punitive exile communicated different political messages at different times.

Discussing banishment in late medieval England in connection with Shakespeare's historical plays, Jane Kingsley-Smith argues that expulsions 'reinforce the identification of king and realm, of body natural and body politic. To say "I banish you" is to say that he embodies land, law and people, and may withdraw these from the offender.'[11] This metaphysical argument calls to mind Kantorowicz's classical study of the legal concept of the King's two bodies, one perishable and the other eternal. If anything, exile reinforces the supremacy of the latter: severing a sick member would undoubtedly impair the body natural but it miraculously strengthens the body politic.[12] In the late medieval period, thus, exile as punishment shored up the sovereign power which in its turn lent it metaphysical weight. Yet, already in Shakespeare's time, this metaphysical doctrine had become an anachronism, superseded by more pragmatic approaches to felony and merely nostalgically recollected in historical imagination. Here comes into view a crucial difference between this outlook and that which obtained in the modern period. Nowadays, namely, exile appears to take away from the sovereign power, as one is likely to ask what power is unable to deal with the offender *intra muros* and is forced to banish him or her instead. Unless there are some specific benefits, the latter is likely to be interpreted as a sign of weakness rather than strength.

So, the pre-eminently modern question is: what is to be gained by applying exile as punishment? In response to this pragmatic question, one could at once stress the sheer economy of exile in comparison to other forms of punishment: it is reliable and cost-effective. Standard punitive measures such as the death penalty, corporal punishment, imprisonment, ignominy and fines involve the courts that pronounce them but they also require, typically over a considerable period of time, other institutions and officials to implement them, including executioners, police officers, medical doctors, probation officers, prison guards, etc. At the very least, it appears that a straightforward expulsion instead of confinement would render the complex apparatus of executive and supervisory agents unnecessary.

In the Foucauldian optic, exile goes against the logic of punitive institutions. By taking part in penal 'enchainment', one disciplines the transgressor and at the same time gets disciplined as a member of a 'chain' of penal institutions, which cannot be achieved in contumacy. Exile is also bound to fall short of meeting the old retributive requirement that the amount of pain inflicted be proportionate to the ill committed. Unlike imprisonment or fine, it inflicts no quantifiable physical pain or psychological distress. Furthermore, by relinquishing all juridical control over the transgressor's actions, the state also renounces all instruments which enable its penal measures to exert any utilitarian function. It cannot prevent because once a sentenced person leaves the territory under the jurisdiction of a sovereign authority, there is nothing to stop him or her from continuing the criminal action. It cannot reform because there is no way to guarantee that eviction would not allow the transgressor to enjoy the benefits of the previous crime. It cannot deter because it subtracts the offender from the view of the public who are supposed to learn from his or her example.

The legal and ethical arguments suggest that the history of exile is, to a large extent, the history of a practice which masquerades as punishment but which is not one and, moreover, cannot be so. We have started the discussion of punitive exile with Shakespeare's *Coriolanus*; are we not better advised to recall the argument of fiends from Milton's *Paradise Lost*? In their consecutive oratories, Lucifer and his companions transform their expulsion into an immense space of freedom and even exultation:

> The mind is its own place, and in itself
> Can make a heav'n of hell, a hell of heav'n.
> [...]

> Here at least
> We shall be free; th' Almighty hath not built
> Here for his envy, will not drive us hence.[13]

Well, in the historical world things do not always work out that way. Moderate optimism may be justified but triumphalism is out of place because the state typically has several subsidiary punishments to spare. Exiles lose significant parts of their economic and social capital through the confiscation of property, the imposition of a stigma, and the political pressure on family members and friends who remain behind. Thomas Hobbes, the sober taxonomist of the monarchy, argued that as soon as anything is seized from the departing person — and, typically, something *is* seized — exile ceases to be a 'mere change of air' and 'is to be reckoned amongst punishments pecuniary'.[14] In any event, pecuniary and other punishments by proxy may accompany exile to a greater or lesser degree but they are usually there and form a broader legal framework for the process.

If exile does not have demonstrable punitive effects — and therefore does not convince as the standard dispensation of the law — one can still argue that it is efficient in those cases when the law has to be suspended in its entirety. If the state of exception suspends laws and plunges the state into the primordial field of the political and if the whole point of that field is, as Schmitt stipulates in *Political Theology* and *The Concept of the Political*, to decide on and then symbolically to produce the public enemy, exile seems a very apposite instrument for that purpose.[15] Whereas assassinating someone will never produce a public enemy (unless he or she has already been declared as such), exiling the same person almost certainly will. Following that person's departure, the enemy–friend distinction between him and those who remain behind is going to be multi-fold: political, in that the exile is a *hostis*; territorial, in that the exile turns into a stranger; and discursive, since the exile will incur moral and aesthetic disgrace. After being identified as public enemies and forced to leave the country, exiles become bad and ugly: from humans they turn into 'stray dogs' in the words of Muammar Gaddafi. Nevertheless, exile does not score so well on Schmitt's second criterion which requires the polity to produce the public enemy in such a way as would enable it to be on the terms of *ius belli* with him, and go for his life when needed.[16] The 'existential negation' of this type of enemy is not a real possibility unless the home polity launches an open war against their host state or, more practically, hires assassins to execute them abroad secretly. To be sure, the latter has been done — one thinks of the executions of the Italian *fuoriusciti* at the orders of Mussolini or of Trotsky by Stalin — but it is a far cry from a functional *ius belli*. The state's right to decide who is a friend and who an enemy is determined by the domestic as well as by diplomatic considerations, and the exile will often play one off against the other.

That the exile is not entirely convincing as a convict and not quite efficient as a public enemy does not mean that in political practice he or she cannot be all of that. Exile has fulfilled a multiplicity of pragmatic purposes and will probably continue to do so in the future. However, these purposes are no longer intrinsically punitive, nor do they support the fundamental functions of sovereignty, as was the case in the Middle Ages. More often than not, exile emerges as a short- or long-term socio-political expedient, as a fall-back option when other measures fail, or simply as a consequence of the climate of fear in an interregnum. These pragmatic developments are retroactively construed as eminently ethical or political facts. In other words, in order to think of the exile as a distant convict or as a public enemy one needs to employ political and literary imagination rather than legal thinking.

Exile and the Force of Imagination: Banishment, Duress, Alienation

Imaginative resources have been applied profusely, in scholarship at least, to overwhelm the intrinsic ethico-political ambiguity of exile. In 1972, the Hungarian-born publicist Paul Tabori published his summa of the histories of exile from antiquity to the twentieth century, *The Anatomy of Exile*. It is a most epitomic title for the most typical book about exile. The notion of anatomy conjures up the image of a coherent organism. Exile is imagined not as a conglomerate of different practices and mindsets but as a single body, that can be observed and described by the sympathetic anatomist just as it was previously exposed to the violence of the state. To be sure, that body has many smaller bodies inside, but, not unlike Hobbes's Leviathan, they all coalesce into one form. Let us, hence, take Tabori's cue and probe that imagined body politic of exiles.

In their studies of exile, modernist and postmodernist scholars tackled several important problems. In the first place, they were concerned with the taxonomies of exile. Bringing together categories of law and popular imagination, they worked to determine whether exile is a distinct form of displacement, to be assessed against other forms such as diaspora, emigration, expatriation, internal displacement, and even tourism, or whether it is an overarching category — a state of affairs or a state of mind — which includes the rest.[17] Then, they were also interested in pinning down the relations between banishment as a biographical fact, literary text as a product of individual imagination, and exile as an intercultural image. The various possible interactions in this triangle occupied much of the literary scholarship on exile.[18] Finally, they searched for a substrate which would transform the different representations of exile into exilic literature, a distinct literary genre that cuts across other genres and spans different periods and cultures. In particular, numerous comparatist studies have identified thematic parallels stretching from antiquity to the twenty-first century and created the now current notion of the literature of exile as a synchronic and diachronic whole, with its recognizable topographies, *topoi* and poetic genealogies.[19] As the notions of home and foreignness came under postmodernist criticism, the studies of exile morphed into postmodern philosophy,[20] deconstructive criticism,[21] memory studies,[22] cultural studies[23] and postcolonial studies.[24] Nevertheless, a key idea has lived on: exile as a non-hegemonic community beyond territorial and ideological confines of nation states. In the process of addressing taxonomical, historical and generic problems, the modernist and postmodernist scholars joined forces to create the exilic anti-Leviathan, an extra-territorial literary body politic that challenges the sovereign power.

Nevertheless, the one aspect of exile which these scholars have not covered so well (if at all) is its *primum mobile*, political force. Browsing through the different historical surveys of exile, such as Paul Tabori's *The Anatomy of Exile*, through edited anthologies of exiled writers' essays, such as Mark Robinson's *Altogether Elsewhere*, as well as through scholarly volumes that explore those writers, such as Susan Rubin Suleiman's *Exile and Creativity*, one gets the impression that they start from a nominal notion of banishment and then proceed to establish as wide a community of exiles as possible, often overriding the key conceptual premise, the presence of force. Here are a few notable examples, placed in their logical rather than chronological order:

> Exile usually means political banishment: A person leaves his or her country to avoid harassment by the state; the state expels an individual for real or imaginary crimes. (Robinson)[25]

> An exile is a person who is compelled to leave his homeland — though the forces that send him on his way may be political, economic, or purely psychological. It does not make an essential difference whether he is expelled by physical force or whether he makes the decision to leave without such an immediate pressure. (Tabori)[26]

> Émigrés, exiles, expatriates, refugees, nomads, cosmopolitans — the meanings of those words vary, as do their connotations. [...] In its narrow sense a political banishment, exile in its broad sense designates every kind of estrangement or displacement, from the physical and geographical to the spiritual. (Rubin Suleiman)[27]

Let us establish briefly what these definitions propose. To Robinson, exile is primarily forceful banishment although one can decide to leave his or her country voluntarily if exposed to harassment and that, too, would count as exile. In Tabori, this definition is significantly broadened and exile, still a geographical displacement, now includes various other forms of compulsion which strictly speaking need not be political, such as economic duress and psychological dissatisfaction. In Rubin Suleiman's definition, political banishment is referenced as the 'narrow' meaning of the word; yet, its broad definition is not merely expansion but transformation under completely different terms: force has now turned into alienation and territory into a discourse.

These definitions illustrate a very important phenomenon in the scholarship of exile: the gradual disappearance of the political force, and its transformation into a spectral force, which is everywhere because it is nowhere. Political force turns into a fictional banishment, then into duress and finally into vague alienation. This is neither a logical error nor a Wittgensteinian game of language, although it may appear so to conceptual purists. This erasure is part of a broader push in modernist and postmodernist thought to articulate non-hegemonic alternatives to the sovereign power: in order to make the anti-Leviathan as numerous and as powerful as possible the net naturally had to be cast as wide as possible.

Actually, whether force is used or not may turn out to be very important to the sovereign and to the exile, especially to the writer. Political agents in control of such decisions often have pragmatic reasons to enforce someone's exile indirectly, i.e. without declaring it, so as to preserve the appearance of legality and to avoid more drastic forms of confrontation that may lead to social unrest or capital punishment. Exiles have their own reasons to call for some force to be openly used because voluntary departure reduces their likelihood of restitution both politically and economically. As he was to be expelled to Alma Ata in 1927, Leon Trotsky was so keen not to allow Stalin and the Politburo to make his exile appear voluntary that he actually forced the agents to use force: they had to dress him up, lift him in their arms and take him away.[28] Furthermore, in the communication between the exile and the sovereign it is also important to know what kind of force has been used: it can be verbal and physical and the two often interact. In the Roman Republic, exile was encoded in word, as the decree of *aquae et ignis interdictio* which denied the proscribed person water and fire and confiscated his property, whereas in the late medieval Italy expulsion was consummated in deed, by the ritualistic burning of exiles' houses and towers.[29] Finally, it is also important to be clear about who used force. To point one's finger simply at the state, as exiles and critics have occasionally done, may blur the picture and exclude all those cases in which none of the structures of the state was formally implicated in exile. The Kristallnacht of 1938, which sparked a fresh wave of the Jewish emigration from Germany, was organized by the SA squads of the Nazi party which imposed itself as a state above the state; in 1993, the Croat writer Dubravka Ugrešić, a staunch critic of nationalism, went into exile after being targeted by a smear campaign in the press, ostracism at work and anonymous phone calls by members of the public, all of whom acted as proxies of the state; Jean–Jacques Rousseau was hounded out of his Swiss haven of Neuchâtel (1765) by local mobs which effectively acted against the state and the decision of asylum granted by the sovereign, Frederick II of Prussia.[30]

Thus, the force of exile is not simply a retrospective abstraction but an actual practice which has its what, how and who. All these strategic decisions on the employment of force create different political prospects for exiles. What is more, they inform different patterns of literary imagination.

Implied Exile and its Rhetoric

As we have seen, exile has consistently been associated with force but the exact kind of force brought to bear on the exile has never been plausibly defined. We have seen that exile is problematic if delivered through the force of the law, be it as a standard legal measure i.e. punishment, or as an extra-legal remedy, part of an exceptional decree. Then again, the force of exile is imagined by exiles and literary scholars as spectral and diffuse, more of a metaphysical than political construct. But where then can the force of exile come from? This book will propose that it is a kind of force that negotiates between the legal and the metaphysical realms: it arises in the interstices of the regular law and is eventually lodged in the imaginative expanses of the intertext. In that sense, my model differs significantly from the proposition of the critical theorists of the Schmittian orientation for whom force works the other way round, arising from theological premises and being consolidated in the different propositions of the law.

Unlike most classical studies on exile, this book has a very specific focus. It is concerned with texts about exile arising from the real experience of exile. Needless to say, many texts about exile have been written by people who had not themselves been in exile — one thinks of Shakespeare — and many people who were in exile chose not to write about it — one may instance Hobbes. While my focus on the texts arising from the lived exile does not discard the influence of these lateral strands of exilic discourse it still insists on the importance of exile as a human experience recollected in literature.

Focusing on the texts arising from exile, this book also frames a particular type of exile which, in my view, allows the best insight into its rhetorical nature. This kind of exile, which I define throughout the book as 'implied', is neither delivered as a statutory punishment nor enforced as part of a state of emergency. It is, rather, triggered within the standard legal system but enacted in extrajudicial context. Furthermore, this implied exile is neither compulsory, because no physical force is delivered and no decree of eviction issued, nor is it voluntary, because some duress is communicated to, and absorbed by, the exile. Rather, implied exile is based on a bilateral and willing communication between the sovereign (or his/her proxy) and the exile.[31] We are, therefore, talking of a very indirect and yet fairly effective exile.

Having defined what implied exile is not, it is of course important to specify it in positive terms: to spell out what it is and provide some salient examples. Under implied exile I subsume all cases of displacement, individual or as part of a wider migratory movement, which display two features: a) they are heteronomous, i.e. they involve a change of legal jurisdiction and political territory; and b) they are retroactive, i.e. the exclusion from the body politic is not communicated a priori but inferred post factum. In a word, this book will be concerned with those instances of exile where a person departs from his or her homeland under duress and subsequently realizes that return is not possible or is associated with a substantial punishment, such as the pain of death or imprisonment.

What are the typical patterns of implied exile? To begin with, one can be charged, rightly or wrongly, with some crime or other, and while the court proceedings are still under way (or even before they have started) he or she can decide to leave the country rather than wait for the verdict to be delivered. In this case, the legal process is conducted in the court and completed in contumacy but the act of exile itself is extrajudicial. Then, in a somewhat different political context, one can also be tempted or actively encouraged to leave the territory of the state and then be prohibited from returning. Another version of the same model is to declare that someone who is already abroad as an expatriate or traveller has forfeited citizenship and, therefore, cannot return. In this case, exile may be a judicial affair but it is phrased indirectly, as foreclosure rather than banishment. Finally, one can be driven into exile by the pressure of various informal groups which may or may not represent the attitudes of the government but which do not act on any formal injunction. Here, the decision to leave is taken by the person affected as a response to the extrajudicial duress.

Therefore, the implied exile explored in this study is heteronomous and retroactive and its principal forms are created by evasion, foreclosure and informal duress. This may look like too narrow a selection considering the vast number of objective and self-propelled displacements covered in the earlier studies of literature in exile. Nevertheless, this selection actually covers some of the most iconic instances of exile: Cicero, Dante, Rousseau and Brecht, to name but a few, all found themselves locked out of their countries in one of these three ways. This means that the argument presented in this book is actually not narrowing down significantly the pool of 'classical' cases of exile but rather proposing to look at them from a different angle.

But what is the point of this reformatting of the good old exile? What is to be gained by getting bogged down in all these legal particulars instead of taking for granted what the exiles — and posterity — thought about their experience? While evasion, foreclosure and lateral duress are very different as personal predicaments and indicate different involvements with the sovereign power they still share the same feature, namely, that a direct legal force has not been employed either in word or in deed to drive the affected person away. The flaming sword or — for those who prefer up-to-date methods — the smoking gun is nowhere to be seen. It has been concealed and de-emphasized. Consequently, it may appear to the exile that he or she has been banished with no force and that any legal duress will have to be proven and emphasized. Bertolt Brecht voices the concern of his fellow writers who left Germany upon Hitler's ascension to power but also of the entire cohort of the implied exiles before and after him:

> Immer fand ich den Namen falsch, den man uns gab: Emigranten.
> Das heißt doch Auswanderer. Aber wir
> Wanderten doch nicht aus, nach freiem Entschluß
> Wählend ein anderes Land, wanderten wir doch auch nicht
> Ein in ein Land, dort zu bleiben, womöglich für immer.
> Sondern wir flohen. Vertriebene sind wir, Verbannte.
> Und kein Heim, ein Exil soll das Land sein, das uns da aufnahm.
>
> [I always found the name false which they gave us: Emigrants.
> That means those who leave their country. But we
> Did not leave, of our own free will
> Choosing another land. Nor did we enter
> Into a land, to stay there, if possible for ever.
> Merely, we fled. We are driven out, banned.
> Not a home, but an exile, shall the land be that took us in.][32]

Therefore, the deficit of force in the legal and political discourse is met with its surplus in the retrospective discourse of exiles about their departure. This phenomenon will henceforth be referred to as the compensatory elicitation of force.

Nevertheless, this book aims to go a step further than merely establishing the counter-proportion of force in the legal and the literary discourse. It intends to show that the concealment of force by the state and its elicitation by the exile typically proceed by certain figurative transfers the use of which implies some practical rhetorical competence in both parties. Hence, one could talk of the figurative encoding of force by the state and its subsequent decoding by the exile.

On the sovereign's end of the chain, force is typically diverted on the basis of contiguity. In terms of chronological (and causal) contiguity, the state may suggest that one's departure was voluntary and wanted and hence represents the grounds for foreclosure from returning (rather than acting as the retroactive pretext for that ban). Then, in terms of spatial and sociopolitical contiguity, the state can delegate the employment of force to its informal proxies (for instance, mobsters) or otherwise direct that force to the exile's proxies (for instance, harass family members, burn books, confiscate assets). In symbolic terms, the state can resort to various figurative phrasings such as the Roman interdiction of water and fire instead of eviction (the *pars pro toto* principle) or specify the minimum radius of the ban instead of defining the destination (the contiguity principle). All these measures display the structure of a well-known figure in the classical rhetoric: metonymy. The one striking difference, though, is that this political metonymy is not a mere decoration of speech but rather the constitutive trope of exile as a political practice.

On the receiving end of the chain, these metonymic displacements of force are decoded by the exiles. This means that they are constitutive not only for the sovereign's perspective on exile but also for exiled subjects' responses to that practice and this dual optic opens up a rhetorical contest. The most obvious way of eliciting force is to follow the original metonymic code and claim that *pars* means *totum* and that the proxy points to the subject concerned. This reconstruction of the chain of signification is what a trained solicitor would do in a restitution process. However, the striking feature of the literary texts of implied exile is that the writers are not content with that straightforward and pragmatic approach. To be sure, even if they were, they would usually not be granted the right to claim back their civic status at the bar. Instead, they pick up elements of the metonymic code and develop them into powerful metaphors of duress. In poetry, a Gorgon that may not be seen is more forceful an image of the sovereign power than an anonymous threatening letter (Brodsky); a conflagration of the city is more forceful than a burnt book (Brecht); a big stone that breaks one's window is more forceful than a pebble (Rousseau).[33]

At this point, one could be tempted to think that the main claim of this book is that the literature of implied exile is all about the exaggeration of force. In a very colloquial sense, it is not entirely incorrect to call this effect exaggeration although the standard rhetorical term amplification would be much more fit for the purpose. Nevertheless, it has to be stressed that the overbidding of force is not flippant posturing but part and parcel of the writer's active political involvement in his or her world, a signal of the commitment to the ongoing polemic with the sovereign power. At the same time, however, this metaphoric construal of force is much more than mere exaggeration. Drawing from its verbal resources, it adds up to a visionary transformation of force and is, hence, part of the way in which all literature achieves its effects. In that respect, a major strand of this argument will be focused on pinpointing the differences between the litigant and literary discourse on exile. Whereas a solicitor may employ metaphors to demonstrate the involvement of force, his key focus — Roman Jakobson would say 'the dominant'[34] — will be metonymy. For a poet, metonymical references may occasionally crop up to substantiate the case but the dominant will be metaphor. The pivotal and, in a sense, serendipitous example in this comparison between the litigant and the literary will be Cicero. Himself an exile, a lawyer of exiles, and the poet of the law, Cicero in his orations fuses litigation and literature and lays down theoretical foundations for the study of the rhetoric of exile, which will be discussed in Chapter 1.

In the specific context of literature, the argument will move through a number of examples taken from the poetry and prose of exiled authors to establish how the metonymic concealment of force was met by its metaphoric amplification. In particular, in four dedicated chapters it will show how this metaphoric force is brought to bear on different levels of the literary text. Thus, Chapter 2 will explore the political deployment and displacement of fire in two major thermopolitical paradigms, the Roman Republic and the Inquisition of the early modern period. It will then proceed to analyse instances of fire imagery in the poetry of Dante, Brecht and Brodsky and link it to those paradigms as well as to the metonymic encoding of fire in their own exile. Chapter 3 will move from the individual poetic images to the socio-political templates that emerge in the works of implied exile. The argument will establish a link between the concealment of force in the political discourse and its reconstruction within a nightmarish, paranoid world of the exiled subjects. In Aeschylus' *Oresteia* and Nabokov's *Pale Fire* exiles turn paranoid; in Rousseau's autobiographic texts, a paranoid exile is accepted into an equally paranoid host community and exiled from it; in Kiš's *Garden, Ashes* and Heym's *The Wandering Jew*, exiles' persecutory imagination gets redeemed — and remedied — in that they are quite literally martyred by their paranoid hosts. The argument will then move from socio-political templates to the figures of textual force, those that are imagined to hold the literary work together or to break it apart. The key image in that sphere will be the paternal metaphor: father emerges as a mnemonic link to the lost fatherland and as the pivot of textual coherence, a form of an in-text Lar. The metaphor will first be explored in the autobiographic texts of Nabokov and Kiš, both of whom see their dead fathers as a guarantors of their identity in exile, and then in the psychoanalytic theory of Freud, in connection with his myth of the primal horde, where stymied sons are exiled by the omnipotent father and return to kill him. Chapter 5, finally, will trace the metaphors of force at the level of language, once again in the lyrical poetry. The case will be made for interlingual (code-switching) poems such as Miloš Crnjanski's 'Lament over Belgrade' as rare and yet epitomic examples of the duress of implied exile. An interlingual poem is divided between the different sections as if they were territorial entities and the poets establish metalingual metaphoric bridges to mitigate the perceived sinister division in their poetic sequence.

My debt to the comparatist studies of exile as the human universal has already been indicated in the previous section; I now need to introduce another close ancestor: research into conceptual metaphors and metonymies and its predecessors in psychology and linguistics. In its heyday, from the late 1970s to to the 1990s, this field attracted a lot of interest and saw some quite dynamic development not least because, like the study of exile, it sought to shed light on a presumed human universal. Just like the scholars of exile, conceptual linguists aimed to discover, catalogue and rationalize ubiquitous windows on the world which structure our knowledge and communication in largely analogous ways. The modern enquiry into metaphor and metonymy started with Freud's discovery of displacement and condensation as pervasive principle of psychic life.[35] It was followed up by Jakobson's analyses of the systemic interactions between metaphor and metonymy along paradigmatic and syntagmatic axes of language.[36] This model was supplemented and, in a sense, displaced by Lacan's study of metaphors and metonymies as elements in the signification chain that project the psychic life as a signified.[37] Lakoff and Johnson transformed the terms of the debate by anchoring their research in the empirically available material determined by cultural and cognitive templates. Crucially, they pointed to the pragmatic role of metaphors in structuring our actions: 'The concept is metaphorically structured, the activity is metaphorically structured, and, consequently, the language is metaphorically structured.'[38]

While honouring these classical studies on metaphor and metonymy, the argument proposed in this book aims to give a new meaning to the old conceptual pair and apply it within a broader political horizon. In particular, while researchers have convincingly shown how these figures inform psychic life, language performance and cognitive processes, much less headway has been made in understanding their function and interactions in politics. By referring to politics, I do not mean political discourses: conceptual linguists and critical discourse analysis have applied some of these findings in the exploration of specimens of political language. Rather, what I have in mind is their use in political practice and articulation and justification of fundamental policies of the sovereign power such as implied exile. If in Lakoff's and Johnson's well-known example argument is conceptualized as war, perhaps the relationship can be reversed and exile can be conceptualized as argument, or, more precisely, as a rhetorical contest. Another point that needs to be stressed is that the conceptual linguists saw metaphor as the elder brother of metonymy and dedicated more effort to it. This study will try to shift the balance in favour of metonymy: it claims that it is the sovereign power's displacements of force on chronological and spatial proxies that prompts the authors to strike back with condensed metaphors of force.

Nonetheless, the gist of the argument should be clear at all times: exile is principally about the ramifications of a human situation rather than the construction of a theoretical platform. Since that human situation sets one's heart on remedying political homelessness, one could resort to an architectonic metaphor. Exile is a mythopoeic edifice built by many generations of master builders. At some point in time this edifice collapsed and revealed various metaphorical beams which used to support the structure and which are now employed to erect other, smaller edifices. This metaphor would be broadly correct, yet not entirely adequate, unless one goes a step further to recognize that tropes were not only integrated as beams but also laid in the foundations of that edifice. We need to understand that exile is not merely generative of figures: it is in itself a figure and, moreover, rhetorical transfers are the conditions of its possibility as a political practice. It is by this internal rhetorical setup that exile prefigures its sundry representations and reflections in other types of discourse.

Notes to the Introduction

1. Paul Graf Yorck von Wartenburg, *Die Katharsis des Aristoteles und der 'Oedipus Coloneus' des Sophokles* (Berlin: Verlag von Wilhelm Hertz, 1866), p. 26 (my translation).
2. *Oedipus Coloneus* v. 207, in Sophocles, *Antigone, The Women of Trachis, Philoctetes, Oedipus at Colonus* (Cambridge, MA, London: Harvard University Press, 1994), pp. 434–35.
3. This point has been put with great precision in the essay by Nigel Rapport and Andrew Dawson, 'Home and Movement: A Polemic', in N. Rapport and A Dawson (eds), *Migrants of Identity: Perception of Home in a World of Movement* (Oxford and New York: Berg, 1998), pp. 19–38.
4. Joseph Brodsky, 'The Condition We Call "Exile"', in John Glad (ed.), *Literature in Exile* (Durham, NC, and London: Duke University Press 1990), p. 101.
5. A representative document codifying this belief is the 'Universal Declaration of Human Rights' adopted by the General Assembly of United Nations in 1948, which in Article 9 declares that no one shall be subjected to exile and in Article 15 that everyone has a basic right to nationality of which 'no one shall be arbitrarily deprived'. Article 3 of The Council of Europe's 'Protocol No. 4 to the Convention for the Protection of Human Rights and Fundamental Freedoms' (1963) also prohibits the expulsion of nationals from the territory of their respective states. Beside these international treaties, protection of the right to citizenship against expulsion is encoded as a provision in the constitutions and constitutional charters of many countries. The Portuguese constitution (1976), for example, guarantees in Article 23 that no Portuguese national shall be expelled or deprived of his or her nationality. Even in conditions of war or armed conflict, when certain statutory civic and human rights are suspended or derogated, the basic right of not being expelled is guaranteed by the relevant international treaties. Thus, Article 49 of the Fourth Geneva Convention (1949) explicitly prohibits both individual and mass expulsions of civilians from the territories of an occupied state to any other territory.
6. Barthes's formulation is: 'the birth of the reader must be at the cost of the death of the Author'. Roland Barthes, 'The Death of the Author', in *Image, Music, Text* (London: Fontana Press, 1977), p. 148.
7. Gustave Flaubert, *Madame Bovary* (Paris: Garnier Frères, 1971), p. 208; translation in Flaubert, *Madame Bovary* (New York, London: W. W. Norton, 2005), p. 163.
8. Paul Ricoeur, *The Rule of Metaphor: The Creation of Meaning in Language* (London and Henley: Routledge 1978), pp. 299–300.
9. *Coriolanus*, III. 3. 96–102, in *The Library Shakespeare*, vol. II (Quarry Bay: Midpoint Press 2005), p. 323.
10. *Laws* IX. 865d–e in Plato, *Complete Works*, ed. by J. M Cooper and D. S. Hutchinson (Indianapolis, IN: Hackett, 1977), pp. 1523–24, Baron de Montesquieu, *The Spirit of the Laws* (New York: Hafner, 1962), pp. 186–87, Jean-Jacques Rousseau, *Discourse on Political Economy and Social Contract* (Oxford: Oxford University Press, 1999), pp. 71–72.
11. Jane Kingsley-Smith, *Shakespeare's Drama of Exile*, ebook (Basingstoke: Palgrave Macmillan, 2003), p. 59.
12. See Ernst H. Kantorowicz, *The King's Two Bodies: A Study in Medieval Political Theology* (Princeton, NJ: Princeton University Press, 1987).
13. John Milton, *Poetical Works* (Oxford and New York: Oxford University Press, 1988), p. 218.
14. Thomas Hobbes, *Leviathan* (Oxford: Oxford University Press 1998), p. 210.
15. Carl Schmitt, *Political Theology: Four Chapters on the Concept of Sovereignty* (Chicago, IL, and London: University of Chicago Press, 2005), pp. 5–15, and *The Concept of the Political* (Chicago, IL, and London: University of Chicago Press, 2007), pp. 25–27.
16. Schmitt, *The Concept of the Political*, pp. 32–34.
17. See, for instance, the neat categorization proposed by Mary McCarthy, 'Exiles, Expatriates and Internal Émigrés', *The Listener*, Thursday 25 November 1971, vol. 86, No. 2226, pp. 705–08 and by Christine Brooke-Rose, 'Exsul' in Susan Rubin Suleiman (ed.), *Exile and Creativity: Signposts, Travelers, Outsiders, Backward Glances* (Durham, NC, and London: Duke University Press, 1998), pp. 9–24.
18. On this problem see the theoretical essays by Joseph Wittlin, 'Sorrow and Grandeur of Exile',

Polish Review, 2 (Spring/Summer 1957), 99–111 and Claudio Guillén, 'On the Literature of Exile and Counter-Exile', *Books Abroad*, 50 (Spring 1976), 271–80. The triangular structural problem has been treated at the interpretative level in numerous writer- and context-specific studies: Louis L. Martz, *Milton: Poet of Exile* (New Haven, CT, and London: Yale University Press, 1986); Isabelle Cielens, *Trois fonctions de l'exil dans les œuvres de fiction d'Albert Camus: initiation, révolte, conflit d'identité* (Uppsala: Almqvist & Wiksell, 1985) and Paul Ilie, *Literature and Inner Exile: Authoritarian Spain, 1939–1975* (Baltimore, MD, and London: Johns Hopkins University Press, 1980).

19. For some exemplary thematic genre analyses, see Harry Levin, 'Literature and Exile', in Harry Levin, *Refractions* (New York: Oxford University Press, 1966), pp. 62–81 and David Bethea, *Joseph Brodsky and the Creation of Exile* (Princeton, NJ: Princeton University Press, 1994). For exilic literature as a formal, language-based genre, see Jo-Marie Claassen, *Displaced Persons: The Literature of Exile from Cicero to Boethius* (London: Duckworth, 1999).

20. The representative texts are: Kenneth White, *L'Esprit nomade* (Paris: Bernard Grasset, 1987), Gilles Deleuze and Félix Guattari, *A Thousand Plateaus: Capitalism and Schizophrenia* (London: Athlone Press, 1988) and Julia Kristeva, 'A New Type of Intellectual: The Dissident', in Toril Moi (ed.), *The Kristeva Reader* (Oxford and Cambridge, MA: Blackwell, 1986), pp. 292–300.

21. See the interpretation of exile as an allegory of aesthetic activity in Michael Seidel, *Exile and the Narrative Imagination* (New Haven, CT, and London: Yale University Press, 1986) and as an allegory of the reading process in Robert D. Newman, *Transgressions of Reading: Narrative Engagement as Exile and Return* (Durham, NC, and London: Duke University Press, 1993).

22. The seminal study in this strand is Svetlana Boym's *The Future of Nostalgia* (New York: Basic Books, 2001) which proposed the distinction between restorative and reflective nostalgia.

23. See Angelika Bammer (ed.), *Displacements: Cultural Identities in Question* (Bloomington and Indianapolis: Indiana University Press, 1994) and Caren Kaplan, *Questions of Travel: Postmodernist Discourses of Displacement* (Durham, NC, and London: Duke University Press, 1996).

24. The key text in this strand was Edward Said, 'Reflections on Exile', *Granta* (Winter 1984–85), pp. 157–72; for follow-up research, see Sophia McClennen, *The Dialectics of Exile: Nation, Time, Language, and Space in Hispanic Literatures* (West Lafayette, IN: Purdue University Press, 2004).

25. Marc Robinson, *Altogether Elsewhere* (Boston, MA, and London: Faber and Faber, 1994), p. xiii.

26. Paul Tabori, *The Anatomy of Exile* (London: Harrap, 1972), p. 37.

27. Susan Rubin Suleiman, 'Introduction', in *Exile and Creativity*, pp. 1–2.

28. Leon Trotsky, *My Life* (New York: Grosset and Dunlop, 1960), pp. 540–41.

29. See Gordon Kelly, *A History of Exile in the Roman Republic* (Cambridge: Cambridge University Press, 2006), pp. 17–19, and Christine Shaw, *The Politics of Exile in Renaissance Italy* (Cambridge: Cambridge University Press, 2000), p. 111.

30. Anthony Read and David Fisher, *Kristallnacht: The Unleashing of the Holocaust* (New York: Peter Bedrick Books, 1989), pp. 56–58; Dubravka Ugrešić, 'A Question of Perspective' in Ugrešić, *Karaoke Culture* (Rochester, NY: Open Letter, 2011), pp. 203–46; Maurice Cranston, *The Solitary Self: Jean-Jacques Rousseau in Exile and Adversity* (London: The Penguin Press; Chicago: University of Chicago Press, 1997), pp. 110–40.

31. 'Implied' exile, as well as its 'rhetoric', are an adaptation from and an homage to a classic study in a different field, narratology. In *The Rhetoric of Fiction* (1961), Wayne Booth coined the term 'the implied author' to designate the central repository of the work's norms which arises from all of its elements and should not be confused for the real author (who may disown his or her work's values or be unaware of them) or the narrator (who may be reliable or unreliable). My use of the word implied in connection with exile is, like in Booth, suggestive of something derivative. Nevertheless, differently from Booth, who sees the implied author objectively contained in the text and disconnected from both the author and the reader, the idea of implied exile is shared between the addresser (the sovereign) and the addressee (the exile) rather than articulated in the political discourse. See Wayne Booth, *The Rhetoric of Fiction* (Chicago and London: Chicago University Press, 1961), pp. 70–77.

32. Bertolt Brecht, *Svendborger Gedichte*, in Brecht, *Gedichte*, vol. IV (Frankfurt am Main: Suhrkamp Verlag, 1961), p. 137. Translated by Tom Kuhn in Kuhn, '"Visit to a Banished Poet": Brecht's *Svendborg Poems* and the Voices of Exile', in Ronald Speirs (ed.), *Brecht's Poetry of Political Exile* (Cambridge: Cambridge University Press, 2000), pp. 49–50.

33. See Joseph Brodsky, *Peremena imperii* (Moscow: Izdatel'stvo Nezavisimaya gazeta, 2001), p. 351. The English translation by Brodsky is taken from Joseph Brodsky, *To Urania: Selected Poems 1965–1985* (London: Penguin Books, 1988), pp. 34–35. See also Bertolt Brecht, *Selected Poems* (New York: Grove Press; London: Evergreen Books, 1959), pp. 170–71, and Jean-Jacques Rousseau, *Correspondance complète de Jean Jacques Rousseau*, vol. XXVI (Oxford: The Voltaire Foundation, 1976), pp. 325–84 (materials on the 'lapidation de Môtiers').

34. See Roman Jakobson, 'The Dominant', in Ladislav Matejka and Krystyna Pomorska (eds), *Readings in Russian Poetics: Formalist and Structuralist Views* (Ann Arbor, MI: Michigan Slavic Publications, 1978), pp. 82–87.

34. Sigmund Freud, *The Interpretation of Dreams*, in *The Standard Edition of the Complete Psychological Works of Sigmund Freud*, vol. IV, ed. by James Strachey (London: The Hogarth Press and the Institute of Psychoanalysis, 1958), pp. 277–309.

35. Roman Jakobson, 'Two Aspects of Language and Two Types of Aphasic Disturbances', in Jakobson, *Language in Literature* (Cambridge, MA, and London: The Belknap Press of Harvard University Press, 1987), pp. 95–114.

36. See Jacques Lacan, *The Seminar of Jacques Lacan (Book 3: Psychoses, 1955–1956)* (London: Routledge, 1993), pp. 214–30.

37. George Lakoff and Mark Johnson, *Metaphors We Live By* (Chicago, IL, and London: Chicago University Press, 2003), p. 5.

CHAPTER 1

Banished With No Force: Implied Exile in Cicero's *Pro Caecina Oratio*

Exile, that paradoxical and galvanizing modernist concept, has been undermined by the very same discursive forces that nourished it throughout the twentieth century. It has become a neutral designator, one of the versatile umbrella terms by which we intend to encompass nearly everything without committing ourselves to anything in particular. One of the main reasons for this peculiar semiotic proliferation is that we have become accustomed to regarding exile as being either imposed on a person by a supra-individual authority or freely chosen by a person as a response to some situation with supra-individual implications. It has been understood that in both cases the motives for departure must transcend personal importance if the event is to qualify as exile. Whatever its convenience, this bold division has its difficulties. In this chapter I will submit that the neat and seemingly unproblematic division of exile into two modal classes of events (enforced and voluntary) needs to be revised. In addition to compulsory exile (banishment) on the one hand, and, voluntary exile (expatriation) on the other, the legal systems of some states have allowed for a third, intermediate model of exile. This form of exile, being neither entirely compulsory nor entirely voluntary, is based on ambiguity and non-definability of proportion between these two categories. The duress is not imposed by physical force, or for that matter juridical decision, but is encoded and decoded by an underlying consensus of all involved agents.

My case for this intermediate form of exile will be based on legal conventions and fictions of the late republican period in Ancient Rome but its implications will be obvious in many other contexts, including modern politics. I will first revisit Giorgio Agamben's analyses of the Roman legal system and, more specifically, his interpretation of *homo sacer*. This concept will be tested against different models of exile that co-existed in the political history of Rome and consequently I will envisage an alternative paradigm, specifically based on what I call the implied, or indirect, exile. I will then present two case studies of implied exile: the convention of *aquae et ignis interdictio* in criminal law, and *deiectio* in property lawsuits. This comparative look into practices of indirect expulsion in the late period of the Roman Republic will reveal how the contesting discourses in two unrelated cases of eviction evolved around the same rhetorical figure, metonymy. In the absence of overt physical force, this figure communicated duress by means of displacement on multiple semantic levels. Furthermore, the subsequent claims for restitution which arose from such departure addressed precisely this metonymical nexus as an instance of unlawful use of force.

Exposition of the Problem: Agamben's Theory of *Homo Sacer* and Exile

The notion of a form of ban as the establishing function of sovereign power appears especially forcefully in Agamben's theory of *homo sacer*, that well-known albeit curiously elusive religious relict in the early history of Roman law. After a long period of virtual disuse, *homo sacer* re-emerged as a syncretistic fusion of several strands of twentieth-century political philosophy. On the one side, Agamben expands Carl Schmitt's classical argument about sovereignty as an unqualified right to decide on the state of exception and proposes that each paradigm needs to delineate its zone of exception in order to legitimize its paradigmatic status.[1] On the other side, Agamben also takes up Walter Benjamin's cryptic concept of mythic violence as 'bloody power over mere life for its own sake' and elaborates with historical examples to reveal its political implications.[2] These two propositions are developed via a properly Foucauldian genealogical approach that looks back to antiquity. The Roman state, by Agamben's account, came into being through a successful definition of those who were deemed to be beyond the pale yet within the reach of law. *Homo sacer* represented an established social figure of bare life that could be destroyed with impunity but could not be sacrificed to the gods. This double stipulation signalled *homo sacer*'s exclusion both from *ius humanum* and from *ius divinum*. Agamben's examples stretch across distant sociopolitical fields and historical periods: *homo sacer* emerges in the guise of the Germanic wolf-man and a Jewish camp inmate to no less extent than in patriarchal family organization and in the funeral rites of the late Roman period.

It is interesting, however, that exile does not feature very prominently, if at all, in this list. The inconspicuousness of historical exile in Agamben's theory is all the more surprising when one considers the extent to which his concept of inclusive exclusion relies on the metaphor of banishment: '*In the city, the banishment of sacred life is more internal than every interiority and more external than every extraneousness. The banishment of sacred life is the sovereign nomos that conditions every rule, the originary spatialization that governs and makes possible every localization and every territorialisation.*'[3] Exile occasionally emerges in the work of Agamben's interpreters, too, albeit in a less emphatic form. Demoted from the privileged position of the metaphor of sovereign ban, exile becomes its sub-class, considered alongside phenomena as diverse as concentration camps, outlawry and the treatment of coma: 'Exiled bare life, like the life of the camp inhabitant, the refugee, the bandit, or the overcomatose body of Karen Quinlan, is without a voice in public affairs and may be killed or kept alive without ceremony and without criminality.'[4]

These quotations are not merely an illustration of the free-floating status of exile in the discourses on sacred life; they also pose deeper questions about the compatibility of the two categories. As a metaphor, exile may well serve the rhetoric of Agamben's theory; as an actual practice, however, it emerges as its critical touchstone. If the essence of sovereignty is constantly to re-create bare life and exercise its power over it, to which extent can exile fulfil this function?

Notwithstanding its complexity, Agamben's theory ties in closely with a distinct and longstanding view of exile that has marked Western political thought from the Old Testament to Rousseau. This tradition sees the political centre as the key agent in the process of enforced displacement and the person in exile as a passive recipient of the measure. More specifically, Agamben considers the ban as a unilaterally determined event in which a nascent sovereign power carves the interstitial space between legal remits in order to create, and dispose of, bare life. The actual, spatial removal of the bearer of bare life is simply a consequence of his or her originary displacement within the symbolical order. One may, thus, expect his *homo sacer* to find fairly successful application in all those types of exile where the displaced person remains under some degree of control of his or her home state. Athenian ostracism is a good case in point. Wherever internal political conflicts threatened to undermine the democratic order of the city-polis, one of the contenders, chosen by popular vote, was required to leave the city for the period of ten years. Likewise, in the Roman Empire, transgressors were relegated from Rome to a distant place within imperial jurisdiction. Colonial powers like England and France to the West as well as Russia and China to the East, established their own topographies of internal exile. In all of these cases, the initial political relation between the banishing power and the exiled was preserved and perpetuated.

Yet, some instances of exile do not fit into this pattern. It is far from clear that a typical Roman exile of the Republican period or for that matter an uprooted refugee from a twentieth-century dictatorial regime would be good candidates for *homo sacer*. Displacement from a polity (expulsion) differs in motives and impact from internment within the confines of that polity (concentration camps). Agamben himself indirectly recognizes this difference by bringing up Pompeius Festus's etymological distinction between what is *extrarius* ('whoever is outside the hearth, the sacrament, and the law') and extraneous ('whoever is from another land').[5] In the case of internal displacement, localization is determined at all times by the need for the sovereign capture of life. In expulsion, however, exclusion assumes a radical form: the authority over bare life is renounced and surrendered to another sovereign power. If this latter, extraneous type of exile is an example of *homo sacer*, by what means does the inclusion take place? If, however, such exile is an exception from *homo sacer* — that is an exception to an exception — why is it so common in originary myths and political practice?

To be sure, Agamben does make a brief and passing mention of *aquae et ignis interdictio*, a convention which allowed suspected transgressors to leave Rome before verdict, and he quotes Cicero's observation that this was by no means a penalty. Adopting a time-honoured view of the legal historian James Strachan-Davidson, Agamben finds no difficulty in claiming that 'the life of the exile or the *aquae et ignis interdictus* borders on the life of *homo sacer*'.[6] Meanwhile, he does not explain how exactly this borderline measure is supposed to reflect a sovereign ban. For one thing, not only is this type of exile extraneous, it is also enacted through a cunning rhetorical interaction. No official order to leave is served and no obvious means of force are employed to hasten departure. Instead, an appropriate framework is created for that person to decide to leave of their own accord. Once they have done so, the second stage of the process implies an *ex post facto* exclusion of that person from the state by means of an official decree in which the decision to leave one's homeland serves as a legal and ethical pretext for the revocation of citizenship. One goal of this chapter will be to start from Agamben's indication about *aquae et ignis interdictio* and follow it through to its implications. Consequently, the validity of the *homo sacer* paradigm will either be confirmed in the context of implied exile or otherwise an alternative model will emerge.

My main interest will not be in the immediate political context of indirect expulsions in the Roman Republic but in implied exile, the rhetorical configuration that enabled those expulsions. As we have already seen, Agamben argued for an interstitial position of *homo sacer*: this figure is extracted both from human and from divine order but still defines the limits of the two. By analogy, the challenge of my argument will be to establish whether indirect exile is confined to the field of political action that involves state institutions and individuals or whether it is also present in other forms of social intercourse, such as transactions between individuals in private law. If the latter were the case, the way would be open for the exploration of implied exile as a rhetorical paradigm in its own right. In practical terms, our interest should be in how legal and practical discourses of different agents are transformed into an individual sense of duress and fear, and how such anxieties are subsequently transformed into a departure that paradoxically appears as both 'forced' and 'voluntary'. To be sure, in most studies, citizenship regulations and real property laws have been addressed as separate remits, which they certainly are. However, the ineluctable conflict over the entitlement to stay in a place and one's removal from that place is apparent in both spheres and therefore calls for a cross-field examination.

Implied Exile 1: *Aquae et ignis interdictio*

An early and striking example of implied exile, the custom of *aquae et ignis interdictio*, was attested in the Roman Republic from the late third to the late first century BCE.[7] Nowadays, a great deal of our knowledge about the origins and course of *aquae et ignis interdictio* remains speculative. To begin with, Roman jurisprudence has left us no topical treatise on this subject. Furthermore, the sketchy narratives and references in the extant sources are marked by interspersed lacunae that have to be reconstructed and by apparent contradictions that have to be resolved. Finally, there is a significant possibility that the observed practice itself was not always consistent, being subject to the vagaries of the political moment as much as to the deceptive fixities of legal frameworks. Nevertheless, in recent philological and legal studies, the key stages of the process have emerged and seem to be beyond reasonable doubt.

Of all contemporaneous sources, the two most significant statements on the indirect nature of exile in the Roman Republic come from Polybius and Cicero. In Book 6 of his *Histories*, Polybius provides a detailed account of the tripartite constitutional arrangement of the Roman Republic, consisting of magistrates elected or nominated by the Senate, the people, and the consuls. In discussing the specific judiciary powers of the plebeian assemblies he makes a passing remark that would prove to be an important account of exile:

> κρίνει μὲν οὖν ὁ δῆμος καὶ διαφόρου πολλάκις, ὅταν ἀξιόχρεων ᾖ τὸ τίμημα τῆς ἀδικίας, καὶ μάλιστα τοὺς τὰς ἐπιφανεῖς ἐσχηκότας ἀρχάς. θανάτου δὲ κρίνει μόνος. καὶ γίνεταί τι περὶ ταύτην τὴν χρείαν παρ' αὐτοῖς ἄξιον ἐπαίνου καὶ μνήμης. τοῖς γὰρ θανάτου κρινομένοις, ἐπὰν καταδικάζωνται, δίδωσι τὴν ἐξουσίαν τὸ παρ' αὐτοῖς ἔθος ἀπαλλάττεσθαι φανερῶς, κἂν ἔτι μία λείπηται φυλὴ τῶν ἐπικυρουσῶν τὴν κρίσιν ἀψηφοφόρητος, ἑκούσιον ἑαυτοῦ καταγνόντα φυγαδείαν. ἔστι δ' ἀσφάλεια τοῖς φεύγουσιν ἔν τε τῇ Νεαπολιτῶν καὶ Πραινεστίνων, ἔτι δὲ Τιβουρίνων πόλει, καὶ ταῖς ἄλλαις, πρὸς ἃς ἔχουσιν ὅρκια.

> [It is by the people, then, in many cases that offences punishable by a fine are tried when the accused have held the highest office; and they are the only court which may try on capital charges. As regards the latter they have a practice which is praiseworthy and should be mentioned. Their usage allows those on trial for their lives when found guilty liberty to depart openly, thus inflicting voluntary exile on themselves, if even only one of the tribes that pronounce the verdict has not yet voted. Such exiles enjoy safety in the territories of Naples, Praeneste, Tibur, and other *civitates foederatae*.][8]

Polybius's account entails two salient points. Firstly, since such departures had to occur before the completion of the popular vote, they appear to have been treated as exceptional legal events that annulled any ongoing proceedings. Secondly, Polybius suggests that the legal mechanisms that open up the possibility of voluntary exile rest entirely with popular jurisdiction, rather than with centumviral courts or with court juries. However, the latter point should not be pushed too far. The unrestricted vote does not imply that there is an intrinsic link between the people and banishment of individuals, such as the one attested in the Athenian institution of ostracism. Rather, the popular institutional setting of voluntary exile arises from the simple fact that it is meant to replace capital punishment. Namely, all cases involving the life and death of a Roman citizen were within the remit of the Roman people and the plebeian assembly, and it is likely that decisions on exile were carried forward in the same institutional setting.

An important supplement to Polybius's historiographical account is found in Cicero's speech *Pro Aulus Caecina Oratio* [*In Defence of Aulus Caecina*] from 69 BCE. That year, Cicero advocated the cause of his friend and client Aulus Caecina in a property dispute and in his speech to the jury court he passed the following comment on exile:

> Exsilium enim non supplicium est sed perfugium portusque supplicii. Nam qui volunt poenam aliquam subterfugere aut calamitatem, eo solum vertunt, hoc est, sedem ac locum mutant. Itaque nulla in lege nostra reperietur, ut apud ceteras civitates, maleficium ullum exsilio esse mulctatum; sed quum homines vincula, neces ignominiasque vitant, quae sunt legibus constitutae, confugiunt quasi ad aram in exsilium. Qui si in civitate legis vim subire vellent, non prius civitatem quam vitam amitterent: quia nolunt, non adimitur iis civitas, sed ab iis relinquitur atque deponitur.

[Exile is not a punishment: it is a harbour of refuge from punishment. Because people want to escape from some punishment or catastrophe, they 'quit their native soil', that is to say, they change the place of their abode. And so, in no statute of ours will you find, as you will in the laws of other states, that exile figures as the punishment for any crime at all; but people seeking to avoid imprisonment, death, or dishonour, when imposed upon them by our laws, take refuge in exile as in a sanctuary. Should they consent to remain within the citizen body and submit to the rigour of the law, they would lose their citizenship only with their lives. But they do not consent; and therefore their citizenship is not taken from them, but is by them abandoned and discarded.][9]

As expected, Cicero does not mention as safe havens the cities of Naples, Tibur, and Praeneste, that became part of the Roman territory after the Social War (91–88 BCE). Apart from this variation, however, there is a significant degree of agreement between the two accounts in that both Polybius and Cicero stress the circumventive nature of departure and its retroactive assessment as exile. However, there is also a certain difference in emphasis. While sidestepping the issue of institutional framework, Cicero sheds light on an aspect of *aquae et ignis interdictio* that eluded Polybius: the consequences of one's exile to his or her citizenship status. Cicero's underlying assumption is that the state is authorized unilaterally to deprive one of citizenship (*capitis diminutio media*) only as a corollary of that person's earlier loss of liberty (*capitis diminutio maxima*) as, for instance, in the case of the approved sale of army deserters into slavery. In the case of voluntary exile, however, the citizenship is not taken by the state but relinquished by the exile himself; the decree of *aquae et ignis interdictio* thus comes as a recognition of that fact.

In addition to Polybius's and Cicero's reports, which encapsulate the phenomenon in its legal and rhetorical principle, there are other historiographical and juristic sources which refer to specific cases of *aquae et ignis interdictio*. These references, when taken together and considered within the general constitutional context of the Roman Republic in the second and first centuries BCE, enable us to reconstruct the process in its main stages. The legal procedures of the Roman Republic envisaged two different pathways for lawsuits. While offences against private interests were often tried within the regular *legis actio*, with the state acting as a minimal mediator, suspected crimes pertaining to the state interests were tried *ex officio*.[10] The latter category implicated mainly Romans of higher social standing who pursued political careers and held public offices particularly vulnerable to the charges of the abuse of power. If such charges were capital, these individuals were customarily left an escape route to avoid the final consequences of the legal process against them. Unless they were incarcerated, which was very rare, they could leave Rome at any moment before the end of their trial and settle down in one of the allied city states. These cities, three of them mentioned by Polybius, were on good terms with Rome but not under direct Roman jurisdiction. In some cases the departure occurred even before the beginning of the trial, at the moment when promulgation of a new law would leave the official exposed to possible charges, and the trial would then not take place. In other cases the departure could be deferred and brought dangerously close to the execution of the penalty: the defendants tried by *iudicium publicum* could even wait for their verdict to be passed before leaving the city for good. Upon their departure, the tribune would formally propose to the plebeian assembly that the decree of *aquae et ignis interdictio* be passed in order to prevent the person under *quaestio* from ever returning to Rome. Such a decree of interdiction effectively banned the person from the polity but it also contained certain concomitant provisions against the defendant's interests. Some of these provisions were fixed (forfeiture of property, a clause preventing the exile's restoration by any legal body in the future), whereas the others were facultative (demolition of residential premises, imposition of a minimum distance for the exile's new domicile). On the other hand, with the ratification of the decree by a senior magistrate, the *interdictus* would be spared any further pursuit — be it legal or physical — and left to his own devices in a new domicile. Unless he decided to return to Rome, where he risked death, his safety was not under threat. In such circumstances, the exile's typical course of action was to assume the citizenship of the host state, a step which would legally cancel his Roman citizenship.[11]

An important question arises from this outline: how clear was the permission or, more precisely, the incentive for the accused to go? We should talk of a range of methods and intensities of duress rather than a specific form and degree. At one end of that spectrum, communication could be extremely subdued and ambiguous and much of the assessment regarding time and circumstances of a possible exile would be down to the accused. At the other end of the spectrum, there were instances of overt encouragement, often accompanied by informal threats as the trial wore on. For instance, much of Cicero's speech *In Catilinam I*, delivered in the Senate to debunk a conspiracy against his consular power, was dedicated to convincing the ringleader, not without irony, that now that his ploy has been foiled he should go into exile of his own rather than continue to inconvenience the republic by forcing it formally to take his life. On both ends of the spectrum, *aquae et ignis interdictio* is not a *poena legis* but a paralegal communicative practice.

Another important problem is highlighted by the historical continuity of *aquae et ignis interdictio* as a convention and its link with other, more explicit forms of expulsion, inasmuch as these were in force in the Roman Republic. The late republican and imperial juristic sources report a number of cases, most of which occurred in the first half of the first century BCE, where *exilium* seems to have become a mandatory punishment (*poena legis*) for certain statutory crimes.[12] The exact chronology of this shift remains undecided. In different studies, the introduction of statutory exile is dated to some point between Sulla's establishment of permanent criminal courts (*quaestiones perpetuae*) in 82/81 BCE[13] and Caesar's and Augustus's *leges Iuliae* in 45 BCE and 18 BCE.[14] In some cases of exile during that period, the wording is equally ambiguous. In 63 BCE, six years after his description of exile, Cicero himself introduced a law against electoral bribery (*lex Tullia de ambitu*) which metes out expulsion as a punishment without, however, explicitly using the expression of *aquae et ignis interdictio*. Whatever the date and terminology of this newly established form of expulsion, it seems that evasive and statutory exile continued to co-exist well into the second half of the first century BCE, when the latter entirely replaced the former. Furthermore, it is likely that in some cases, where *aquae et ignis interdictio* was intended as a statutory punishment, the defendants actually decided to leave

Rome before the end (and possibly even before the beginning) of their trial. Upon their departure, the decree of *aquae et ignis interdictio* may have been passed not as a punishment, but according to the default procedure as described above.

Even if we reconstruct the sequence of actions in this implied exile and its link with direct banishment, some lingering questions remain unresolved. Despite the overarching consistency of Polybius's and Cicero's accounts, the metaphors they use to describe the punitive aspects of *aquae et ignis interdictio* have entirely different implications. Polybius, on the one hand, suggests that through this convention the state hands over its right of the administration of punishment to the defendants, who respond by 'inflicting voluntary exile on themselves'. On the other hand, Cicero has no doubt that *aquae et ignis interdictio* does not represent a penalty but 'a harbour of refuge from punishment'. If the ethical appraisals of *aquae et ignis interdictio* are diametrically opposed, it seems dubious that there could have been any consensus over the principle of justice and/or the political goal behind this process.

New questions arise if we assume that during the second and the first century BCE, *aquae et ignis interdictio* was a legal convention in its own right rather than a transitional stage leading to direct expulsion as a statutory punishment. What is the possible rationale for having transgressors effectively excluded from the country's legal system rather than dealing with them within that system? And, just as importantly, why would the defendants be allowed to exclude themselves indirectly from the system through exile rather than be excluded through a direct intervention of the state ordaining exile as a penal measure?

In classical studies, there have been two major attempts at addressing these questions; both were based on linking *aquae et ignis interdictio* to the wider political and cultural context of the Roman Republic. The first one is advocated by Richard Bauman who, in his pioneering study of human rights in Rome, states that the roots of *aquae et ignis interdictio* are not legal but philosophical. Exile is said to have derived from the concept of *humanitas*, the Roman amalgamate of the Greek ideas of human kindness (φιλανθρωπία) and education (παιδεία). According to Bauman, in the second century BCE, the ideology of mutual civility in human interactions gained ground in Roman political thought through the influence of the Stoic philosopher Panaetius and the historian Polybius, both of whom were personal friends of the powerful consul Scipio Aemilianus Africanus.[15] Bauman sees the replacement of capital punishment by indirect exile as a momentous development in the institutionalization of that ideology: '*Humanitas Romana* was the source of one of Rome's greatest contributions to human rights, in the shape of the right of voluntary exile'.[16]

In his book *A History of Exile in the Roman Republic*, one of few studies focusing on exile in the Republican period, Gordon Kelly offers an alternative explanation by arguing that *exilium* initially arose from a distinctively Roman Republican concept of political life, 'an outgrowth of the civic ideal of *concordia*'. To Kelly, exile is bilateral action aimed at maintaining the stability of the state above and beyond any factional conflict:

> To this end, *exilium* performed a very specific function: it acted as a 'safety valve' to prevent public disputes among elite citizens from turning into armed

> civil conflict. [...] Exile allowed the losers in political struggles to be perma-
> nently removed from the state without disturbing the overall social fabric.
> Without the safety of exile, politically active Romans who were faced with
> capital punishment would have been disposed to 'fight to the finish' and to turn
> to open violence to save their lives.[17]

For present purposes, there is no need to adjudicate between the two arguments. Even though Bauman's and Kelly's theories present valid historical insights into the shaping force of Roman legal thinking, they effectively deal only with the first of the two open questions, the political and ethical value of exile in relation to other penalties in Roman criminal proceedings. However, the likely philanthropic concerns and then political expediency of a defendant's removal instead of physical destruction still do not account for why exile should be declared retroactively, after departure.

If historians' opinions on *aquae et ignis interdictio* remain so divided, can Agamben's theory of *homo sacer* shed any light on the political rationale of this practice? As we have already argued, extraneous exile is not the primary field of Agamben's interest and the validity of his theoretical model in this specific context has yet to be ascertained. To be sure, some aspects of *aquae et ignis interdictio* seem to epitomize the mechanism of the sovereign exception to no less extent than other examples Agamben cites. One's right to leave Rome during criminal proceedings may conceal political encouragement to do so: exile is tantamount to a subtraction from the legal system of the Republic. Furthermore, it can also be argued that the impending death penalty still 'applies to the exceptional case in no longer applying and in withdrawing from it'.[18] For denial of water and fire as well as the licence to kill the exile should he or she ever return may be understood as unmistakable attributes of *homo sacer*. The privation of two basic amenities of sacrificial and ablution rituals signals exclusion from *ius divinum* and the obliteration of the exile's life without implication of homicide excludes him or her from the realm of *ius humanum*.

However, pushing the analogy between *homo sacer* and *aquae et ignis interdictus* further than this apparent resemblance would mean stretching Agamben's concept beyond its heuristic limit. For each point of similarity between the two types of ban, there is a differential caveat. The sovereign exception is instituted and the exile is subtracted from the regular penal law; however, in a centrifugal turn, the exile is also displaced from the sovereign power's realm of influence and surrendered to another sovereign realm. The ritual ban and physical death are imposed on the exile and thereby his bare life is framed; yet, this violence is purely rhetorical since it is conditional on his return to Rome which, as a matter of course, is not expected to happen. Thus, if we maintain Agamben's premise that *sacratio* is driven by inclusive exclusion, we are compelled to recognize that in the case of implied exile, which is heteronomous and retrospective, the inclusion is either abortive or not intended at all. The earlier option would leave us with *homo sacer* as the best available mould for shaping our understanding of *aquae et ignis interdictio*; the latter would go against Agamben's cue and necessitate a wholly different approach to the link between politics and force.

Implied Exile 2: *Deiectio* in the Caecina Case

In order to address the inherent ambiguity of exile, I will look more closely at the Caecina speech, the underlying context of Cicero's statement which has been disregarded by Agamben as well as by historians of exile. Albeit patently dealing with a private property dispute under provisions of civil procedure, this case has significant implications for our perception of exile, since its essential argument relies on the assumption of a rhetorical and bilateral quality of expulsion.

As the Caecina speech falls into the group of relatively straightforward cases of Cicero, I will only briefly reconstruct its main points as they transpire in his discourse. Namely, upon her death, a woman by the name of Caesennia leaves 23/24 of her property in her will to her second husband, Aulus Caecina, and another 1/72 to her acquaintance and legal proxy, Aebutius, as an acknowledgment of his help. This leaves Caecina in *de facto* possession of the largest part of the legacy including the disputed estate. However, Aebutius, dissatisfied with his share, questions Caecina's ownership of an estate at the vicinity of Tarquinii by making two claims: a) Caecina cannot be Caesennia's heir for statutory reasons as he is a Volaterran, and the Volaterrans, due to restrictions on their citizenship status, have only limited right to inheritance; and b) Caecina cannot inherit the said estate in particular because it is not owned by Caesennia but by Aebutius who allegedly bought it at an auction and merely allowed her to enjoy her life interest in it, as specified by the will of her first husband, M. Fulcinius.

In such cases, the way to bring the contesting claims to legal resolution would require one side assuming the capacity of plaintiff and agreeing to be formally ejected from the property by the defendant and then requesting that the praetor issue an injunction order (*interdictum*). It is important to stress that such evictions were entirely consensual: the contesting sides merely enacted their dispute in the presence of witnesses and thereby transformed it into legal discourse of litigation (*litis contestatio*). Once the contesting claims were made clear and the legal course for the process determined, the praetor would appoint a judge (*iudex*) or a panel (*recuperatores*) who were acceptable to both sides and whose duty it was to examine the case, weigh the arguments of both sides, and render a final verdict.

However, what ensued in Caecina's case represents a significant detour from the regular judicial course of action. In the initial arrangement, Caecina agreed to assume the role of evictee, who is denied possession and has to summon the court to attest his right. Aebutius, consequently, agreed to assume the role of defender who protects his property from the intruder. However, when on the agreed date Caecina and his witnesses approached the disputed estate in order to get formally ejected, they were prevented from entering by a group of men summoned by Aebutius and instructed by his friend Aulus Terentius. As soon as Caecina's group approached the vicinity of the estate, these men started throwing stones and spears at them. At first, Caecina considered resistance, but quickly changed his mind and fled from the vicinity of the estate without entering it.

Facing the stalemate, Caecina was left with no other recourse except to apply to the duty praetor to endorse a different form of process which would lead to an injunction (*interdictum*) ordering Aebutius to restore him to the place from which he was forcefully expelled (*de vi armata*). The text of that injunction, obviously aimed at discouraging armed conflicts in the settling of private property disputes, stipulates that the restitution will be considered if and only if the expulsion can be confirmed to have involved four specific circumstances. Namely, the plaintiff should be restored to the place whence a) 'you, or your household, or your agent' b) 'by force' c) 'through men collected together' or 'armed' d) (were) 'ejected'.[19] Of these four circumstances, (a) and (c) are beyond dispute in the Caecina case because they are duly recognized by Aebutius and his witnesses. However, they denied that their actions involved the elements (b) and (d), arguing that they could not have ejected Caecina because they would have not let him enter in the first place and that no force was used because there was no armed or physical contact with Caecina and his witnesses. Thus, Caecina's legal action was countered by Aebutius's claim that he had restored, meaning that he considers the matter to have been already settled.

At this stage, Caecina engaged Cicero to bring his case to the attention of a board of recuperators, a form of jury usually appointed by *praetor peregrinus* in all cases involving non-citizens or citizens with restricted status. The case need not necessarily have been without precedent in the juridical history of Rome, but Cicero does not mention any such analogies and the essential argument should be ascribed to him. The most striking feature of his speech is that his emphasis is not on establishing Caecina's ownership of the disputed estate on the strength of Caesennia's will. We can conjecture that Cicero may have reckoned that the loss of documents would prevent him from presenting a sufficiently convincing argument in favour of Caecina's ownership. An even more pressing reason for Cicero's abandonment of the property dispute is to be found in the fact that the injunction *de vi armata* is not so much about the ownership itself but about the prohibition of the use of force in bringing ownership disputes to juridical attention. Cicero's key rhetorical target is, thus, to demonstrate that Aebutius's treatment of Caecina is a case of violent expulsion by all four terms of the injunction, and particularly by the two disputed ones. This strategy was devised in view of the immediate goal of having Caecina restored to the estate but, as we will see shortly, it also presented Cicero with an opportunity to address some broad questions of political theory concerning the nature of force and eviction.

Let us now draw some theoretical implications of this case. Caecina and Aebutius were engaged in a wager of law, a standard form of legal contest in which norms and proceedings are clearly stated. The wager is conditional upon a specific kind of coordination which is cooperative and at the same time agonistic: Caecina will be allowed to cross the threshold of the estate and, in turn, will allow himself to be banished from it. However, Aebutius prevents him from entering the estate and thus forecloses the wager. Here again we establish a tentative analogy with Agamben's theory of the political; after all, analogical thought is often the driving force of his argument. Caecina's situation bears a remarkable similarity to the state of exception which Agamben links back to senatorial *iustitium*, 'when the law stands still, just as [the sun does] in solstice'.[20] Just as in *senatus consultum ultimum*, when the acting consul is summoned and authorized to defend the Republic, Aebutius felt that the estate was endangered and that extraordinary measures should be taken to ensure that no intruder would take control of it.

Yet, this initial point of similarity is also where the analogy between Cicero and Agamben ends. In Caecina's approach and retreat, the law is in force at all times; however, it is neither applied, as in the regular state of affairs, nor suspended, as in the *senatus consultum ultimum*. What Aebutius creates on the disputed estate is not 'a space devoid of law, a zone of anomie in which all legal determinations [...] are deactivated'.[21] On the contrary, the law is asserted in its effect; this occurs through the change of place rather than within a confined space. By the same token, Aebutius's sovereign privilege would not consist in extricating Caecina from the aegis of law, but in enforcing his abandonment of that protection. Aebutius's plan for an all-out exclusion of Caecina is not a distorted version of *sacratio*, but a stratagem in its own right.

Paradoxical though it may appear, with direct exile both the expeller and the expelled become recognized by law and step into its domain. I believe I am not mistaken in assuming that it is this type of recognition that Agamben could qualify as inclusive exclusion. However, in implied exile, one side leaves the realm of law without being banished and all grounds for inclusion are cut off. Even if we allow for the assumption that implied exile may have originated in the ancient custom of *sacratio*, it must be admitted that in time it evolved into something different from both the historical practice and Agamben's interpretation of that practice. At this point, then, we need to part company with Agamben's mechanisms of exception and look for other explanatory models.

Force as Rhetoric vs. Rhetoric as Force: Cicero's Counter–Metonymic Argument on Implied Exile

What, if anything, do the two models of indirect expulsion have in common? To be sure, Cicero did not see any apparent analogical link between the injunction dealing with expulsion *de vi armata* and *aquae et ignis interdictio*. He mentions the latter only towards the end of his speech and tangentially, in order to refute Aebutius's claim that Caecina is a Vollaterran, and that as such he has no right to inheritance. Cicero's argument is that, once acquired, citizenship comprises a set of inalienable rights that cannot be taken away through exile nor disputed by claims that naturalized citizens such as Vollaterrans are not full citizens.

However, the fact that Cicero did not argue for a link between the two cases does not imply that no such analogy can be established. Instead of taking the standard deductive approach that separates forms of criminal suits from civil suits, I propose that we tentatively think in terms of how exile alerts us to the actual analogies between the two realms. Granted, a comparative enquiry of the kind I propose is not an uncharted field in legal history; at least, it has not been so since Strachan-Davidson's hypothesis on the symmetrical devolution of juridical power in public and private suits.[22] The starting point for comparison, however, will not be the procedural arrangement of magistrates but their shared strategic use of implied exile in both realms. In Roman jurisdiction, property law represents a set of legal norms and practices which regulate the right of a qualifying person to use a piece of land, including his/her unrestricted right to access and stay on that land. Roman citizenship law represents, by analogy, a set of legal norms and practices which regulate a qualifying person's status and functional membership in the Roman Republic, including the unrestricted right to access and stay within the territory of that republic. To be sure, in both of these legal contexts, non-qualifying individuals may also be entitled to access, but their stay is restricted and they are subject to removal.

Furthermore, there is a clear symmetry between the respective demands made upon exiles by the plebeian assembly and upon Caecina by Aebutius. Both requests display the same disjunctive pattern that would underlie Austin's definition law some nineteen centuries later: command backed by threats.[23] The decree of *aquae et ignis interdictio* necessitated keeping clear of Rome and, by a similar token, Aebutius forewarned Caecina to keep clear of the disputed property. In the case where the duties arising from the orders were broken, the ultimate punishment would be meted out on the trespasser. Significantly, these commands with concomitant threats were not articulated as a requirement to leave, and there was no direct link with banishment, be it punitive or procedural. Caecina and his witnesses were expelled from an estate that was adjacent to the one which they wanted to access. In *aquae et ignis interdictio*, a parallel development is observable: the decree declared that if the *interdictus* is seen returning anywhere within the fixed distance of four hundred miles, anyone is authorized to mete out the death penalty.[24] In other words, one is declared interdicted not only from the city of Rome and its vicinity but also from the adjacent areas in Italy.[25] This enmity was noticed by Kelly who correctly remarks that 'a proscribed man was considered a public enemy (*hostis*), and though he may flee from Roman territory, he was never afforded a safe resting place'.[26]

This analogy between property law and citizenship law is not to be taken too far: its implications are heuristic rather than structural. The key difference, of course, is between the two types of admittance claims: the reserved, personalized one in the case of possession (and usufruct) and the distributive, shared one in the case of civil membership. Another important opposition is in heterogeneous types of legal actions aimed at addressing contentious aspects of the status. In the case of ownership, the remedy consisted in a routine vindication through the plaintiff's summoning of the defendant to the court (*rei vindicatio*). In the case of citizenship, legislative decisions were voted out in the plebeian assembly and such motions were conditional upon a wider political support for the exile's cause.

Another proviso concerns the concept of force. In his dialogue *De legibus* [*The Laws*], written in the late 50s, Cicero warned against the dangers implicit in the use of unlawful force:

> nihil est enim exitiosius civitatibus, nihil tam contrarium iuri ac legibus, nihil minus et civile est et humanum quam composita et constituta re publica quicquam agi per vim

> [Nothing is more destructive to governments, nothing is in such complete opposition to justice and law, nothing is less suitable for civilized men, than the use of violence in a State which has a fixed and definite constitution][27]

Yet, what exactly qualified as legitimate law-preserving force was open to dispute.

Namely, the force emanating from the law was unstable in that it was applied unevenly in different spheres of legal practice of the Roman Republic. On the one hand, the legal norms of the first century BCE routinely envisaged the use of force in corporal punishments such as flogging and in capital punishment. On the other hand, they discouraged, or at least treated as problematic, any use of force in ensuring a citizen's departure from Rome, or for that matter from a piece of disputed land. In addition to this, the act of banishment had different implications in property law and civil law respectively. The legal system allowed and even encouraged procedural eviction in the realm of the law of property but it apparently prohibited, or at least discouraged, direct banishment by decree in citizenship law.

It was Aebutius's exploitation of the intrinsic ambiguity of eviction that prompted Cicero to make a case for Caecina's restitution on the grounds of expulsion by force. Even more importantly, Aebutius's manoeuvre enabled Cicero to articulate some broader assertions about the nature of exile. Namely, in order to win the case for Caecina, he had to argue that eviction and force are not substantive but rhetorically encoded phenomena.

In the first place, Cicero severs the conventional link between use of force and physical contact with its target by arguing that the latter is not indispensable for the former. In other words, for force to be employed, Aebutius need not hit and injure Caecina with spears and stones, or for that matter exert any direct physical pressure to remove him from the contested estate. All it takes is to deploy instruments of force in a way that suggests that they might be used to inflict pain and discomfort or, alternatively, to present a threat to the same effect by mere bodily posture. Thus, according to Cicero, the real touchstone for the presence of force in any specific situation is the extent to which it removes an individual from his habitual state of mind:

> Etenim, recuperatores, non ea sola vis est quae ad corpus nostrum vitamque pervenit, sed etiam multo maior ea, quae periculo mortis iniecto formidine animum perterritum loco saepe et certo de statu demovet.

> [In truth, gentlemen, force which touches our persons or our lives is not the only form of force: much more serious is the force which removes a man from a definite position or situation by exposing him to the danger of death and striking terror into his mind.][28]

It is impossible to overlook how far-reaching the implications of this argument are. Cicero effectively detaches the issue of force from the realm of verifiable and quantifiable impact on the objects and bodies of the perceptible world and transfers it into the realm of subjective experience. To be sure, in both realms the performative aspect of force is related to a form of reluctant displacement, but in the latter case the removal is a figurative rather than spatial category. In the physical sense the use of force effectively achieves expulsion by prompting a person to leave a place where he or she is exposed to existential threat or pain; in the psychological sense the force expels one from a state of composure into a state of fear and agitation. Cicero makes the vital claim that it is this subjective perception that matters in determining the presence and use of force. For if one held to the objective criterion only, a number of cases where force is conveyed by rhetorical means would pass unnoticed. Furthermore, the social impact of such objectivist focus would be even more pernicious, for the contending sides would be stimulated to go beyond the formal eviction and resolve their dispute by open conflict with unforeseeable consequences.[29]

The second component of Cicero's argument addresses the concept of eviction by revisiting its implied semantic content in law. In order to show that Caecina meets the set criteria for restitution, Cicero has to prove that it makes no substantial difference whether he had already crossed the boundaries of the estate, or was about to cross them when Aebutius expelled him. In both cases, the evictor's purpose is to ensure that the person claiming the right of access is not present within the estate, and it is consistent with the law that this purpose should be confirmed or refuted through a subsequent legal process:

> Quid hoc ab illo differt, ut ille cogatur restituere qui ingressum expulerit, ille qui ingredientem reppulerit non cogatur?
>
> [What difference is there between the two cases such as to enforce the restitution of a man who has been expelled after making entry but not to enforce that of a man who has been expelled as he was making entry?][30]

As in Cicero's previous link between the objective use and subjective perception of force, here, too, the demand for the equivalence of legal rights to restitution stems from the putative analogy of the two respective sets of circumstances. The difficulty with this latter parallel, however, is that it runs against the common semantic acceptation of the term *deiectus*, which is normally seen as the outbound movement implying a crossing of boundaries. In order to support his thesis that to eject a person can mean both to expel him *and* to withstand, Cicero has recourse to a complex semantic argument. He firstly argues that the etymological bearing of *deiectus* itself is already too restrictive for any sensible legal practice because it encompasses only the one who is thrown (*iectus*) downwards (*de*), from a higher to a lower surface.[31] Since the magistrates have already tacitly recognized the restrictive nature of the term *deiectus* by including cases of expulsion from all surfaces without regard to their level, there is no reason why it could not be expanded further to include other associated cases. The first situation to be included in this way, Cicero argues, is eviction by withstanding entrance. Here again, the rationale is linguistic: the standard text of legal injunction states *unde deiecisti* [whence you have ejected] and in the vernacular Latin the word *unde* 'utrumque declarat, ex quo loco et a quo loco' [covers two cases, both the place out of which and the place away from which I was driven].[32]

The two parts of Cicero's argument — on force and on expulsion — have their specific strengths and can be considered separately. However, since in practice force and expulsion are coextensive, Cicero's claims can also be integrated into single amalgamated assertions where the two terms predicate each other. Thus, force would comprise any threatening gesture which either compels us to leave or prevents us from reaching a place. And *vice versa*, it is possible to assert that anything constitutes expulsion that by application of force either compels our bodies to leave a place through physical pressure or displaces our minds from secure position through the induction of fear.

In addition to their empirical inseparability and logical fusibility, Cicero's claims on force and expulsion have yet another common feature: they are not based on a literal reading of the injunction but on rhetorical transfers that go beyond the text. The credo behind this discursive turn is made clear by Cicero: 'si in verbis ius constituamus, omnem utilitatem nos huius interdicti, dum versuti et callidi volumus esse, amissuros' [if we make Right dependent upon words, we shall be losing all benefit from it as long as we like to exercise our ingenuity and cunning].[33] Cicero considers the legal text as a trope that targets some core textual meaning, which itself covers a specific situation, but that also urges an exercise of rhetorical ingenuity and cunning to see to which other situations it should apply by the principle of figurative transfer.

In the case of Caecina's injunction, Cicero relies on the artifice of metonymy, the figure in which 'the mapping or connection between two things is within the same conceptual domain',[34] as distinct from metaphor, which involves connection of two things belonging to two different domains.[35] For to claim that the subjective perception of force, as signalled by the emotion of fear, precedes the manifest deployment of force is to make consequence (reaction) pass as cause (event). Likewise, to state that the place from which one tried to access another place is to be considered as equivalent to the target place itself is to make the former pass as the latter on the grounds of their spatial proximity. Both types of transfer were known in antiquity and epitomized by definitions and examples in a number of rhetorical compendia, including *Rhetorica ad Herennium*, which is now attributed to Cicero.[36] However, the pragmatic context of metonymy in the Caecina case is where Cicero's rhetorical practice steps beyond this theory. While in the conventional view the term B substitutes for the term A to ornament the style, 'in ornatu orationis',[37] Cicero applies metonymical transfer to Caecina's encounter for pragmatic goals. He aims to show that B (Aebutius's actions) is tantamount to A (the text of the injunction) and that neither of the two terms should have any legal supremacy over the other.

It stands to reason that what was decoded through metonymy must have been first encoded by someone as such. Had Aebutius opted to use force in the way prescribed by law, he would have allowed Caecina to cross the threshold of the disputed estate and then would have formally evicted him from it. Such a course of action would have inevitably made him liable to litigation where he would have had to make a case for his ownership of the estate and at the same time invalidate Caecina's case for reclaiming it. In other words, his adherence to the principle of legitimate (lawfully declared and applied) force would have indicated his commitment to whichever legal consequences might arise from that action. Instead, after some deliberation, Aebutius opted for a more circumventive, metonymic approach that enabled him to communicate force to Caecina while at the same time concealing it from any scrutiny of law. In every important aspect, Aebutius applied force by way of some form of displacement. The stones were thrown towards the estate *adjacent* to the disputed one, to the effect that Caecina did not even think of crossing the boundary; the vicious threats were uttered to make Caecina aware of what awaited him *if* he was found within the disputed estate; the armed men were said to have been under the formal command of Aebutius's *acquaintance* Aulus Terentius (not 'of his household'). None of these actions affected Caecina directly; yet the violent intention was conveyed to him by Aebutius in the guise of an enacted metonymic figure.

To be sure, metonymic reasoning is ubiquitous, but its use in law has some important implications. Here, Cicero's argument transcends the limits of his immediate juristic goal and delves deeply into the realm of political theory. It would be worth recalling that in his landmark essay, 'Violence and the Word', possibly the most lucid anatomy of legal violence, Robert Cover presented an embryonic theory of the juridical use of metonymy. Namely, he argues that interpretative deliberation and physical punishment are necessarily interlocked in a cooperative network, in which responsibility for violence is displaced from one actor to another. A judge's decision will always remain open for scrutiny by another judge or a panel of judges and any sentence will further involve other actors such as wardens, guards or doctors.[38] However, he also stresses that certain legal systems have been characterized by a special 'incapacity or unwillingness to ensure a strong, virtually certain link between judicial utterance and violent deed'.[39] In such cases, there may be a further displacement, one from executive authorities to informal groups, as is seen in the cases of lynching. True, Cover never mentions metonymy and instead prefers to talk of 'bonded interpretation'. Yet, even so, it is obvious that he identifies legal process as a set of relays in need of coordination and that he conceives of these displacements not as an anomaly but as an intrinsic feature of the law.

However, Cicero's argument in the Caecina case sheds light on another form of displacement that would be disregarded by Cover. Metonymic transfer need not involve only the magistrates — or for that matter accomplices — who decide on and commit legal violence. In cases where hesitation is particularly strong, it may also displace the penalty from its target, the alleged offender, and still retain punitive implications in the realm of the signified. By showing through two metonymic transfers that Caecina was expelled by force, Cicero suggested that force and expulsion themselves are rhetorical phenomena. In the injunctions regulating property contests as well as in criminal lawsuits, force need not find a way round the laws; it can also be applied through these laws and at the same time be concealed by them.

The importance of this turn emerges with especial clarity in the light of the polarized approaches to force in modern legal theory. Drawing on Plato, the foundationalist school in jurisprudence denounces any excursion into rhetoric as a form of force imposed on the pristine language of the law.[40] Legal theorists as different as H. L. A. Hart and Ronald Dworkin considered it fundamentally important to posit a settled field of reference, or at least a process, in which legal discourse would be regulated by certain interpretative strictures.[41] This anti-rhetorical claim was supported by the equally important foundational axiom that legitimate force is external and subservient to law rather than the other way round (as with illegitimate force). Individual acts of violence were seen as essentially different from coercive measures of law but also as a threat to the existence of legal system.[42] While the legal foundationalists committed themselves to the idea of a double divide separating law from force and from rhetoric, the relativist school denied the existence of any distinct borders between these realms. Stanley Fish thus frames force as an arbitrary imposition of coercion that is active both in acts of physical violence and in acts of legal interpretation: 'if it is the business of law to protect the individual from coercion that is random, unpredictable, and arbitrary, then the individual is no less at risk when he is at the mercy of an interpreting court than when he is at the mercy of an armed assailant.'[43] Fish's statement is taken up by Derrida, who in his essay 'Force of Law' linked force and interpretation: 'The very emergence of justice and law, the founding and justifying moment that institutes law implies a performative force, which is always an interpretative force [...] that in itself is neither just nor unjust and that no justice and no previous law with its founding anterior moment could guarantee or contradict or validate.'[44] For the anti-foundationalists, the distinction between legitimate and illegitimate force is thus itself a product of force. The interpretative barrier supposedly protecting objective meaning from rhetorical incursions is raised by rhetorical claims.

The value of Cicero's argument consists in his subtle and effective mediation between the two positions. To be sure, this mediation is not without its own contradictions. While attempting to prove that the figurative turn in legal interpretation is a form of force and that this is a good thing, Cicero falls back on the conventional notion of a settled, intended meaning behind every legal text.[45] In addition to this hermeneutic ambiguity, Cicero reserves for himself the discretion of using both edges of the rhetorical sword in his assessment of force in implied exile. On the one hand, he claims that the decree of *aquae et ignis interdictio* involves no force on the part of legal system, and merely acknowledges the status already chosen by the *interdictus*. On the other hand, he argues that Aebutius's foreclosure of the disputed estate, which differs from procedural eviction, is an obvious example of private violence threatening the foundations of law.

Yet, despite these ambiguities — or precisely through them — the argument of *Pro Caecina* transcends paradigmatic conceptualizations of force and rhetoric, and alerts us to the intrinsic connectedness of indirect expulsion and metonymy. On the one hand, as we have seen, the foundationalist model delineates an empire of law threatened by illegitimate violence coming from outside while the anti-foundationalist model, on the other hand, sees law as a realm created by an act of banishment, with performative force displacing contesting sources of coercion. In opposition to these models, the kind of force framed in *Pro Caecina* effectively prevents incursion, while at the same time disavowing implications of direct banishment. The metonymic force is not a sovereign power constituting the legal subject; it is what displaces the subject from the realm of accountability without itself being held accountable for that course of action.

Cross-Case Implications: Metonymical Strategies in Cicero's Exile 58–57 BCE

Up to this point we have argued that in the late Republican period the application of metonymic force resulted in parallel examples of implied exile both in criminal and in private law. In the last part of the argument, I will maintain that the metonymic force was not locked within these separate remits and that it effectively mediated between them. More specifically, a metonymic chain was created in which citizenship claims were displaced into the realm of property law and then into divine law. In arguing for this metalegal displacement, I will refer to a case that involves elements of indirect expulsion from private property as well as from state territory.

In 58 BCE, eleven years after his speech for Caecina, Cicero was himself subjected to indirect expulsion. The story of his exile is so well known that one need not recapitulate it beyond its main points. The charge against Cicero was not related to ongoing political matters, but harked back to his role as consul in crushing of the Catilinarian conspiracy in 64–63 BCE. Catiline and his fellow ringleaders mounted a popular revolt in the provinces while simultaneously trying to assassinate Cicero in Rome.[46] Upon the advice of the Senate, Cicero took personal responsibility for quenching the rebellion: when some of the conspirators were arrested in Rome he ordered that they be executed without a trial.[47]

Five years later, his main opponent among the *populares*, P. Clodius Pulcher, served as a tribune and, as one of the first acts, passed a retroactive law in the plebeian assembly according to which anyone who put a Roman citizen to death without a trial was to be put on trial in turn (*lex Clodia de capite civis Romani*).[48] After realizing that the law was being promulgated to strike him personally, Cicero left Rome days before the scheduled vote. After a short sojourn in the town of Vibo, he made his way to the coastal town of Brundisium from where he crossed the Adriatic sea by boat to Dyrrachium and, later, to Thessalonica.[49] In response to his departure, a decree of *aquae et ignis interdictio* was passed in Rome, by which he was outlawed, his property confiscated, and any future discussion of his return in any of the assemblies prohibited.[50] The bill was soon amended to specify that he must keep no less than four hundred miles from the city, an unusually rigorous stipulation. As this included the whole of Italy as well as Sicily, the closest safe-haven for Cicero was Western Greece.[51] To ensure that Cicero never returned to his house on the Palatine hill, Clodius went as far as to take personal charge of the exile's forfeited estate. Under the terms of the decree, he arranged for its consecration as a shrine of the goddess Libertas. Prior to this formal expropriation, parts of the property were reportedly looted and put to the torch by Clodius's mobs.

A year later, after the tribune elections led to Clodius's departure from office, a sustained campaign by Cicero's supporters in Rome started yielding results. After unsuccessful attempts in the Senate and the plebeian assembly,[52] the decree of *aquae et ignis interdictio* was eventually revoked in the *comitia centuriata*. Cicero was greeted to a triumphant welcome on the streets of Brundisium and Rome and gave speeches of thanks to the Senate and the Roman people.[53] However, while the bill of restitution provided for Cicero's return to his former status, the Palatine house remained under the sway of religious jurisdiction and he had to make a further appeal to the pontiffs to revoke its conversion into Libertas's shrine, which was ultimately granted.[54]

Having mastered both force as rhetoric and rhetoric as force, Cicero carries forward these ambiguities into his new domicile to become 'the personage most versatile in his writings about exile', as Jo-Marie Claassen aptly described him.[55] His correspondence with Atticus during the exile and speeches he delivered after his return to Rome provide ample material for understanding the circumventive nature of implied exile, its deferred personal impact as well as its link with the forfeiture of property.

In the first place, the very term *aquae et ignis interdictio* is based on a peculiar verbal spin. There is an important symbolic element in the selection of water and fire as these are considered not only in their function of nourishing individual existence but also in their function of social integration. However, this metaphoric figure is framed by a metonymic transfer. What the law declared was the prohibition of the use of water and fire, and the supplement *et tectis* was often added to the effect that the person in exile could not be sheltered either. The practical implication was the prohibition of entrance to any place in the territory of the Roman Republic. In other words, denial of selected portions of the natural and communal life of the state is supposed to warn the exile off from treading into the state as a whole. The rhetorical turn which is now known as synecdoche, indicating the whole of some entity by focusing on one of its parts (and vice versa), was a recognized trope in traditional rhetoric and considered alongside cases of metonymy.[56] As one would have expected, in his early post-exilic speech *De domo sua*, Cicero addresses precisely this metonymic encoding of exile when he accuses Clodius of using equivocal formulation to conceal force: 'Tulisti de me, ne reciperer, non ut exirem: quem tu ipse non poteras dicere non licere esse Romae [...] poena est, qui receperit: quam omnes neglexerunt: eiectio nusquam est' [In your measure you forbade that anyone should give me shelter, not that I should leave the city; for not even you could assert that I had no right to be in Rome [...] penalties are enacted against all who harboured me, and these penalties were universally set at naught; there is no mention anywhere of my being turned out].[57] Obviously, what Cicero says about shelter applies to water and fire, too: there is a penalty for providing fire and water to an exile but not the explicit ordinance that he should leave Rome.

An important difference arises when this metonymic encoding is compared to the designations of the standard punishments in the penal system of the Roman Republic. By their very names, most penalties linked the transgressor to the coercive imperium of the magistrates in a fairly unambiguous way. Among such chastisements figured deportation to an island (*deportatio in insulam*), forced labour in mines (*opus metalli*), beating (*verbera*) and incarceration (*carcer*) of slaves. Among these, capital punishment (*poena capitis*) may at first view appear as an exceptional metonymic label in that it takes a part of the body, the head (*caput*), for the human life as a whole. In an etymological respect, however, it does not stem from a metonymical transfer but has a literal meaning, since the death penalty was performed on the condemned person's head which was cut off by an axe. Furthermore, the axe itself was not a randomly chosen instrument of execution; it implied an obvious allusion to the emblematic image of the magistrates' coercion power — a fasces with an axe in the middle.[58] In this case, too, the link between the agent, the instrument and the object of punishment is quite apparent, even if it is conveyed through a mixture of strictly denotative and metaphoric signs.

In opposition to this straightforward approach, *aquae et ignis interdictio* represents a displacement: a person is displaced from the territory of the Roman Republic but the concept of punishment is also displaced from its place in the judicial administrative chain. Metonymical reference to water and fire is, I submit, a signal of a more fundamental metonymy. For exile is supposed to provide a functional substitute for capital punishment in two ways: a) by coming before the sentence in the temporal sequence and, thereby, supplanting it; and b) by transferring the responsibility for enforcement from the state onto the transgressor. This inversion in time and agency is certainly not what the conventional punishment does or aims at. Theodor Mommsen, in his classic textbook on Roman penal law, defined punishment as the 'infliction of harm to some person according to a legal or habitual norm and through state-approved sentence, in recognition of a transgression previously committed by him'.[59] If we apply the terms of Mommsen's definition to *aquae et ignis interdictio*, as practised in the first century BCE, we see that all the key elements are missing: the measure was not applied in the wake of a sentence, it did not necessarily involve any transgression, and its place in the system of punitive norms was unclear. Furthermore, the harm was not administered by the state; instead, it was deemed to have been self-inflicted by the person concerned through voluntary departure from Rome.

This inward turn can neatly be illustrated by Cicero's discursive construction of force during his eighteen months of exile. In his letters to Atticus from Brundisium and Thessalonica, he expresses an intense anxiety that lacerates (*lacerat*) and tortures (*conficit*) him:

> Reliqua quam mihi timenda sint video, nec quid scribam habeo et omnia timeo, nec tam miserum est quicquam, quod non in nostram fortunam cadere videatur.
>
> [I see how threatening the future is, though I have not the heart to write. I am afraid of everything; there is no misfortune that does not seem to fall to my lot][60]

In another letter he even avows that he has been considering suicide: 'Quod me a vitam vocas, unum efficis, ut a me manus abstineam' [Your pleas to me not to think of suicide have one result that I refrain from laying violent hands on myself].[61] To be sure, there are strong indications that in this and other letters from exile Cicero exaggerated his plight and that his distress never went so far as to prevent him from considering rational solutions to his state. Still, throughout these epistles the grief is mixed with an awareness of a penalty (*poena*) and guilt (*culpa*).[62] Had Cicero attempted to take his own life, it would have epitomized the intrinsically metonymic effect of implied exile, by which the objective punitive process of the state is forestalled only to open the way for the accused party to internalize the coercion and experience punishment in the subjective realm.[63]

Whereas Cicero's exilic epistles testify to the metonymic internalization of force, in his post-exilic speeches in Rome he unravels the rhetoricity of coercion and traces it back to its objective sources. Thus, in *De domo sua*, he replicates his Caecina argument by claiming that his departure was effectively an eviction that involved all conceivable indicators of force:

> hunc tu civem ferro et armis et exercitus terrore et consulum scelere et
> audacissimorum hominum minis, servorum dilectu, obsessione templorum,
> occupatione fori, oppressione curiae, domo et patria

> [was this the citizen whose retirement from his home and country [...] you
> endeavoured to procure by the power of the sword, by the menace of an army,
> by the guilt of the consuls, by the threats of desperadoes, by a levy of slaves,
> by a blockade of the temples, by a seizure of the forum, and by the stifling of
> the senate.][64]

The violent excesses listed in this tirade have one thing in common: not one
of them actually happened, at least not before Cicero's departure. His rhetorical
ratio is a metonymical one and in accordance with what he said in *Pro Caecina*:
the effect (fear) is taken to stand for the cause (use of force). Indirect expulsion is
consequently denounced as an instance of disguised unlawful force which should
be made accountable by law. There is one striking difference, though: the plea in
Pro Caecina was articulated to redress a situation arising from indirect expulsion
in property law rather in citizenship law. More specifically, Cicero claimed that
preventing one by means of armed force from crossing the boundaries of a piece of
land was next to a direct expulsion; in the case of *aquae et ignis interdictio*, however,
political and legal duress resulting in departure was not seen as an expulsion but as a
free act of the involved citizen. In the later speech, addressing his own exile, Cicero
transfers the very same metonymic argument from the realm of property law into
the juridico-political context of *aquae et ignis interdictio*. A striking piece of evidence
of rhetoric as enforcement in performance, this metalegal displacement integrates
the two contiguous aspects of law.

Meanwhile, the same metalegal rhetoric works in the opposite direction, too:
in the way in which the exile is warned not to return to Rome. The one feature
of Cicero's exile where citizenship law and property law are not only mutually
analogous but also overlap is the expropriation of his Palatine house, which
was carried out under terms of *aquae et ignis interdictio*. As a consequence of its
consecration as a shrine to Libertas, the place was exempt from the general property
restitution accorded to Cicero upon his return; instead, it was consigned to the realm
of religious law on the grounds of the sacrosanctity of shrines. The metonymical
rationale of Clodius's manoeuvre is barely concealed: Cicero cannot take possession
of his house, not because he is banished from it but because it lies alongside Clodius's
estate. The counter-analogy with Agamben's *homo sacer* is nowhere more apparent
than here. In Agamben's interpretation, *sacratio* extracts one simultaneously from
public law and religious law thus creating a zone of indistinction in which bare life
will be at the disposal of sovereign power at all times. Metonymic force renounces
the commitment of biopolitical control: instead, it removes a person from one realm
— spatial as well as legal — into another, thus foreclosing his or her return.

Clearly, Cicero's recovery of his house depended on his ability to show that
Clodius's actions were based on rhetorical communication and concealment of
metonymic force. Cicero uses rhetoric as force to press the pontiffs to recognize
that Clodius's consecration was null and void in a two-fold sense. It was undertaken
in contravention of auspices, which recognized the inviolability of the hearth,

and also in breach of public laws, which explicitly prohibited bills *ad hominem*. Unsurprisingly, Cicero has recourse to his long-standing argument from *Pro Caecina* and claims that prohibiting the proprietor from access to property amounts to forceful banishment. The only marked difference from his earlier speech is that this time the banishment is enacted by gods rather than by humans: 'Ista tua pulcra Libertas deos penates et familiares meos lares expulit, ut se ipsa tamquam in captivis sedibus collocaret?' [Did your darling Liberty drive out my household gods and the spirits of my family, that she might establish herself in what was virtually a captive's dwelling?].[65] In this case, the metonymic construction of force from implied exile is articulated, with a hint of pathos, as an allegorical theomachia between the encroachment of the thoroughly political Liberty and a righteous defensive stance of the indigenous Penates and Lares.

However, Cicero's claim to restitution of his Palatine house has another rhetorical pillar. He argues that the importance of household gods and hearth is such that his expulsion from the house is tantamount to the banishment from the republic which has just been reversed:

> Nam nunc quidem, pontifices, non solum domo, de qua cognostis, sed tota urbe careo, in quam videor esse restitutus. Urbis enim celeberrimae et maximae partes adversum illud non monumentum, sed vulnus patriae contuentur. [...] cum mihi conspectum morte magis vitandum fugiendumque esse

> [For as it is, gentlemen, I am deprived not alone of my house, which is the subject of your inquiry, but of the whole city, to which, on a superficial view, I have been restored. For the chiefest and most frequented districts of the city are confronted by the vision of what I will not describe as a memorial, but rather as a scar upon our country. [...] I must needs shun and avoid the sight of this more than death][66]

It is not difficult to see how this bold figure reflects Cicero's earlier arguments on implied exile raised in *Pro Caecina*. The partially restored exile cannot suffer to see his house dishonoured and the laws of Rome blatantly sidestepped; he is impelled to flee from the vicinity of the estate as if facing mortal danger, thus replicating the initial exile. Therefore, the restitution of an exile to his former status without full restoration of his property rights is not only an unjust concession to the rhetoric of concealed force, but is, as such, incomplete. Any such restriction on previous property rights is also overtly opposed to the principle of restitution because it perpetuates the fear of death that accompanies *aquae et ignis interdictio*.

Cicero's claim to the pontiffs can thus be summarized as follows. The prohibition of a person from access to and possession of a property represents in the first place an act of expulsion from that property. If the property in question is also one's domicile, the very same warning off the property is in the second degree equal to banishment from the state. One will not fail to note that these metonymies represent an exact inversion of the contiguity transfers already employed by Clodius, who used force as rhetoric to make two points. The prohibition of a person — in this case Cicero — from access to and possession of an estate which he abandoned is a legal act of foreclosure, inasmuch as the property has been displaced into the realm of religious law. Likewise, even if the said property was previously the exile's domicile, his or her restitution to a whole (the state) does not necessitate restitution to any single part of that whole (property).

Where, then, is the difference between force as rhetoric and rhetoric as enforcement of law? It may seem somewhat disconcerting that such decisive difference, if there is one, is not likely to be found in their respective structures: both rely on metonymic transfers. It is at least equally perplexing that force as rhetoric and rhetoric as force need not be set off from each other by different agents, either: we have already seen how they can be juggled by the same person, Cicero, in the same text, *Pro Caecina*. Instead, I would suggest that what differentiates the two lines of legal action is their pragmatic orientation. There is behind every lawsuit an intricate set of communal values and cultural associations that legal assertions, antagonized though they may be, aim to elicit.[67] Metonymic force, as applied by Clodius in *aquae et ignis interdictio* and by Aebutius in *deiectio*, uses this communal resource for the paradoxical purpose of parting irrevocably with a member of community. Rhetoric as a way to enforce law, on the other hand, does not seek to achieve a symmetrical effect of exile. Its primary goal is to re-establish the sense of community undermined by indirect expulsion and it does so through the only possible medium — the field of discourse. Having said that, one should add that there need not be anything intrinsically legitimate, or for that matter just, about this vindication. Whatever the relative weight of Cicero's arguments, we may safely assume that there were a number of other cases where the grounds for restitution were just as dubious as the means of imposition of implied exile. Yet a key difference remains: while the implied signified of force as rhetoric is severance and exclusion, rhetoric as force aims at inclusion, even if it be an exclusive one, and legal recognition, even if on gratuitous terms.

In an ironic way, the exceptional status of *homo sacer* in the Roman legal system has led to its becoming a heuristic paradigm that covers a range of situations where exemption is instrumental to sovereign inclusion. However, one juridico-political phenomenon steadily resists the interpretative rewards of the *homo sacer* model: implied (extraneous and retroactive) exile. Whereas *homo sacer* stands for the unilateral capture of bare life by a sovereign order, exile represents a bilaterally driven subtraction of that life from the order. In the Roman Republic, empirical cases of the implied exile have been attested both in the realm of criminal law, through retroactive decrees of *aquae et ignis interdictio*, and in civil law, through occasional evasions of procedural eviction. Those who took the role of agents of indirect expulsion relied on force as rhetoric: in their attempts to hinder an absent person's return, they used metonymy to impart force to that person and at the same time to conceal that force from any subsequent legal review. On the opposite end of the chain, the indirect expellees relied on rhetoric as enforcement: in their demands for restitution, they used metonymy to decipher the rhetorical code of implied exile and prove that it was in effect a forceful expulsion. A legal limbo reminiscent of Agamben's state of exception was created but then immediately filled with metonymic claims aiming at entirely different goals: foreclosure or restitution. The metonymic nexus suggests that the rational motive for application of *aquae et ignis interdictio* was similar to the one that disposed Aebutius to prevent Caecina from accessing the estate rather than to evict him formally. In both cases, relying on force as rhetoric was more opportune than having recourse to legitimate force or to illegitimate coercion. Namely, both lawful and unlawful force necessitated one's commitment to bearing out any juridico-political consequences that might arise from their use. The rhetorically encoded force required no such commitment: it was metonymically displaced and its traces had to be retrieved through an interpretative process which was, ultimately, bound to present itself as another, contesting and contestable form of force. Finally, in cases where displacement was not only in terms of space (state territory or estate) but also from one legal remit into another (public and religious law), restitutive interpretation generated such metonymies as deemed likely to override the double foreclosure of the exile.

Notes to Chapter 1

1. Carl Schmitt, *Political Theology: Four Chapters on the Concept of Sovereignty* (Chicago, IL, and London: University of Chicago Press, 2005), pp. 5–15; Giorgio Agamben, *Homo Sacer: Sovereign Power and Bare Life* (Stanford, CA: Stanford University Press, 1998), pp. 17–25.
2. Walter Benjamin, 'Critique of Violence', in *Selected Writings (Volume 1: 1913–1926)* (Cambridge, MA, and London: The Belknap Press of Harvard University Press, 1996), p. 250.
3. Agamben, *Homo Sacer*, p. 111
4. Thomas Carl Wall, 'Au hasard', in Andrew Norris (ed), *Politics, Metaphysics and Death: Essays on Giorgio Agamben's 'Homo Sacer'* (Durham, NC, and London: Duke University Press, 2005), pp. 39–40.
5. Agamben, *Homo sacer*, p. 110.
6. Ibid., p. 110. See also James Leigh Strachan-Davidson, *Problems of the Roman Criminal Law*, vol. II (Oxford: Clarendon Press, 1912), pp. 31–34.
7. The second century BCE should not be understood as *terminus post quem* for the emergence of direct or for that matter indirect (implied) exile, but as the earliest period with reliable historiographical records of that practice. The legend has it that the Roman Republic was established by the expulsion of the last king Tarquin the Proud in 509 BCE. For their part, Livy and Plutarch relate several cases of the exile of military leaders during the early period of the Republic, including Coriolanus (*c.* 491 BCE) and Camillus (391 BCE). However, the authenticity of these accounts — resonant though they proved to be — is dubious. On the other side of the time span, the military conquests and territorial expansion of Rome into the Mediterranean during the first century had made it more difficult to enact exile beyond the borders and the internal relegation seems to have been the measure of choice.
8. Polybius, *The Histories* VI. 14. 6–8 (London and Cambridge, MA: Harvard University Press 1972), pp. 300–03. In my quotations from classical texts, I have tended to use Loeb editions of Harvard University Press for their bilingual versions.
9. Cicero, *Pro Caecina* 100 in *Pro lege Manilia, Pro Caecina, Pro Cluentio, Pro Rabirio perduellionis* (Cambridge, MA, and London: Harvard University Press, 2000), pp. 198–99 (henceforth listed as *Pro Caecina*).
10. A. H. J. Greenidge, *The Legal Procedure of Cicero's Time* (Oxford: Clarendon Press, 1901), pp. 6–8.
11. While exile seems to have represented a *de facto* right, there were some cases where the citizens were prevented from using it. For a concise list of such restrictions, see Gordon P. Kelly, *A History of Exile in the Roman Republic* (Cambridge: Cambridge University Press, 2006), pp. 20–25.
12. Most of these references to exile as statutory punishment are found in the *Codex Iustinianus* and are quotations from the late imperial juristic sources which come after the Republican period, such as Marcianus, Ulpian, Macer, and Modestinus. See Marcian, *Institutes*, book 14, Ulpian, *Edict*, book 37, Modestinus, *Punishments*, book 3, Macer, *Criminal Proceedings*, book 1 in *The*

Digest of Justinian, ed. and trans. by Theodor Mommsen, vol. IV (Philadelphia: University of Pennsylvania Press, 1985), pp. 819–20, 820–21, 829–30, 830–31.

13. See Theodor Mommsen, *Römisches Strafrecht* (Graz: Akademische Druck- U. Verlagsanstalt, 1955), pp. 73, 965–67, 971–73; Greenidge, *The Legal Procedure of Cicero's Time*, p. 513; Ernst Ludwig Grasmück, *Exilium: Untersuchungen zur Verbannung in der Antike* (Paderborn: Ferdinand Schöningh, 1978), p. 106, and Richard A. Bauman, *Human Rights in Ancient Rome* (London: Routledge, 2000), pp. 45–46.

14. Kelly, *A History of Exile in the Roman Republic*, pp. 44–45.

15. Richard A. Bauman, *Crime and Punishment in Ancient Rome* (London and New York: Routledge, 1996), pp. 13–14.

16. Richard A. Bauman, *Human Rights in Ancient Rome*, p. 44.

17. Kelly, *A History of Exile in the Roman Republic*, p. 13.

18. Agamben, *Homo sacer*, p. 82.

19. The text of the injunction reads: 'Unde tu aut familia aut procurator tuus illum vi hominibus coactis armatisve deiecisti, eo restituas.' See Greenidge, *The Legal Procedure of Cicero's Time*, p. 215.

20. Giorgio Agamben, *State of Exception* (Chicago, IL, and London: Chicago University Press, 2005), p. 41.

21. Ibid, p. 50.

22. Strachan-Davidson, *Problems of the Roman Criminal Law*, vol. II, pp. 43–50.

23. John Austin, *The Province of Jurisprudence Determined* (Cambridge: Cambridge University Press, 2001), pp. 21–25.

24. The credibility of this death threat is difficult to ascertain. We do not know of a single case where an exile was put to death in this way; but, on the other hand, the sources do not give any case where individual return was attempted without a prior agreement on restitution in one of the assemblies of Rome.

25. Cicero, *Letters to Atticus*, vol. I (London: William Heinemann; Cambridge, MA: Harvard University Press, 1956), pp. 198–99.

26. Kelly, *A History of Exile in the Roman Republic*, p. 3.

27. *De legibus* III. xviii. 42 in Cicero, *De re publica/De legibus*, (Cambridge, MA, and London: Harvard University Press, 1994), pp. 508–09. For an anthropological evolutionary version of the same argument, see: Cicero, *Pro Sestio* 91–92 (London: William Heinemann; Cambridge, MA: Harvard University Press, 1984), pp. 158–61.

28. *Pro Caecina* 42, pp. 138–39.

29. Ibid., 46–47, pp. 142–45.

30. Ibid., 39, pp. 136–37. A good example of an imperial re-interpretation of this argument is Ulpian's discussion of the interdict in *Edict*, book 69 in Mommsen (ed.), *The Digest of Justinian*, pp. 582–85.

31. *Pro Caecina* 50, pp. 146–47.

32. Ibid, 87, pp. 184–85.

33. Ibid, 55, pp. 150–51.

34. Raymond W. Gibbs, *The Poetics of Mind: Figurative Thought, Language and Understanding* (Cambridge: Cambridge University Press, 1994), p. 322.

35. Although metonymy is usually seen as a province of literary criticism, the most important insights into this figure have come from applied linguistics. Classical linguistic analyses of metonymy in relation to other cognitive and rhetorical models are found in Roman Jakobson, 'Two Aspects of Language and Two Types of Aphasic Disturbances', in Jakobson, *Language in Literature* (Cambridge, MA, and London: Belknap Press of Harvard University Press, 1987), pp. 95–114 and George Lakoff, *Women, Fire, and Dangerous Things: What Categories Reveal about the Mind* (Chicago, IL: Chicago University Press, 1990), pp. 77–90.

36. Cicero, *Rhetorica ad Herennium* IV. 32. 43 (London: William Heinemann; Cambridge, MA: Harvard University Press, 1995), pp. 104–05. Before Cicero, Aristotle somewhat misleadingly discussed instances of what we nowadays define as metonymy under the heading of metaphor in *Poetics* xxi (London and Cambridge, MA: Harvard University Press, 1995), p. 105 and *Treatise on Rhetoric* III. 10 (London: Bell & Daldy, 1872), pp. 236–39. A few other instances of merging

metaphor and metonymy are found in Demetrius's treatise *On Style* 272–80 (London and Cambridge, MA: Harvard University Press, 1995), pp. 504–09. On the other hand, rhetoricians later than Cicero, such as Quintilian, elaborate further on distinctive types of metonymy; see Quintilian, *Institutio oratoria* VIII. 6. 23–29 (Cambridge, MA, and London: Harvard University Press, 2001), pp. 437–41.

37. Cicero, *De Oratore* III. 167 (London: William Heinemann; Cambridge, MA: Harvard University Press, 1942), pp. 132–33.

38. Robert Cover, 'Violence and the Word', *Yale Law Journal*, 95.8 (1986), 1601-29 (pp. 1624–28).

39. Ibid, p. 1624.

40. In Plato's *Gorgias*, rhetoricians are likened to tyrants who 'kill whoever they want to, expropriate, and expel from the cities whoever they think fit'. However, the rhetorician's access to a position of power, be it in jury courts or in mobs, does not entail the real power. For killing, exiling and despoiling in the name of mere opinions (δόξα) means sacrificing the ultimate good which one firstly needs to know (ἐπιστήμη) before being able to yearn for it. Plato, *Gorgias* 466c (Oxford: Clarendon Press, 1979), p. 35.

41. H. L. A. Hart, *The Concept of Law* (Oxford: Oxford University Press, 1997), p. 12; Ronald Dworkin, 'Law as Interpretation', *Critical Inquiry*, 9 (1982), 179–200, and Dworkin, *Law's Empire* (Oxford: Hart Publishing, 1998), pp. 176–275.

42. For a critical analysis of this position, see Benjamin's 'Critique of Violence', pp. 238–39.

43. Stanley Fish, *Doing What Comes Naturally: Change, Rhetoric, and the Practice of Theory in Literary and Legal Studies* (Oxford: Clarendon Press, 1989), p. 505.

44. Jacques Derrida, 'Force de loi: le "fondement mystique de l'autorité"', *Cardozo Law Review*, 11.5–6 (1990), 920–1044 (pp. 940–43).

45. Cicero, *Pro Caecina* 51–56, pp. 146–53.

46. See *In Catilinam* I. 5–11, in Cicero, *In Catilinam I–IV, Pro Murena, Pro Sulla, Pro Flacco* (London: William Heinemann; Cambridge, MA: Harvard University Press, 1989), pp. 36–45; Sallust, *The Jugurthine War/The Conspiracy of Catiline* (London: Penguin, 1963), pp. 194–95; Plutarch, *The Life of Cicero* 18 (Warminster: Aris & Philips, 1988), pp. 84–87.

47. The senatorial decision by which this extraordinary authority is vested in the acting consul to defend the republic is referred to as *senatus consultum ultimum*, or the last decree of the Senate (Sallust, *De coniurat.* 196). The first-hand account of the arrest and execution of the conspirators is found in Cicero, *In Catilinam* III. 4–6, IV, pp. 102–07, 134–65. See also Sallust, *Jugurthine War/ The Conspiracy of Catiline*, pp. 209–10, 227 and Plutarch's biography of Cicero (19–22, pp. 86–95).

48. Most ancient sources second Cicero's views in promulgating a highly unfavourable image of Clodius as a ruthless schemer and of his laws as barely concealed *privilegia* against specific persons. See Velleius Paterculus, *Compendium of Roman History* (New York: G. P. Putnam's Sons, 1924), pp. 147–51; Plutarch, *The Life of Cicero* 30–33, pp. 107–15 and Cassius Dio, *Dio's Roman History* 38. 12–16, vol. III (Cambridge: Harvard University Press, 1993), pp. 221–33. Modern scholars disagree over which statutory punishment was envisaged by Clodius's law. While on the one hand Greenidge argues that it was *aquae et ignis interdictio* (*The Legal Procedure of Cicero's Time*, p. 359), Kelly, on the other hand, suggests that the extant sources do not provide us with enough grounds to speculate on the penalty and that in particular it is unlikely that *aquae et ignis interdictio* would have been applied in that period (*A History of Exile in the Roman Republic*, pp. 226–28).

49. See *Ad Atticum* III. 2–4, 7–8, pp. 196–99, 202–09; Clement Lawrence Smith, 'Cicero's Journey into Exile', *Harvard Studies in Classical Philology*, 7 (1896), 65–84 and Kelly, *A History of Exile in the Roman Republic*, pp. 110–25.

50. *Ad Atticum* III. 12, 15, 23, pp. 216–19, 222–33, 246–53.

51. Ibid., III. 4, pp. 198–99.

52. Ibid., III. 24, pp. 252–55.

53. Ibid., IV. 1, pp. 258–65 and Cicero, *Pro Archia, Post reditum in Senatu, Post reditum ad quirites, De domo sua, De haruspicum responsis, Pro Plancio* (Cambridge, MA, and London: Harvard University Press, 1993), pp. 48–131.

54. Cicero, *De domo sua*, pp. 132–311.

55. Jo-Marie Claassen, *Displaced Persons: The Literature of Exile from Cicero to Boethius* (London: Duckworth, 1999), p. 27.

56. *De oratore* III. 168, pp.132–35.

57. *De domo sua*, 51, pp. 196–97.

58. Mommsen, *Römisches Strafrecht*, pp. 916–17.

59. Ibid, p. 897.

60. *Ad Atticum* III. 8, pp. 206–07.

61. Ibid., III. 7, pp. 202–03.

62. Ibid., III. 8, 10, 14, 15, pp. 204–09, 212–15, 220–33. A similar model of indirect expulsion as a vicarious punishment is found in Cassius Dio's account of Cicero's exile: 'Then at least he departed, against his will and with the shame and ill-repute of having gone into exile voluntarily, as if conscience-stricken.' See *Dio's Roman History* 38.17, vol. III, p. 235.

63. A highly illuminating contrast to this despondent self-denigration is found in the grandiose self-image Cicero presented in *Pro Sestio*. In this speech, delivered soon after his restitution in 57 BCE, Cicero shows how quickly he has regained all psychological confidence and civic pride. At this stage, he thinks of his exilic ordeal not as penalty for an elusive guilt, but as a deliberate sacrifice for the safety of the entirety of Rome (*Pro Sestio*, 42–50, pp. 88–101). A later, philosophically adorned version of Cicero's exile is found in Philiscus's dialogue with Cicero in Cassius Dio's *Roman History*. Since the two personages lived in different times, the lengthy dialogue is entirely fictional, but it still illustrates the heroic ethos with which Cicero's exile would be invested in late antiquity. See: Cassius Dio, *Dio's Roman History* 38.25, vol. III, p. 251.

64. *De domo sua* 5, pp. 138–39.

65. Ibid., 108, pp. 262–63.

66. Ibid., 146, pp. 306–09.

67. In this respect, James Boyd White was right to draw a distinction between, on the one hand, 'constitutive' rhetoric, which generates and integrates law and legal community, and, on the other hand, 'instrumental' rhetoric, which uses communal resources as a means for *ad hoc* persuasion. See James Boyd White, *Heracles' Bow: Essays on the Rhetoric and Poetics of the Law* (London and Madison: University of Wisconsin Press, 1985), pp. 28–48.

CHAPTER 2

Firebrands of the City: Vicarious Functions of Fire in Exile

The most typical feature of implied exile is not a direct application of force but its displacement. This indirectness is clearly visible in those cases where it is produced through evasion, retroactively imposed as ban on return, enforced through informal pressure or, very frequently, through the combination of the three. Implied exile showcases to the highest degree the political stakes of excluding a member of the state from its jurisdiction: constitutionality, biopolitical rationale, the management of the public response, and possible restitution claims all need to be taken into consideration. The rhetorical manoeuver of implied exile is essentially a metonymical one — cause for effect, vicinity for locus, part for the whole until one is locked out legally, spatially and discursively — and so is the litigant strategy of his or her restitution. The mainstay of this strategy is to threaten bodily destruction (pain of death) in case of return while at the same time hinting at one's civic death in exile. The one conspicuous method of destroying both life and property is fire, which is noted for convenience (ease of setting and economy) as well as for its pervasive and transformative impact (combustion). Fire, therefore, deserves close attention, not as an instrument of a direct exile or for that matter as part of a larger anthropological store of symbols that also happen to be relevant in exile but as a constituent element in the rhetorical mechanism of implied exile. This chapter will firstly situate the rhetoric of fire within contemporary theories of fire and home in on its different uses in indirect displacements. It will then frame the performative link between fire practices and citizenship practices and explore how it is refracted in two different metonymic codes of exile, one stemming from the Roman Republic and the other from the period of the Inquisitions. Finally, the argument will be rounded off with the analysis of three 'fiery' poems by three implied exiles, Dante Alighieri, Bertolt Brecht and Joseph Brodsky, in order to show how the metonymic drivers from the political context are countered by metaphoric condensation in the poetic text. In this effervescent construal of flaming imagery, the exile will, once again, turn out to be more of a *homo faber*, man the maker, than a *homo sacer*, the proscribed man.

The Flaming Sword and its Metonymic Detours

In the biblical history, the first exile was an act of overwhelmingly forceful banishment and it was marked by the *in situ* deployment of fire: 'After he drove the man out, he placed on the east side of the Garden of Eden cherubim and a flaming sword flashing back and forth to guard the way to the tree of life.'[1] The cherubim's flaming sword, a centennial challenge for mimetic painters, is one of the best examples of what can be called the transcendental rhetoric of exile. From the human perspective, fire is a numinous amplification of the cold blade of the sword; from the divine vantage point, it is a suitably moderated, material token of the spiritual calorific economy that informs the universe. The same fire will appear in the book of the Revelation after the opening of the seventh seal: dispensed from a censer, it will announce the end of the world and, consequently, terminate humanity's earthly exile.[2] The imaginative association of exile and fire is also encountered in some of the most important works of epic poetry. Embarrassed by the lameness of her son, Hephaestus, Hera precipitated him from Olympus into the sea. During his nine years of exile, Hephaestus did not linger in idleness but mastered fire and became a consummate blacksmith. The supreme, if somewhat perfidious, evidence of his craft was a golden throne with invisible fetters which he cunningly sent to Hera as a gift from his smithy. When Hera sat on it she remained tied by the chains and the gods, unable to release her, dispatched Ares to bring Hephaestus back to Olympus by force but he was chased away by fire from Hephaestus's smithy.[3] In this Homeric account, differently from the biblical myth, the exile appropriates fire and is in his turn empowered by it.

Homer's account of Hephaestus's submarine exile is just one of the versions of a popular and well-elaborated myth that circulated throughout the ancient world in many versions and genres. Many centuries later, one of these variants was taken up by John Milton who wove it into his *Paradise Lost*, the syncretistic narrative that brings together the theomachia of the Homeric world and the providential narrative of the Scripture. Hephaestus, now called by his Italian nickname Mulciber, is a denizen of Hell and his primary skill is architecture, which is obvious from his masterwork, the palace of Pandemonium wherein 'by subtle magic many a row | of starry lamps and blazing cressets fed | with naphtha and asphaltus yielded light | as from a sky.'[4] There is in this elaborate contraption a mixture of blasphemy and nostalgia: Hephaestus's real fall, the reader is told, was not from Olympus but from Heaven, it was accompanied by fiery hail, and ended not in the sea or on the island of Lemnos, but in the fire and brimstone of Hell. In the myths of genesis and epics, fire seems to be made purposely for exile: it is a direct vehicle of expulsion, or a spell in exile (as pastime or punishment), or an instrument of homecoming. In this manner, it contributes to the key stages in the cycle of the imagining of force in exile. To be sure, fire is not encountered in all myths of exile and exile is not featured in all legends of fire, but the association is frequent enough to cut a recognizable *topos*.

Nevertheless, the Jahwist, Homer and Milton have something more specific in common: they describe metaphysical rather than political exile and refer to divine rather than empirical fires. In the historical world, exile should be much less forceful because the kind of sovereignty created on earth is, by the tenets of creed, much more fragile. Likewise, fire in nature is a limited resource because it needs combustibles to feed upon and combustibles are commodities: they have their geopolitical distribution and economic value. It is at this empirical touchstone that some important contrasts between natural fire and anthropogenic exile emerge. Physically, fire is started by friction (rubbing) and operates by the assimilation of a contiguous area whereas exile works by disruption and displacement. Socially, and etymologically, too, fire is the *focus* of human liaison in space and in time (hearth, altar) and the seal of impregnation (punitive brand); both of these functions are ostensibly severed in exile. Anthropologically, in primordial communities, fire is used to chase away wild beasts and spirits rather than fellow humans: it marks the boundaries of the human world with zoological and spiritual realms.

Therefore, banishing one solely by the dread of fire against the body may well be a coveted mythical image but it is not a viable political strategy. Actually, many autocrats would probably describe the idea as positively ludicrous for, should it come to that, are there not more efficient means, such as the threat of firearms or forcible transportation to the border? Extracted from its biblical context, the notion of the flaming sword can at best be a powerful poetic motif, as in William Blake's poems and engravings, and, at its worst, a frightening pretence, as in the Ku Klux Klan's rituals with the flaming cross. In most of the everyday references, it will remain somewhere in between pure imagination and full-blown action: an expression of our lingering expectation for the political exile to be more forceful — more fiery, as it were — than it actually is. However, if banishment by fire is so unlikely in reality, why has it impressed itself so forcefully upon myth, literary imagination and popular culture? What follows cannot resolve this question completely. Yet, it can propose historical contexts and rhetorical templates with which to address that question in the future.

To claim that expulsion by flame is a metaphysical hypothesis — perhaps an obvious point in itself — is still not to say that fire cannot be instrumental and even formative power in politics, as an actual force or as a metaphor thereof. Needless to say, as a versatile and captivating phenomenon, fire has been a perennial subject of interest for speculative thinkers who have sought to integrate it into their ontological and political theories. Thus, the pre-Socratic cosmological speculations frame fire either as one of the two foundational elements, as in Parmenides, as one of the four, as in Empedocles, or as the sole principle of the world, as the eternal and pervasive flame, in Heraclitus.[5] There is, then, the redemptive fire of the fathers of the church who, following Saint Augustine, posit it not at the beginning but rather at the end of the world, as a tool of trial and judgment that saves the righteous and devours the wicked.[6] The purifying fire of the alchemists, defined in the writings of Paracelsus as the melting Vulcanus, operates somewhere in between the beginning and the end of the world, in the recesses of the matter, where it effects a mysterious, ennobling transformation of substances into one another (minerals into metals).[7] The disciplined, rationalistic fire of the Enlightenment (and of modernity) is assigned a definite place in the chain of causes and effects in the nature and of components in the technological process; Chevalier de Jaucourt's article in the *Encyclopédie* quickly references a few philosophical ideas on fire and then indulges in a thorough description of the proto-model of steam engine and various other machines that rely on thermal energy.[8] One should not disregard the narrative fire of the speculative ethnographers, such as James Frazer, in whose view the originary myths of the taming of blaze across the world provide an interpretative lamp to illuminate the shared substrate of humanity before the emergence of the civilization.[9] Finally, the eschatology, alchemy and technology of fire would reach a sinister synthesis in light of the Holocaust: the crematoriums of the Third Reich transform humanity into a burnt offering to an unresponsive god and reduce their common substrate to a community of ashes. In Elie Wiesel's haunting words, 'Never shall I forget those flames which consumed my faith forever', fire comes across as the catachresis of memory of an entire civilization, an event that cannot possibly be remembered and even less forgotten.[10]

Nevertheless, these speculative approaches, imaginative though they are, do not really help in addressing the specific construal of fire in exile. Most theorists of fire have focused either on the pragmatic functions of fire, i.e. what rational goals are achieved with it, or on the abstract symbolism of fire, i.e. what fire means. Thus, the functionalist Reyner Banham can speculate that a savage tribe can reach a clearing with a lot of fallen branches and timber and either use it to build a wind-break and settle ('structural solution') or burn it and continue to move ('power-operated solution'), but are such deliberations not determined in advance by certain symbolic codes of which even most savage tribes are possessed (e.g. settledness, nomadism, expulsion, migration)?[11] Likewise, the humanistic symbolist Northrop Frye may well associate fire in all cultures with border and touchstone on the way to 'the heaven of the apocalyptic world [...] the city of gold' but how does this explain the political function of fire in very specific acts of exile within this world?[12] To make things more complex, literary texts, especially those emerging from exile, are amphibian structures. Such texts have a very concrete function in the exile's rhetorical contest with the state and, as part of that contest, also generate powerful symbols of force. In that imaginative elicitation of force, they often have recourse to stock symbols of direct banishment, such as the flaming sword from the Bible, or conflagration in Virgil's *Aeneid*.

The metaphysics of fire eventually came to be challenged by interdisciplinary approaches that brought together symbol and function in an interactive relationship. The key claim of Stephen Pyne's monumental study, *Vestal Fire*, is that civilization may be imagined to have started by banishment from the garden by flaming sword but its earthly history is determined by a sustained effort to banish fire from the garden, i.e. to shore up its agricultural core against natural wildfire and anthropogenic incendiarism.[13] Luis Fernández-Galiano, a theorist of architecture, articulates the same argument in the context of urban planning: despite the fact that fire was the key element in the Roman foundational rituals for major cities in Europe it ended up banished from those central spaces, reduced from open hearths and altars to fireplaces, furnaces and chimneys, and finally supplanted by central heating.[14] Psychiatrist studies into arsons associated fire with nostalgia, which is within the realm of the expellee rather than that of the expeller. Karl Jaspers in his doctoral dissertation *Homesickness and Crime* [*Heimweh und Verbrechen*, 1909], reviews urban arsons perpetrated by peasant-born nannies who, lacking other means to articulate their gender and class duress, resorted to desperate measures in the hope that a sudden blaze would sever links with host families and allow them to return to their parental home in the countryside.[15] Thus, rather than having fire serving as a weapon of banishment, these theorists reverse roles. Fire is conceptualized as the target of banishment and also as a weapon for the exile's return.

In addition to these reversals of roles within the traditional narrative of direct banishment, fire has also been connected to indirect displacement. It has been compellingly argued that the dread of fire is socially mediated rather than direct: it banishes by a prior ban, rather than by direct exposure to the heat. In his seminal treatise *The Psychoanalysis of Fire*, Gaston Bachelard insists that adults teach the child to avoid open fire by prior social prohibition ('Stay clear of fire!'), and that the empirical evidence (the child has its fingers burnt on fire) is furnished later on and merely confirms the ban. Actually, adults will apply a gamut of coercive measures to prevent the child from even contemplating any physical contact with fire: for instance, they will raise their voice and even slap their fingers. Although in *aquae et ignis interdictio* fire is denied rather than imposed, the metonymic structure of the ban is essentially the same. The avoidance of the object of the ban is based on interdiction rather than on expulsion and the force of fire is effervescently imagined by the child before it decides to take the risk and submit to it.[16] In a broader social context, this is reflected in Bentham's situation of 'the neighbour's house on fire': although not under direct threat, one is apprehensive and runs out by a metonymic reasoning as fire could spread to one's own house and then engulf everyone in it.[17] Or, alternatively, one could simply be asked to leave. Historians of urban incendiarism have observed that one of the most frequent strategies of fighting spreading fires has been to destroy the residential areas thought to be in the way of the blaze so as to deprive it of combustibles. Residents' responses to this strategy were not always understanding and call to mind the ambiguous situation of the implied exile: they are not exactly evicted from their homes by fire-fighting units, because there is a real fire out there, and not exactly by fire, because it has not reached their home yet and could in theory be put out.[18]

At this point, we can venture to define the rhetorical paradox of natural fire. It may well be receptacle for various metaphorical meanings but its essential mechanism of spreading and emitting heat is a metonymical one. Objects catch fire by contiguity and humans are displaced by fire in the same manner. Different metaphorical meanings of fire express humans' perennial fascination with its force but are also instances of semiotic fire-fighting. They aim to control its dangerous metonymic force by encapsulating it in pre-defined frameworks of meaning.

Bonfire: Towards a Thermopolitical Model of Exile

Now if fire operates by displacement and deferral in nature as well as in everyday social life it is reasonable to assume that it can exercise the same role in some of the exceptional forms of that life such as political exile. That fire has often been used as an instrument of the rhetorical encoding of force in exile should come as no surprise given its implicit association with the state. An exercise in analogical thinking yields interesting connections between fire and different models of the state. For one thing, some physical qualities of fire seem to suit well the political model of the absolute monarchy. Hobbes's commonwealth can be imagined as the dauntless Leviathan that arises from the sea but also as a central thermic resource which generates protective heat and the light of common sense but which, nevertheless, may not be touched; the sovereign is mortal, i.e. can be extinguished like fire but still represents an immortal idea (symbol). For another thing, some of the modern, contract-based political theories could be re-articulated in thermodynamic terms. Locke's model of the state could be conceptualized as a collaborative combustion, a process that involves both levies and benefits: decisions have to be made on which materials are to be used, from which realm (public or private) and in which quantity, and this has to be followed up by the practical organization of supplying those materials to the incineration point. Finally, in more recent approaches of the critical theorists such as Foucault and Agamben, the apparent disappearance of fire from the urban spaces and interiors — the process which historians of urbanism described as banishment — could actually be represented as its concealment or, in political terms, its symbolic capture and sinister rationalization. Apparently, as a conceptual model of the state, fire would have something to offer to political theorists of very different shadings.

To be sure, these speculative thermic analogies have not been as popular with theorists as the common metaphors of the ship of the state introduced by Plato and the body politic articulated (and visualized) in Hobbes's *Leviathan*, or, for that matter, the family proposed by Rousseau, or the garden, nourished in the Islamic tradition. In the alchemist's workshop fire purifies but in the philosopher's study it may create a mess. Their reasoning was that metaphors for the state should be straightforward and highlight what states are all about: control, coherence and splendour. Fire is, however, unpredictable and dangerous, and therefore irrational. As a matter of fact, in most of the classic political treatises fire appears fairly rarely and is typically imagined as the fire of strife, indicating insidious civic discord, or as the state of being inflamed, a token of perilous particularism. In both of these cases, obviously, fire connotes something completely opposite to the political coordination and hierarchy that are requisite for sovereignty. Neither has the fire-state model been paid due recognition by the main theorists of conceptual metaphors: they relegate fire to the tribal outlook (Lakoff) or envisage it only as correlate of emotion or situation but not of a cooperative structure (Kövecses).[19]

Actually, the link between fire and politics has not been perpetuated in the verbal discourse but in performance. Above any symbolism, fire practices have conveyed the related ideas of imagined community (Anderson), stabilized the boundaries between 'friends' and 'enemies' (Schmitt), and negotiated between private and public (Habermas). Take, for instance, the bonfire. It can be staged at the incentive of the state or as a protest against that state but in any event it prompts participants to display pre-eminently political attitudes in the public space and is often accompanied by speech-acts. Thereby, the bonfire represents a performative political statement from the very first flames to the last glows. What is more, the performative aspect of fire is not limited only to the time between ignition and extinction of the flames. Prior to incineration, participants need to supply materials and make appropriate arrangements which usually involve permission from the authorities.[20] Afterwards, as the schedule of bonfires underscores the national calendar, participants are prompted to look back at the previous solemnities, make comparisons, and, crucially, to remember.[21] Thus, performative involvement with the sovereign power is not limited to the actual maintenance of the flame but also to the preparation and remembrance of bonfires. In addition to bonfires, eternal flames, torch and candle processions, and fireworks all provide additional opportunities for the performative deployment of fire and the exercise of the relevant set of civic virtues and activities or for the articulation of alternative sets.

Fire, therefore, emerges as the symbolic and performative correlate of the state. Having earlier pinned down the rhetorical paradox of natural fire, we can now identify the rhetorical paradox of political fire, which can also be defined as 'thermo-political'. On the one hand, within the symbolic order of the polity, fire is linked to sovereignty in positive terms, as the epitome of its sovereign power and its political memory, but also in negative terms, as a threat to it. On the other hand, this token of the sovereign power cannot possibly be brought to bear on exile *in praesentia* because he or she has already left. Consequently, fire is displaced from the target — metonymized — in a way that communicates force and forecloses one's return. Therefore, as a thermopolitical figure operating at the interstice of practice and speech, fire informs the rhetorical contest between the state and the exile. In what follows, I will proceed to establish two broad metonymical paradigms of delivering fire to an exile. In the first of these paradigms, which I associate with the Roman republican period, fire is imagined as a standing feature of the polity in political, sacerdotal and ethical sense, and exile is encoded as denial of this element on a *pars pro toto* basis under the pretext of avoiding conflagration. In the second paradigm, which emerges in late medieval and early modern Europe, fire is broken down into two components, light, which is reserved for the spiritual world, and heat, which is brought to bear on bodies or, *in contumaciam*, on different contiguous objects.

Metonymic Fire 1: Denial of Heat to the Exile

In the Roman Republic, the notion of calorific equilibrium within the state was never articulated explicitly, but as a conceptual model it was very widespread throughout antiquity and in a peculiar way representative of Rome's political life. For one thing, fire was a ubiquitous presence in the life of each citizen: the kindling of the hearth marked one's birth and the pyre consummated one's earthly trail and the life in-between was punctuated with rites of passage and festivities involving fire. For another, fire was central to the three pillars of political theology of Rome: the hearth with the ancestral *Lares* focusing on *patria potestas*, public altars devoted to specific gods and served by *flamines*, and the sacred flame at Vesta's temple, safeguarded by the Vestal Virgins. All these fire practices and loci underscored the civic identity of the individual citizens and the political rhythm of the Republic, providing stability within variation and coherence within diversity. This central position of fire within the diachronic as well as synchronic dimensions of the Republic made the notion of the interdiction of fire, together with water, the most forceful articulation of exile.

It would also have been evident to Cicero and his contemporaries that this thermic regime could veer towards overheating or underheating. The Aristotelian theory, later picked up and developed by the Stoics, framed the golden mean as the ideal state which, in empirical reality, was not always easy to preserve. Only nature — the realm of the divine — had an unfailing regulatory system, known as world-heat (*mundi ardor*), while all other entities, individual and corporate, could be exposed to a detrimental surplus or an undue want of heat. Essentially, the same argument applied to an organism, which needs moderate heat for motion, to a kilt, which needs it for production, and by extension to politics, which can either fail to ignite the audience, if the orator lacks the glow of passion, or inflame it to unrest — possibly arson — if he is too fiery. This pattern also had its field of application, if by unstated consensus, in urban fire practices. For instance, whereas the eternal fire at the Vestal Virgins' altar should never be extinguished, lest a cataclysm — usually conflagration, but also invasion or earthquake — befalls the city, fire regulations required that flames in the urban space should always be kept in check and never allowed to turn into a blaze.

In 52 BCE, five years after the oratories about the Palatine house discussed in the previous chapter, Cicero delivered another speech concerning enforced displacement. This time, however, his own exile was not the main subject and came to be invoked only for strategic reasons, to raise pathos and refresh memories. The speech was delivered in a special court of inquiry rather than in the Senate, and turned upon the impending exile of Milo, Cicero's friend and protégé. By a twist of irony, the popular tribune Milo, who formed a vital part of the network of support that secured Cicero's restitution in 57 BCE, now stood accused of the murder of his arch-rival, Clodius. In mid-January 53 BCE, the two mob-barons and their slave retinues had chanced to meet on the Appian Way, not far from Rome. An argument ensued, followed by a fracas in which arms were used. Clodius was critically wounded and taken to a nearby tavern, from where he was dragged out again and finished off by Milo's men. His mutilated body was apparently left on the road and discovered by a senator who happened to be passing by, and who instructed his men to take it to Rome. After a brief period of private mourning within the enclosure of his house on the Palatine, Clodius's body was carried by his supporters to the forum with a view to displaying far and wide the brutality of the crime of the previous night. Amidst uproar, the procession with the bier then repaired to the last post, the Senate house. Inside the Senate, Clodius's loyalists improvised a funeral pyre from wooden benches and other pieces of furniture. However, as the body of the rabble supremo was surrendered to flames, the fire got out of control and engulfed the building itself, causing more mayhem. From the Senate house, fire spread to the adjacent Basilica Porcia and a few houses in the vicinity were also looted and put to the torch. In the meantime, after the massacre on the Appian Way, Milo made signs of preparing to go into exile, but to everyone's surprise returned to Rome on the night of the fire in the Senate to await the fallout.

In his speech *Pro T. Annio Milone Oratio* [*In Defence of T. Annius Milo*], Cicero made a case for the acquittal of Milo on the grounds of self-defence: his client's personal responsibility for the death of Clodius was taken for fact, but the circumstances behind that fact became the matter of a pitched legal battle. Whatever the weight of Cicero's argument, the outcome of the trial was not favourable. Milo was pronounced guilty of the murder, charged with the abuse of power on several counts, and went into exile. A decree of *aquae et ignis interdictio* was duly recorded.[22]

It may have been peculiarly inhibiting for Cicero that the subject of the trial — the incident on the Appian Way and the defence of Milo — geared his argument away from the legal particulars of the incident in the Senate house. Roman funerals, elaborate amalgams of religious and class representations, were legally codified by several layers of strict regulations, from the Twelve Tables to *leges Corneliae*. Likewise, from the earliest period of Roman legal history, arson was equated with murder and punished accordingly, while accidents involving fire were punishable by statutory penalties in proportion to the level of negligence, the location of the blaze and the extent of damage. Cicero would have had a good case to make about the reckless obsequies of Clodius, which were in breach of both funeral rules and arson laws.[23] On a more personal level, the conflagration in the Senate bore resemblances to the Catilinarian conspiracy in which part of the ploy involved insurgents setting fires at twelve different strategic points in the city. The multiple conflagrations were supposed to create mayhem and help the conspirators to get access to and kill Cicero and the second consul, as well as their retinues. It is in those dramatic circumstances that Cicero evoked the figure of the reckless arsonist who is determined to set alight the city as well as the entire world. It must have struck Cicero as rather ironic that the living conspirators failed to set the city alight yet the dead Clodius effectively succeeded in burning the Senate. The analogies between the two forms of violence against the Republic were all too clear and made the rhetorical exploitation of the Senate fire worthwhile.

Balancing the formal exigencies of the trial and personal remembrance, Cicero opted not to dwell on the very demonstrable breaches of law during Clodius's funeral. Instead, he went on to represent the fire in the Senate as the very epitome of conspiracy against the law. The movements and designs of Clodius's friends and supporters following his death are likened to an ominous gathering of torches or firebrands which eventually light up a catastrophic blaze. This complex metonymy has elements of both synecdoche and contiguity transfer: instead of contributing offerings for the sacrificial fire at the public altar, the malcontents turn into torches that destroy the shrine of justice and are fused together in that conflagration. The transfer also has distinct psychological implications. The spectacle of conflagration is so startling that it moves the spectator's mind, as in the Caecina case, outside his habitual self-control: 'movet me quippe lumen curiae' [I declare I am unmanned by that shining — ay, that burning — light of the Senate-house!].[24] The very thought of his friend's exile produces very many sorrows ('dolores'), to such an extent that he himself cannot feel restored to his homeland seeing his restorer about to be expelled.[25] The impact of fire is, thus, associated with the force of exile: in the past, it sent Cicero into exile and it will now lead to Milo's expulsion unless it is stopped.

Inasmuch as it sparks the fire in the Senate, the pyre is also the ultimate crime of the dead Clodius. The conflagration is a natural sequel and the logical completion of what he started during his life, 'ut eam mortuus incenderet, quam vivus everterat' [in order that he might burn in death what in life he had overthrown!].[26] The metaphoric ornamentation should not occlude the underlying metonymic rationale: the dead Clodius emerges as the murderer of the Republic whose misdeed is rightly punished in advance by Milo.

At a more fundamental level, however, Cicero sought to integrate these metonymies within a wider conceptual displacement. Milo stood trial for the murder of Clodius and, far from being exposed to physical threat by fire, actually decided to return to Rome after hearing the news. However, Cicero wanted it to appear as if he was about to be banished because of or, more precisely, *by* the fire in the Senate.[27] In *Pro Milone*, thus, fire flares up into something sinister that illuminates not only the case itself but also the political system that produced it. In the period of political crisis, civic participation ceases to be a duty and becomes licence, an endlessly multiplied act of torch-bringing (*faces urbis*) which sparks the blaze in the Senate-state (*lumen curiae*).[28] However, the contest emerges as to who these torch-bringers are. From the perspective of the departing exile, the torch-bringers are arsonists who set alight the Senate, even with their own corpses, and capture the state. From the vantage point of the jury and the state, it is the torch-bringers who should be made to go into exile and be denied, through a decree of *aquae et ignis interdictio*, the political fire which they misused. Thus, as the body politic is exposed to overheating the biopolitical body of the exile suffers from underheating.

Metonymic Fire 2: Imposition of Heat on the Exile's Effigy

In the early modern period, Cicero's model of underheating and overheating is encountered in the rhetoric of Christian mysticism where the equilibrium disappears and one has the choice of either burning with a great love for God or turning cold and being alienated from Him.[29] On the whole, this period confronts us with a completely different rhetorical configuration of fire in exile. The versatility of fire as a natural phenomenon, as well as its many accrued symbolic connotations, chimed in with the Renaissance image of man as a free creature at the centre of the universe. Just as fire can engulf anything so man too can project himself into any imaginable form and organize a model state according to his needs and inclinations. What is more, as a token of his privileged status among other creatures, and differently from his pagan predecessors, this man is aware of having a soul, a tender immaterial flame responsive to the summoning flares of the Creator's fire. This concordance, alongside the wholesale adoption and dissemination of the apparatus of the Classical rhetoric, ensured a degree of continuity with the tropology of fire of Cicero's time. For one thing, firebrands of the state get an occasional cautionary mention in Machiavelli, Bacon and Hobbes, among others. For another, Erasmus, Jean Bodin and even Savonarola make tentative parallels between the state and the flame. As Shakespeare's Coriolanus prepares to mete out a Doomsday on Rome fire is seen, at the hearth of Aufidius, but even more imagined, as the general conflagration of the city, as the charred, indiscriminate mass of coal left after combustion and as the pile of noisome chaff that is about to be incinerated.[30]

However, there are some significant changes. Fire's light travels fast and reaches relatively far but its heat is slower and gets dissipated before it reaches very far. Exile may well discern the light from distance but eventually succumbs to underheating. The Christian doctrine of the eternal world performed a radical revision of the natural phenomenon and assigned the by-products of combustion to two ontologically and ethically opposed realms. On the one hand, Heaven is a place dominated by light and neutral to any specific temperature; on the other hand, Hell is a place of absolute heat which is plunged into darkness or at least deprived of any light of its own. Poised between these realms of absolute light and heat is the terrestrial temporal world which is too fragile and inconsequential to receive either of the two in their full scope and intensity. The most one can expect to get of that eschatological blaze in this world is a charitably tempered heat, as in the real fire in the oven, or a figurative rendition, as in the notion of baptism of fire.

In that respect, another momentous change is to be noticed in that period: humans themselves come to be included in the category of combustibles. Consequently, exiles receive the metonymic code of force through a different channel. Rather than being denied fire, they get too much of it.

Like exile, burning at the stake as well as its correlates — flammable shirt, pouring of molten metal, immersion into a burning liquid — existed as a method of punishment for much of the recorded history. In Ancient Rome, the pyre was typically reserved for the dead and was only considered for living persons as an unusual and ultimately ignominious punishment. Although it had been enshrined in the Twelve Tables as a mandatory punishment for arsonists as a typical provision of *lex talionis* it only came to be applied more frequently in the imperial period, against Christians.[31] As marker of civic otherness, it was adequate to demonstrate the resilience of a martyr — on the pyre, Lawrence of Rome was said to have exclaimed: 'Now turn me and eat me' — but never the honour of a Roman citizen.[32] In the Middle Ages, however, the era which virtually rooted out the cremation of the dead, the burning of living transgressors became firstly a non-codified practice, favoured by mobs and secular princes, and later, during the Inquisitions, a standard penalty for recalcitrant or lapsed heretics, witches, and Jews returned to Mosaic faith after baptism. Jews themselves were, strictly speaking, outside the Inquisition's purview and, in spite of periodical mass burnings, were normally considered for expulsion by secular authorities.

As in the cremation rituals in Rome, in medieval and early modern Europe fire was preferred for its performative and visual effects, namely the spectacle of building the pyre, conducting the procession through the streets, and surrendering the condemned to the flames. Unlike in Rome, however, the late medieval pyres seemed to possess impeccable dogmatic integrity. For one thing, the stake was not a 'blood sentence' such as the church formally renounced — *Ecclesia abhorret a sanguine* — but it still effectively prevented resurrection by the thorough obliteration of the heretic's body. Furthermore, burning at the stake counter-analogically linked the punishment of the heretics to the suffering of early Christian martyrs as well as analogically to the eternal agony of the wicked in Hell. Finally, the stake also displayed a rudimentary form of gender sensitivity since it spared women the ordeal of having to be hanged and quartered, a feature which was of no small importance during the era of witch trials. This convinced Pope Lucius III, concerned about the spread of Cathars and Waldensians in the Western Europe, to legislate indirectly in its favour (bull *Ad abolendam*, 1184) and the secular ruler, the Holy Roman Emperor Frederick Barbarossa, went on to specify the method (1224).

Obviously, the prospect of death on the stake was an incentive for suspected heretics to flee before the proceedings into other realms where the Inquisition did not operate or where it was, at least, not so strong. Such evasions were possible but not always likely: most of the accused lacked the flexible cultural outlook, social infrastructure and financial resources necessary for distant migration and, as pointed out by Hamilton, 'went into hiding in their own villages, or became outlaws in the wilder parts of their own regions, and they were easily recaptured.'[33] Even much further afield, hiding seemed difficult because the Inquisition sent notices of absentees to the different local tribunals and, in Lea's words, 'it was a mere matter of convenience whether he should be tried where he was caught or sent back.'[34] Three groups, however, could still avail themselves of exile: those who had by chance or by premonition expatriated themselves before the proceedings, young men without families who could join mercenary armies, and members of the clergy willing to abandon their habit or nobility willing to pay out their freedom by relinquishing parts of their property. Periodically, this evacuation took on an organized character and the historians of late medieval period stress the role of *nuncii hereticorum* [the guides of heretics], vocational chaperons who, in exchange for remuneration, escorted individual and groups to safe havens, facilitated their settlement in the existing colonies, and acted as messengers between settled exiles and those left at home.[35] The Inquisition, for its part, strictly processed every suspect and made no concessions to those who for whatever reason were unavailable. Regardless of the motives and the chosen method of departure, such people were left a twelve-month period to present themselves, failing which they were declared impenitent heretics and passed to the secular court to be condemned *in absentia*. Thus, as in Rome, exile is interpreted by the Inquisition as a substitute for the death penalty.

However, while in *aquae et ignis interdictio* death would be merely implied, as the underheating far away from the central political fire, in the Inquisition the dispensation and public perception of a typical *auto-da-fé* necessitated different forms of figurative reasoning. Three groups of heretics were incinerated together *ad majorem Dei gloriam* but were processed by different metonymic transfers. Remanded heretics were burnt *in praesentia*: the destruction of the body provided the spiritual exorcism of the devil. Those on run were processed *in absentia*: the burning of an effigy represented the material conjuration of the condemned. The procedure with the dead partook of both methods: deceased persons suspected of heresy were exhumed and their bones, placed in boxes, were burnt in lieu of living personae. In the case of those who are actually burnt at the stake, fire is imagined as their exile from one jurisdiction to another, which we could term 'burning as displacement'. In the case of those who are already in exile, fire is administered to various substitutes, both generated (effigies) and retrieved (books, belongings), a phenomenon which can be designated as 'displaced burning'. Therefore, a typical *auto-da-fé* has a fundamentally metonymic structure: the church at the same time shirks responsibility for the death of those whom it has in capture and communicates force to those whom it does not hold.

Let us look more closely into the first group, those who die at the stake. Although the stake differed from exile in that it fixed the sentenced to the punitive spot, in the legal discourse and popular imagination of the time execution by burning interacted with several forms of displacement. Legally, after repeated admonitions, the impenitent heretic is deemed to be driven away from the ecclesiastical court and surrendered to the secular court (in the official jargon, 'relaxed to the secular arm') which for its part surrenders him or her to the flames and the Lord's jurisdiction. Spatially, the trials were conducted *intra muros* but burnings typically took place outside the city for the reasons of safety; facilitating a quick dispersal of ashes, and thereby preventing any cult from being founded on relics, was also of importance. Spiritually, burning is the ultimate tool of exorcism: while the heretic is considered excommunicated the devil is driven away from his or her body. Finally, devils themselves get their fair share of fire, but later. Their dismal dwelling on earth is not a privilege over humans, who are dispatched to Inferno, but rather a deferred burning. While in exile, argues Aquinas in Question 64 of the doctrinal part of the *Summa*, the demons are also tormented by a foretaste of the infernal blaze decreed on them. Although in the darksome realm of earth they are not directly confined by fires, they nonetheless suffer 'since they know that the imprisonment awaits them [...] *They take the fire of hell [ignem gehennæ] with them wherever they go.'*[36] Therefore, in the thermopolitical model of the *autos-da-fé*, fire is imagined as displacement, in the juridical space of the law, in the actual space of the city, and in the eschatological space of the divine history.

We now turn to the second major cohort represented at the *autos-da-fé*, namely the absentees. The Inquisition wants them, like devils, to 'carry the fire of hell with them wherever they go.' Just as the burning of the living was imagined as displacement from several domains, so too the burning of the absent was displaced onto various substitute objects. The burning of simulacra had an important precedent in the apotheosis rituals of late imperial Rome, where three-dimensional wax effigies of the emperors were included in the cremation of the emperor's body on the pyre.[37] Under the Spanish Inquisition, however, the custom became associated with those who were absent. Each capitally sentenced absentee had to be represented on the stage, by bones if he or she was dead, or in effigy if in exile. The exigencies of decorum were never forgotten: exiles' effigies 'are made half length, to be carried on poles by porters' and 'wear mitres with flames and sanbenitos with flames on one side and, on the other, the name, residence and crime of the culprit'.[38]

It is interesting to note that in the secular context effigies were used during the royal funerals, between the death of the old king and his burial, which was the moment of the investiture of the new king. In accordance with the legal fiction of the King's two bodies, the effigy guaranteed the continuity of the imperishable body politic, because 'the dead king-in-effigy possessed the attributes of royalty: the crown, the scepter, and *main de justice.'*[39] This is in sharp contrast with the approach to heretics in exile. While in the royal funerals effigy survives the king and ensures the continuity of sovereignty, in *autos-da-fé* exile survives the effigy. Thus, the effigy is not merely a token of magical investment — although this may have been its original, pre-political function — but an indicator of the biopolitical extremes of sovereignty. In the case of the royal effigy, it is absolute power stretching beyond the limits of biological life; and in *auto-da-fé*, absolute disempowerment where even bare life is cancelled by a non-biological surrogate.

The metonymic displacement of burning was enhanced outside the institutional framework of the Inquisition. Some elements of this rhetorical model coexisted with the Inquisition, as popular persecutory practices, and were indirectly supported by it; some other fire practices evolved without its support and even in opposition to it; still others were assimilated by the secular arm in the early modern period. For instance, in addition to puppets, exiles' portraits also made for good effigies: that of Martin Luther was burnt in Worms in 1521 sending out the message about what awaited him should he return there from Wittenberg, but also giving rise to the myth of the 'incombustible Luther' among his supporters as the likeness was said to have resisted flames.[40] Then, there are books, of course. The chilling reminder of Hassan, the wise old Moor of Heine's *Almansor*, that where books are burnt men will also burn in the end, had actually been a grim reality in Europe for nearly two centuries preceding the Reconquista.[41] French mystic writer Marguerite Porete, Czech reformer Jan Hus and English historian William Thomas were all burnt shortly before or after their books; Spanish humanist Michael Servetus was literally burnt *by* his books which were attached to him on the stake. With the decline of the Inquisition, autos-da-fé went secular and books took on the role of effigies for absent writers. Another form of metonymic diversion is to visit fire upon the exile's habitats and belongings. Economically, destroying exiles' assets seems counterintuitive and it was not applied by the Inquisition, which sought to confiscate them. Yet, the burning of property still used to happen as part of a broader political contest, and independently of the ordainments of the Inquisition, by 'ritualistic destruction of a defeated enemy's property' or as 'a feature of factional violence' that, in conjunction with looting, pushed families into exile.[42] In such cases, the long-term benefits of making habitats unliveable, and therefore not claimable in any restitution push, have often been deemed to outweigh the economic and political advantages which come with the reallocation of those homes to members of the victorious group.

Hitherto, we have identified two thermopolitical tropes of exile: overheating/ underheating in the Roman Republic, and burning as displacement/displacement of burning during the Inquisitions. Both tropes are patently metonymical. In the first case, in order to avoid the overheating of the whole one has to underheat (deny heat to) one of its parts by way of exile. In the second case, the burning of a man-made model-effigy provides fuel, real and imaginative, for the destruction of the actual object — the natural body.

Several points are to be made in connection with the two thermopolitical models of exile developed here. To begin with, they should not be seen merely as retroactive figurative descriptions of two forms of exile. Rather, they frame in thermopolitical terms the constitutive metonymies that produced those forms of exile in the first place. It is fair to say that they represent the condition of possibility of the exile: on the one hand, they are a vital part of the strategy of shirking responsibility for one's departure or death and at the same time they communicate force in a strikingly efficient manner. Secondly, the two models are not fortuitous vis-à-vis their historical contexts but, as we have seen, have a solid anchorage in the political rituals and the religious systems of the time. Furthermore, they are tentatively developed in different verbal forms and genres: whereas the one articulates political threat as arson the other frames it as the pyre. Thirdly, although anchored in two rather different historical periods, the two models should not be seen as exclusively attached to them. To say that the culturally preponderant responses to exile are likely to gravitate to one of the two models, depending on the political driver of the time, is still not to suggest that these templates cannot coexist in the same time and even in the imagination of the same exile.

This final point is of decisive importance for the understanding of imaginative responses to the metonymical encoding of fire. For instance, the Roman poet Ovid compares his birthday sacrifice to the pyre of death while at the same time describing Tomis, his place of exile, as cold and dreary.[43] Giordano Bruno, who during his service as a young monk at the Dominican cloister in Naples was accused of the Aryan heresy and had fled the city, remained aware of the pending threat of the pyre during his years of wandering. Yet, in *The Ash Wednesday Supper* (1584), written before his ill-starred return to Italy, he envisioned torches rather than the stake: 'fifty or a hundred torches [...] even though he had to march at midday, would not be lacking if he should come to die in a Roman Catholic land.'[44] This paradox of poetic imagination, which in its reaction to the thermopolitical drivers of political duress fuses them and eventually gets beyond them, will occupy us in the final section of this chapter.

Arsonists in Imagination: Exile as *Homo faber*

The technological advances and social tensions of modernity enhanced the role of fire as a mediator between citizenry and the state. Fire has been a vehicle of political protest against the state, as in arsons; it was also a principal method in the warfare of one state against the other, as in incendiary ammunition; finally, it was an instrument of obliteration of citizens at the hands of their own state, as in the crematoria of the Third Reich. Being applied ever more broadly and efficiently, fire was also used metonymically, to enforce and symbolically encode exile, as seen in different rituals with effigies. In the light of the two world wars, the burning senate of Cicero's oratory and the burning body of autos-da-fé take on sinister connotations which exiled poets seek to unravel.

Despite his bold imaginative thrusts, Cicero was a politician and jurist and in his outlook exile and restitution were primarily linked to the discursive order of law and politics. He could afford to switch *ad libitum* between torch and blaze, as well as between political body and body politic, adjusting the image to the rhetorical exigencies of the moment. Those sentenced for heresy did not have an opportunity for litigation. Not only were they to be burnt but they also faced, as in contemporary staged trials, interrogations that pressed the points of dogma and discouraged imaginative involvement. What way of dealing with metonymical force would appear meaningful to a writer who, following his or her exile, remains alive but typically cannot argue their case at the bar? Such a writer, to whom force has been deviously communicated but punishment and restoration denied, is driven to purely imaginative means of restitution. In particular, he or she is likely to rekindle fire in poetry, as a compensatory metaphor of punishment, a latter-day correlate of the flaming sword. These poetic metaphors can be applied against the exile's own body in an act of self-infliction, against the perceived persecutor in an act of vengeance, and finally, against the universe in an act of visionary transformation.

I will focus on the kind of poetry usually described as lyrical — seemingly an unlikely context for the imagery of force — and briefly discuss three poems, by Dante Alighieri, Bertolt Brecht and Joseph Brodsky. All of these poems arise from some form of implied exile and all of them feature fire both in the political context and in the poetic text. In addition to the fact that their exile was of substantial length, the one tendency these poets shared was the elicitation of force in their autobiographic pronouncements. In the titles of his epistles, Dante used to call himself simply an 'exul immeritus', an undeserved exile.[45] Brecht insisted that the label 'emigrants', routinely attached to his dissident compatriots in Western Europe, was a misnomer because 'wir flohen. Vertriebene sind wir, Verbannte. | Und kein Heim, ein Exil soll das Land sein, das uns aufnahm' [we fled. We are driven out, banned. | Not a home, but an exile, shall the land be that took us in].[46] Brodsky was said to have carried a crumpled paper with a vicious anti-Semitic message which he readily showed to anyone who asked him why he did not return to Russia after the end of the Communist era.[47] Consequently, while in their personal poetic cosmologies fire may have occupied very different places — the highest, Empyrean heaven in Dante,[48] the deep-seated fire of strife in Brecht,[49] and the domesticated image of fire as both tongue and pen in Brodsky[50] — in their political itineraries it also had a specific role as a vicarious punitive instrument.

In the political life of Italian cities during the thirteenth and fourteenth century, it was a common policy for the families of the defeated faction to be driven out or, more frequently, tacitly allowed to leave the city to avoid being caught and executed. Once they had left — or even as they were leaving — their palaces and houses were burnt. It was no less rare that popes intervened into the Italian political affairs by excommunicating entire cities. During the contests between the Guelphs and the Ghibelines in Florence, the latter were expelled (1266) and took hold in Pisa and Siena; in return, Florence itself was put under the papal interdict. Around 1300, when the Guelph party itself split into two factions, white and black, clustering around the houses of Cerchi and Donati, Florence was again left divided. At that time Dante serves a number of important diplomatic roles including the ambassador and the Prior and takes the side of the White Guelphs. The circumstances of his exile are difficult to ascertain but it appears that he left Florence in early 1302 for a diplomatic mission and his opponents might have taken advantage of his absence. While he was away, Dante was charged with misusing public funds for an anti-Black cause, placed under ban and sentenced in contumacy to death by burning.[51]

In the love poetry of Dante's epoch, passion is most frequently portrayed in a fairly conventional way, as a wound afflicted by the Scythian archer, Amor, and also as rain in the heart. However, in some of the poems of Dante's contemporaries, an internal fire sustains all stages of love, from disquieting pleasure to desire filled with longing to the great joy. The metaphor of the flaming heart ('core ardendo') originated in the prophetic tradition of the Old Testament and the apostolate of the Christian faith, where it stood for the excess of longing for God, and was secularized in the troubadour poetry, where it reflected the excess of amorous passion; it was then taken up in the *dolce stil novo*. In the poems of Dante's peers Guido Guinizelli and Guido Cavalcanti, fire in the heart is an allayed version of the incandescence emanating from the stars or a vehicle of communication between their earthly correlates, lovers.[52] At the beginning of Dante's *Vita nuova*, too, the inception of love is announced by an act of fiery cannibalism: Beatrice eats the poet's flaming heart presented by Amor's bountiful hand.[53] Yet, the flaming heart of courtly love and the *dolce stil novo* is not a metaphor but merely an emblem: fire neither explicates love nor expands its semantic field. It is but a fixed predicate that signals a community of genre to no less extent than the one of passion.

In an early self-portrayal as an exile, 'Tre donne intorno al cor mi son venute' [Around My Heart Three Ladies Have Descended] the poet is visited by three despondent female figures, moral abstractions subsequently named as Duty, Largess and Temperance. Expelled from the world in the same way in which Dante was expelled from Florence, they come to Amor residing in his heart for reassurance and consolation. The encounter ends on a more upbeat note: both the poet and the personified virtues find relief and comfort in talking to each other. The three ladies learn that their exile will soon come to an end since Amor's arrows would discover a more hospitable home for them; the poet realizes that his exile must be an honour if he is frequented by such noble refugees. The poem is highly stylized and, at least at first view, bears all the hallmark features of *dolce stil novo*: the bitter-sweet languishing mood, allegorical personifications of virtues, meticulous metre and rhyme. Yet, on a different level, the emergence of fire in the second half of the poem strikes an unexpectedly poignant realistic tone:

> ché, se giudizio o forca di destino
>   vuol pur che il mondo versi
>   i bianchi fiori in persi,
> cader co' buoni è pur di lode degno.
>
> E se non che de gli occhi miei 'l bel segno
> per lontananza m'è tolto dal viso,
>   che m'have in foco miso,
> lieve mi conterei ciò che m'è grave.
>
>   Ma questo foco m'have
> già consumato sì l'ossa e la polpa,
> che Morte al petto m'ha posto la chiave.
>   Onde s'io ebbi colpa,
> più lune ha volto il sol poi che fu spenta,
> se colpa muore perché l'uom si penta.
>
> [For if God's will or destiny decrees
>   the world may hues reverse,
>   changing white flowers to perse,
> 'tis glory to share ruin with the true.

> If distance had not taken from my view
> the lovely target of my eyes' desire
>   which set my heart on fire,
> light I should count what heavy seems to me.
>
>   But now to such degree
> this fire upon my bones and flesh has preyed
> that to my bosom Death has set his key.
>   Wherein if fault I made,
> since it was quenched, how many moons have passed!
> if fault by penitence can die at last.][54]

Judging by the lofty descriptor, 'the fair goal of my eyes', it would appear that these lines hardly go beyond the customary praise of the adored lady and the conventional metaphor of flaming heart that had lingered in European literature since the time of the Septuagint. Yet, the fire of longing which the ladies have rekindled in the poet and which works by proximity is combined with the fire of nostalgia which is ignited by distance. This blaze burns the poet's bones and flesh disturbingly echoing the terms of his death sentence pronounced in Florence in contumacy. This political subtext is neatly highlighted by what precedes and follows the image of corporeal pyre. In the first stanza of the quote, the white flowers change to perse signalling a profound decline of human sympathy and justice. However, in Dante's personal standing, this ubiquitous change of emotional hue, deplorable as it is, intertwines with more pressing concerns: Florence (the 'blooming' city) has recently seen the switch of power from the Bianchi (White Guelphs) to the Neri (Black Guelphs). The death by burning to which the latter sentenced Dante would impose the same darkening effect on his body and make it the site of a clash of forces external to it. The punitive aspect of burning is reinforced by the last stanza of the quote where fire is put down to a guilt ('colpa') that required many months of penance. In the lack of direct penal measures, implied exile is reinvented as a vicarious punishment and supplied with a cause (sin) and an instrument (fire).

Let us now look at the second example. At the time of his exile from Germany, Brecht had already established his profile as the country's foremost avant-garde playwright and adhered to the tenets of Marxist ideology, making them an integral part of his poetics of epic theatre. The advance of the National Socialist party and the fall of Weimar Republic put an end to his theatrical rebellion in Germany. Following Hitler's appointment as the German Chancellor and the fire in the Reichstag in early 1933, Brecht left Berlin for Vienna and subsequently visited several other capitals. He finally took residence perilously near the German shore, in Svendborg, on the Danish island of Fyn. For the next six years, until Denmark's agreement with the Axis Powers in 1939, the insulated township would serve as the hub for Brecht's theatrical enterprise as well as for Marxist intellectuals in Western Europe.[55] Back in Germany, his citizenship was promptly revoked and on 13 May 1933 his books were burnt in public places, together with those of other opponents of the Nazi regime. The ritual was carried out in a strictly defined order and the authors whose books were burnt were called out individually or in groups whereupon the following formula (*Feuerspruch*) was used: 'Ich übergebe der Flamme die Schriften von...' [I surrender to the flame the works of...].[56]

Notwithstanding the burning of books, the semiosis of fire was rife in other forms of discourse. The documentary film by Leni Riefenstahl, *Triumph des Willens* [*Triumph of the Will*, 1935], lends the Nazi torch processions with fire a proper mythopoeic form: the spectator attests to a dazzling, harmonious merger of the torch, multiplied in a myriad of quivering but resolute flambeaux, and the blaze, a powerful bonfire illuminating the night sky. In *Olympia* (1938), a torch, kindled in the mighty fire of Ancient Greek spirit, is being carried through space, and effectively through millennia, by a series of athletes until it reaches, in 1936, the packed Olympic stadium in Berlin and is hosted by Hitler. In addition to these staged pyres, the German propaganda machine before and during Brecht's exile also made use of uncontrolled combustion disguising it in suitable figurative shapes. On 27 February 1933, the Reichstag was set on fire, allegedly by Communist conspirators, and almost completely burnt down. In the Nazi press, the conflagration was received with a mixture of outrage and hidden fascination: while the Nazi officials condemned the blaze as 'a beacon for the Bolshevik rebellion' a reporter of *Völkischer Beobachter*, the daily newspaper of the NSDAP, was struck by its apocalyptic appearance that called for a much broader range of metaphors: 'All of a sudden the firmament is perfused with violet red and [...] one sees bloody-garish flames that invade, like a formidable torch, the black night sky. The dome of the Reichstag smoulders and glows like a chimney.'[57] In 1937, the world's largest zeppelin, Hindenburg, caught fire on its cross-Atlantic flight and crashed near Lakehurst, New Jersey, burning to death 35 passengers and crew and killing another member of the ground personnel. The real footage of the disaster was screened in newsreel programmes on both sides of the Atlantic causing worldwide sensation and references to a man-made inferno. In the airship's home, Germany, Hitler described the disaster as a blow of destiny and the press proceeded to vow new airships and consecrate the death of the pilot, Ernst Lehmann, as a heroic sacrifice: 'he died just as he lived, as the luminous paragon of the fighter'.[58]

Brecht's collection *Svendborger Gedichte* [*Svendborg Poems*, 1939] contains many hidden flames, but three poems are worth mentioning specifically. In 'Der Schuh des Empedokles' [The Shoe of Empedocles], Brecht presents a speculative narrative in verse about the death of the philosopher Empedocles of Agrigento. Bored with the triviality of his earthly renown, Empedocles commits suicide by precipitating himself stealthily into the burning crater of Aetna. At the moment when his disappearance is about to be taken as a proof of his apotheosis, a leather shoe is discovered near the crater and identified as his, which casts doubt on the nascent creed. The second poem, 'Bücherverbrennung' [The Burning of Books], is more closely linked to Brecht's exile. A distinguished poet, who can reasonably be identified as an exile from the Nazi Germany, explores the list of books forbidden in his homeland and realizes that his name and books are missing. Annoyed by what he sees as a lapse of memory on the part of the authorities, he sends them a letter requesting that his books be burned on the pyre together with those of all the other dissenters. Finally, in 'Gleichnis des Budha vom brennenden Haus' [The Buddha's Parable of the Burning House], the sage relates how he recently noticed that the roof of a house was ablaze and how he went inside to warn everyone to move out.

However, the residents remained curiously unmoved by the danger and instead of rushing out they asked him whether he was sure that it was their house burning and what the weather outside was like. At this point, the Buddha concluded that they could not be helped and left the house and its occupants to their destiny. In 'The Shoe of Empedocles', 'The Burning of Books' and 'The Buddha's Parable', fire is an intrinsically material phenomenon, evading all metaphysical implications, even when it becomes a political expedient. The Nazi bonfire is instrumental to keeping the opponents in exile, but it is also a re-enactment of expulsion, albeit metonymically displaced. For combustion is not meant to destroy the poet's body: instead, fire takes an oblique direction and its flames snatch the poet's books. Nevertheless, the agents who administer fire are not entirely in control of it. By means of a secondary metonymy, the whole place they live in eventually catches fire and threatens to burn the burners. The only thing the poet can do is to learn from the Buddha and leave the house lest he, too, dies in flames.

If Brecht's exile was encoded as the burning of his books, one would expect his return to be the same, by means of burning books. Indeed, in his later exilic poem 'Die Rückkehr' [The Return], written during the peak of the World War Two air battles, Brecht conjures up a striking apocalyptic vision in which his homecoming follows closely the allied planes bombarding German cities:

Die Rückkehr

Die Vaterstadt, wie finde ich sie doch?
Folgend den Bomberschwärmen
Komm ich nach Haus.
Wo denn liegt sie? Wo die ungeheuren
Gebirge von Rauch stehn.
Das in den Feuern dort
Ist sie.

Die Vaterstadt, wie empfängt sie mich wohl?
Vor mir kommen die Bomber. Tödliche Schwärme
Melden euch meine Rückkehr. Feuersbrünste
Gehen dem Sohn voraus.

[*The Return*

The city of my fathers, how can I find it?
Following the swarms of bombers
I come home.
Where does it lie? Yonder where huge
Mountains of smoke arise.
There in the flames
It stands.

The city of my fathers, how shall it receive me?
The bombers arrive before me. Deadly swarms
Announce my approach. Conflagrations
Precede the son's return.][59]

What links the bomber planes and Brecht's verses is their shared goal: they are supposed to bring fire, by material explosion or by inflammatory impact, and this joint fire is meant to open up the way for return. One cannot fail to note the peculiarly metonymic form of this fusion: the poems are not compared to the bomber planes, they are following their advance. The image of the fiery verse is vindicated both by Brecht's revolutionary ethos and by actual generic features of his exilic poems. Even with the full awareness of Brecht's didactic slant, one is still surprised by the brutal directness of his poems. Brecht does not hesitate to address his reader directly, nor does he abstain from cursing his enemies. Thereby, he appropriates the totalitarian spectacle of the burning of books and transforms it into his own action of disobedience, a book that burns.

The third example of the metaphoric condensation of fire is from Joseph Brodsky and is rather different from the previous two. After Stalin's era, many political dissidents, especially those of Jewish ancestry, were not interned or for that matter banished but rather made to leave by a cunning manoeuvre. They were encouraged to submit an application for emigration and then in a shorter and simplified procedure issued an exit visa to move to Israel. Once they moved out of the state, legal decrees were passed to revoke their citizenship and make their entry into the territory under Soviet jurisdiction impossible. In May 1972, Brodsky, a political dissident and internal exile of many years, was informed that he would be issued an exit visa for Israel if he applied for it. His reply that he had no wish to leave was met by a barely concealed threat: the following winter could turn out to be very cold; on another occasion, he was told by a KGB agent that the winter could become very hot for him. For Brodsky, who by that time had experienced imprisonment, forceful hospitalization and exile, this could not be a good augury. Incidentally, at that time he also received an invitation to become a poet in residence at the University of Michigan, Ann Arbor, which he accepted, not least because of the new circumstances. In June 1972, he was booked a place on an Aeroflot flight for Vienna, stripped of his manuscripts at the airport check point, and sent off abroad, in an indeterminate status, as 'neither a refugee nor a refu-Jew'.[60] Cold winters in Michigan, where Brodsky was to spend seven years, are not rare and those in Venice, his elective poetic homeland, can also be quite chilly. In a visionary transformation of the thermopolitical code of his exile, which possibly played both on denial of fire and on exposure to it, Brodsky will represent his predicament as a galactic freeze so big that it burns.

Unlike Brecht's lyric, any discussion of exile and fire in connection with Brodsky would need to take into consideration not only how poetry absorbs political rhetoric but also how it ultimately eludes it. It would indeed be difficult to find a poet more reluctant to put his own exile into verse, and at the same time more indifferent to blaze, than Brodsky. In his poetic credo, enlarging on exile, especially if it leads to disregard of more important, metaphysical matters that await poetic revelation, would mean nailing down a vision to a paltry accident of biography. It would be much ado about nothing at best and a sort of spiritual self-castration at worst. By the similar token, obsession with fire and other powerful elemental forces is a Romanticist *faux pas*. Fire is simply too overwhelming and too involved: its deployment in a poem would scorch the life of small things and infinitesimal motions — of a fir-tree needle, splinters of red-speckled eggshell, a myopic bumblebee — whose fleeting and unobtrusive epiphanies are the very substance of poetry. Hence, references to exile and conflagration, jointly or in isolation, are quite rare in Brodsky's poetry. They are not of interest in themselves and can only serve as a starting point for a journey in imagination, a free drift in space and time. Thus, for example, in 'Пятая годовщина' [The Fifth Anniversary], a poem which ostensibly recollects his exile from the USSR to America, the journey actually spans wondrously from galactic realms discerning 'падучая звезда, тем паче — астероид' [a falling star, or worse, a planet] to an oneiric Middle East with 'пальма в Палестине' [a palm in Palestine] to a mythical encounter with 'чугунный лик Горгоны' [a black cast-iron Gorgon].[61] Fire, when it appears, is typically subdued, contained within chimneys and lamps and made subservient to the visionary motions of the poet's mind. For instance, in 'Roman Elegies' the act of writing is likened to burning black Cyrillic letters into the pristine white of the paper with pen serving both as a searing taper and an illuminating lantern.[62]

In an essay on Dante and Montale, Brodsky claims that art should imitate life only in what extends beyond that life i.e. in severance and death, 'that realm of which life supplies no notion'.[63] However, once exile has been encoded, metonymically, as death — in flames or of cold — it can also find a circuitous way into poetry and be raised to 'a higher degree of lyricism'.[64] We now know from multiple contexts and examples that such an encoding indeed has existed and what is more has driven the practices of implied exile. We also know that this encoding was employed in Brodsky's exile, as he was threatened a severe winter in Leningrad, and it is sensible to assume that it fed his poetic idiom and mythology. It is apposite to look at his poem 'Еклога 4-ja (зимняя)' [Eclogue IV: Winter] which, as it happens, brings together calorific and exilic tropes. In its eerily atmospheric scenery, the poem seems to conjure Bruegel's universal winter landscape rather than Virgil's 'messianic' Fourth Eclogue quoted in the epigraph. The temperature of human body is set against a galactic freeze in nature:

> Сильный мороз суть откровенье телу
> о его грядущей температуре
> либо—вздох Земли о ее богатом
> галактическом прошлом, о злом морозе.

>   [A bitter, brittle
> cold represents, as it were, a message
> to the body of its final temperature
> or — the earth itself, sighing out of habit
> for its galactic past, its sub-zero horrors.]

Later on, the first of the two possibilities is reasserted with more detail and emphasis:

> Время есть холод. Всякое тело, рано
> или поздно, становится пищею телескопа:
> остывает с годами, удаляется от светила.

> [Time equals cold. Each body, sooner
> or later, falls prey to a telescope. With the years,
> it moves away from the luminary, grows colder.][65]

What comes across here is a powerful heliotropic metaphor of individual physio-logical cycle as a gradual distancing from the sun and the concomitant decline of body temperature. It is a semiotic cognate of the principal calorific template of exile in which one discerns the source of fire from distance but cannot receive its heat. Remembrance is there, in the form of distant light, but the main resource of sustenance, heat, is taken away. Cold is also a token of the heavenly realm, or *magnus ordo saeclorum*: snow is parachuted from the sky to invade hills and dales, cities and hamlets, and angels 'как по льду | скользят белофиннами в маскхалатах' [are linking in white camouflage like Finnish marksmen].[66] Then, finally, the same cold produces, by a preternatural paradox that obtains in poetry, the sensation of heat, similar to that of burning. The poet is 'нанизан на холод, как гусь на вертел' [skewered by cold like a grilled-goose portion]; cold 'обжигает ваш мозг, как пальчик / шалуна из русского стихотворенья' [burns your brain like the index finger | of a scamp from popular Russian verses] and 'слюна, как полтина, обжигает язык' [saliva suddenly burns its cozy | tongue, like that coin].[67]

Arising from exile, the poems by Dante, Brecht and Brodsky raise the funda-mental problem of compatibility between lyrical poetry and the imagining of force. Is poetry at all amenable to the rhetorical contest without a substantial adulteration of its verbal mechanism? Firstly, exile implies a chronological narrative with more or less clearly defined agential roles and poetry traditionally relies on a stasis or at least on alternating temporal frameworks. Secondly, the rhetorical communication between the state and the exile proceeds by monosemous transfers whereas poetry rests on polysemy and ambiguity. Thirdly, the individual human body is captured, and when need arises ejected, by the body politic whereas in poetry the primary frame of reference is nothing less than nature and the universe. In sum, the imagining of force in exile is necessarily narrative, unambiguous and political whereas the force of poetry is extratemporal, elusive and all-embracing.

Nevertheless, the three poems demonstrate, in different ways, that there does not have to be any contradiction between the two discourses. The poets were clearly exposed to the rhetorical mechanism of implied exile which involved the metonymic encoding of fire. Fire was, namely, displaced from their bodies in several ways: temporally, as a pyre threatened in case of return; spatially, as onto books; or conceptually, as a threat of freezing. Fire was also featured in the broader political context and in the literary tradition of their time. Their exilic poems take up elements of this punitive rhetoric: fire emerges as a pyre in the heart, as a conflagration of the city, as a glacial snap so intense that it burns. Nevertheless, these metaphors are not simply a reactive formation or a compensatory response to that rhetoric. While they complement the punitive narrative encoded by their respective polities they also extend its range of imagery and transcend its realm. Fire is not a metonymic ruse but a metaphoric tool that opens up to ever wider realms encompassing the nature and the universe i.e. all times and all places: the incombustible blaze of love in Dante, the Second Coming in Brecht, and the Ice Age in Brodsky. This forceful transcendence is part and parcel of literary metaphor and also its *differentia specifica* relative to the discourse of litigation exemplified by Cicero.

Therefore, fires of poetic imagination which are ignited in response to the displaced fires of implied exile inform us about the poets' political temperament and poetic range but also about the essential analogies and contrasts between litigant and literary discourse. This point could also be illustrated by a parable from philosophy which, as we know, explored fire as a natural phenomenon and resorted to it as an explanatory principle. In his *Philosophy of Right*, G. W. F. Hegel used a literally *illuminating* example of a criminal who has incidental access to the universal: the arsonist. In Hegel's opinion, although driven by a blind and probably momentary passion for revenge, a person who sets light to a house aims to ignite something larger and more durable than his burning match and the spot touched by it, namely the entire edifice. Objective circumstances will determine the outcome of the plan — the fire may stop burning or spread to other houses — but his wish to burn that house is what matters.[68] This keen desire to reach out to the universal is enough to bring him above the particularism of his immediate motives and objective givens but at the same time it throws into relief his greater personal responsibility before the law. The poet in exile is the arsonist in imagination: barred from restitution and relinquished of legal responsibility, he re-kindles fires that were set alight back home. Thereby, he takes revenge not so much over his being in exile as over the devious encoding of force in that exile. Yet, by virtue of his desire to reach out to the universal, his fiery metaphors gain in strength as well as in spread and eventually flare up within the larger and more durable structure which is his own literary edifice and indeed the entire intertext. Obviously, the direction of the blaze will not be entirely within his control but will also depend on the readers: some firebrands will continue to glow in isolation whereas others will take unexpected ways in the process of interpretation.

Thus, to conclude, the culturally dominant representations typically frame exile as direct banishment and fire regularly appears as a principal instrument, or as accompaniment, of that measure. This association is not surprising because fire has been imagined as a metaphysical backdrop, political epitome and performative vehicle of sovereignty. Nevertheless, the social and political practices surveyed in this chapter indicate that, more often than not, exile has been indirect and implied and fire, when used, has been delivered metonymically. This devious dispensation of fire can be verbal or physical, or both, and can be encoded either as all-out denial (the principle *pars pro toto*) or as burning of substitute objects (the contiguity principle). In the Roman Republic, where fire had a central place in the public rituals and in the individual life cycle, a notion of thermic equilibrium was developed which shunned extremes: conflagration indicated the political crisis of the city and underheating was associated with exile. In the late medieval and the early modern period, fire was spiritually shared between God and man and also divided into constituent components, light which permeated Heaven and heat which scorched Hell. Consequently, the material fire of the *autos-da-fé* was a thoroughly rhetorical construct which successively exiled the condemned from the spiritual to the secular to the divine jurisdiction, while at the same time displacing the very act of burning actual exiles onto various effigies. Exiles' imagination thus had two punitive templates to work upon: the burning sphere, from which they are cast off, and the stake, to which they are attached in effigy. In responding to this metonymic code, poets construct compensatory metaphors of force which elicit this metonymized fire and bring it to bear: it may be self-inflicted as in Dante, turned against the state as in Brecht or self-denied as in Brodsky. Nevertheless, although they may have been kindled in the personal polemical context of exile, those metaphors of force eventually evade the pitfalls of resentment and revenge and turn into self-contained metaphysical images not unlike that of the biblical flaming sword.

Notes to Chapter 2

1. Genesis 3. 24 in *Holy Bible: New International Version* (London: Hodder and Stoughton, 2000), p. 6.
2. Revelation 8. 5 in Ibid., p. 1253.
3. *Iliad* XVIII. 394–403 in Homer, *The Iliad*, vol. II (Cambridge, MA, London: Harvard University Press, 1993), pp. 316–17.
4. *Paradise Lost* I. 726–30, in John Milton, *Poetical Works* (Oxford: Oxford University Press, 1988), p. 230.
5. See James Warren, *Presocratics* (London: Routledge, 2014), pp. 137–38 and Heraclitus, Fr. 37, 40 in Heraclitus, *The Art and Thought of Heraclitus*, ed. by Charles H. Kahn (Cambridge: Cambridge University Press, 1979), pp. 45, 47.
6. *De civ. dei* 16. 24, in Augustine, *The City of God Against the Pagans* (Cambridge: Cambridge University Press, 1998), p. 734.
7. Paracelsus, *Schriften Theophrasts von Hohenheim genannt Paracelsus*, ed. by Hans Kayser (Leipzig: Im Insel-Verlag, 1921), p. 336.
8. Louis de Jaucourt, 'Feu', in Denis Diderot (ed.), *Encyclopédie ou dictionnaire raisonné des sciences, des arts et des métiers*, 1756, facsimile edition, vol. VI (Stuttgart-Bad Cannstatt: Friedrich Frommann Verlag, 1967), pp. 599–647.
9. James George Frazer, *Myths of the Origin of Fire: An Essay* (London: Macmillan, 1930).
10. Elie Wiesel, *Night* (London: Penguin, 1981), p. 45.
11. Reyner Banham, *The Architecture of the Well-Tempered Environment* (London: The Architectural Press, 1969), p. 19.
12. Northrop Frye, *Anatomy of Criticism: Four Essays* (Princeton, NJ: Princeton University Press, 1957), pp. 145–46.
13. Stephen Pyne, *Vestal Fire: An Environmental History, Told through Fire, of Europe and Europe's Encounter with the World*, ebook (Seattle: University of Washington School of Law, 2002), p. 165.
14. See Luis Fernández-Galiano, *Fire and Memory: On Architecture and Energy* (Cambridge, MA, and London: The MIT Press, 2000), pp. 213–25.
15. See: Karl Jaspers, *Heimweh und Verbrechen* (Munich: Belleville, 1996).
16. Gaston Bachelard, *The Psychoanalysis of Fire* (London: Routledge & Kegan Paul, 1964), p. 11.
17. The example was made famous by Jeremy Bentham who used it to illustrate the difference between, on the one hand, motives in *esse* (external, the real fire, and internal, the real apprehension) and, on the other hand, the motives in prospect (the hypothetical spreading of fire). See: Jeremy Bentham, *The Principles of Morals and Legislation* (New York: Prometheus Books, 1988), pp. 99–101.
18. On the blowing up of houses during the Great Fire of London, see Samuel Pepys' first-hand account in Robert Latham and William Matthews (eds), *The Diary of Samuel Pepys*, vol. VII (London: G. Bell and Sons Ltd, 1972), p. 275.
19. George Lakoff, *Women, Fire, and Dangerous Things: What Categories Reveal about the Mind* (Chicago, IL, and London: Chicago University Press, 1990), pp. 91–114, and Zoltán Kövecses, 'The Scope of Metaphor', in Antonio Barcelona (ed.), *Metaphor and Metonymy at the Crossroads: A Cognitive Perspective*, ebook (Berlin: De Gruyter Mouton, 2003), pp. 84–90.
20. See, for example, the account of bonfires in early modern England in David Cressy, *Bonfires and Bells* (Stroud: Sutton Publishing, 2004), p. 80.

21. Ibid., p. 86.

22. See Cicero, *Pro T. Annio Milone Oratio* and 'Appendix to the Speech on Behalf of Titus Annius Milo', in *Pro Milone* (Cambridge, MA: Harvard University Press and London: William Heinemann, 1972), pp. 1–136. For a detailed account of the legal process, see James S. Ruebel, 'The Trial of Milo in 52 BC: A Chronological Study', in *Transactions of the American Philological Association*, 109 (1979), pp. 231–49.

23. For a succinct account of the Roman funerary rites in the republican and imperial period, see Jocelyn M. C. Toynbee, *Death and Burial in the Roman World* (London: Thames and Hudson, 1971), pp. 33–64.

24. *Pro Milone*, 33, pp. 42–43.

25. Ibid, 103, pp. 120–21.

26. Ibid., 90, pp. 108–09.

27. Ibid., 90–91, pp. 106–09.

28. Ibid., 33, pp. 42–43.

29. Saint Teresa of Avila describes fire as a token of unity between the Lord, who holds the fire, and His creature, who is imparted a spark. If neglected, the spark will become cold; if rekindled by prayer, it 'begins to kindle the great fire which (as I shall say in due course) sends forth the flames of that most ardent love of God with which his majesty endows the souls of the perfect.' Little heat is, thus, little burning for God and hence means exile which is, here again, implied rather than declared. See Saint Teresa of Avila, *The Life of St. Teresa* in *The Complete Works of Saint Teresa of Jesus*, vol. I, ed. by E. Allison Peers (London and New York: Sheed and Ward, 1944), p. 90.

30. See: Niccolò Machiavelli, *History of Florence* III. 13 in Machiavelli, *The Chief Works and Others*, vol. III (Durham, NC: Duke University Press, 1965), p. 1161; Francis Bacon, 'Of Seditions and Troubles' in Bacon, *Essays* (London: J. M. Dent & Sons, 1972), p. 44; Erasmus, *Adagia*, I. ii. 16 in *Collected Works of Erasmus*, vol. 31 (Toronto: University of Toronto Press, 1982), p. 161; Jean Bodin, *Les six livres de la république* III. 8 (Lyons: Imprimerie de Jean de Tournes, 1579), p. 331; Girolamo Savonarola, *Selected Writings of Girolamo Savonarola* (New Haven and London: Yale University Press, 2006), pp. 244-58, 291. For fire imagery in Shakespeare's *Coriolanus*, see: *Coriolanus*, iv. 3. 17–22; iv. 6. 75–79, 85, 115–17, 137–38; v. 1. 22–31, 63; v. 2. 7–8, 43–45, 66–67 in *The Library Shakespeare*, vol. II (Quarry Bay: Midpoint Press, 2005), pp. 326, 329–33.

31. Theodor Mommsen, *Römisches Strafrecht* (Graz: Akademische Druck-u. Verlagsanstalt, 1955), p. 923.

32. St Ambrose, *De officiis* XLII 207, ebook (Oxford: Oxford University Press, 2004), pp. 238–39.

33. Bernard Hamilton, *The Medieval Inquisition* (London: Edward Arnold, 1981), p. 56.

34. Henry Charles Lea, *A History of the Inquisition of the Middle Ages*, vol. I (New York: Harper & Brothers, 1888), p. 394.

35. Jean Guiraud, *Histoire de l'inquisition au Moyen Âge*, vol. II (Paris: Éditions Auguste Picard, 1938), p. 249.

36. St Thomas Aquinas, *Summa theologiae*, vol. IX (London: Blackfriars and Eyre & Spottiswoode, 1963), pp. 296–99 (original emphasis).

37. Douglas Davis, *Death, Ritual and Belief: The Rhetoric of Funerary Rites* (London and New York: Continuum, 2002), p. 129.

38. Henry Charles Lea, *A History of the Inquisition in Spain*, vol. III (London and New York: Macmillan, 1922), p. 215.

39. Ralph E. Giesey, *The Royal Funeral Ceremony in Renaissance France* (Geneva: E. Droz, 1960), p. 48. See also Ernst H. Kantorowicz, *The King's Two Bodies: A Study in Medieval Political Theology* (Princeton, NJ: Princeton University Press, 1987), pp. 419–37.

40. See R. W. Scribner, *Popular Culture and Popular Movements in Reformation Germany* (London: The Hambledon Press, 1987), pp. 323–53.

41. Heinrich Heine, *Almansor*, in *Historisch-kritische Gesamtausgabe*, vol. V (Hamburg: Hoffmann und Campe, 1994), p. 16. The practice actually dates back to antiquity but its medieval history, nearly as old as the Inquisition itself, was solemnly launched in France in 1234 with the public incineration of the works by the speculative philosopher Moses Maimonides (1135–1204), at the behest of Jewish conservatives who wanted the inquisitors to help them root out their own

heresiarchs. Against the wishes of the Jewish community, however, the church then focused on the Talmud itself and after a formal disputation in Paris (1240) ordained the destruction of the holy book. See Léon Poliakov, *The History of Anti-Semitism Volume I: From the Time of Christ to the Court Jews* (London: Elek Books, 1966), pp. 68–71.

42. Christine Shaw, *The Politics of Exile in Renaissance Italy* (Cambridge: Cambridge University Press, 2000), p. 114.

43. *Tristia* III. 13. 13–24; *Ex Ponto* IV. 9. 53–54, in Ovid, *Tristia, Ex Ponto*, pp. 150–53, 458–59. For other examples of *sermo absentis* as a standard rhetorical locus in antiquity, see Jo-Marie Claassen, *Displaced Persons: The Literature of Exile from Cicero to Bethius* (London: Duckworth, 1999), pp. 103–30.

44. Giordano Bruno, *The Ash Wednesday Supper* (Hamden, CT: Archon Books, 1977), p. 225.

45. Dante, *Epistolae* (Oxford: Clarendon Press, 1920), pp. 15, 22, 47, 66.

46. See Bertolt Brecht, *Svendborger Gedichte*, in Brecht, *Gedichte*, vol. IV (Frankfurt auf Main: Suhrkamp Verlag, 1961), p. 137. Translation in Kuhn, 'Visit to a Banished Poet: Brecht's *Svendborg Poems* and the Voices of Exile' in Ronald Speirs (ed.), *Brecht's Poetry of Political Exile* (Cambridge: Cambridge University Press, 2000), pp. 49–50.

47. See Salomon Volkov, *Conversations with Joseph Brodsky: A Poet's Journey through the Twentieth Century* (New York: Free Press, 1998), pp. 286–87, and Dubravka Ugrešić, 'The Writer in Exile', in Ugrešić, *Thank You for Not Reading* (London: Dalkey Archive Press, 2003), p. 133.

48. *Paradiso*, XXXI v. 13, 118–38, XXXIII v. 115–20, in Dante, *The Divine Comedy: Paradiso* (London: Routledge and Princeton, NJ: Princeton University Press, 1975), pp. 346–47, 354–55, 378–79.

49. Bertolt Brecht, 'Der Schuh des Empedokles', in Brecht, *Gedichte*, vol. IV, pp. 47–50.

50. Joseph Brodsky, 'Rimskie élegii' in Brodsky, *Peremena imperii* (Moskva: Izdatel'stvo Nezavisimaya gazeta, 2001), p. 403.

51. For a detailed account of the events leading to Dante's exile and his first years as an exile, see William Anderson, *Dante the Maker* (London, Boston, MA, and Henley: Routledge & Kegan Paul, 1980), pp. 145–64.

52. See Guido Guinizelli, 'Al cor gentil...' and Guido Cavalcanti, 'XI' and 'XLIV' in Gianfranco Contini (ed.), *Poeti del Duecento*, vol. II (Milan and Naples: Riccardo Ricciardi, 1960), pp. 460–64, 504, 553. For Ezra Pound's translation of Cavalcanti, see Hugh Kenner (ed.), *The Translations of Ezra Pound* (London: Faber and Faber, 1953), pp. 58–59, 98–99.

53. Dante, *La vita nuova e il Canzoniere* (Milan: Ulrico Hoepli, 1921), p. 70.

54. Dante, Ode 19 (CIV), v. 77–90 in *The Odes of Dante* (Oxford: Clarendon Press, 1963), pp. 210–13.

55. See Martin Esslin, *Brecht: A Choice of Evils* (London: Methuen Ltd, 1980), pp. 53–76.

56. Ulrich Walberer (ed.), *10. Mai 1933: Bücherverbrennung in Deutschland und die Folgen* (Frankfurt am Main: Fischer Taschenbuch Verlag, 1983), p. 115.

57. *Völkischer Beobachter*, 1 March 1933, p. 1. My translation.

58. Ibid., 9 May 1937, p. 2. My translation.

59. Bertolt Brecht, *Selected Poems* (New York: Grove Press; London: Evergreen Books, 1959), pp. 170–71.

60. Brodsky's punning self-appraisal, in a statement to a *Time* journalist. See 'A Poet's Second Exile', *Time*, 19 June 1972, p. 28.

61. Joseph Brodsky, *Peremena imperii*, pp. 348–51. Translation in Joseph Brodsky, *To Urania: Selected Poems 1965–1985* (London: Penguin Books, 1988), pp. 32–35.

62. Brodsky, *Peremena imperii*, p. 403; *To Urania*, pp. 65–66.

63. Joseph Brodsky, 'In the Shadow of Dante' in Brodsky, *Less than One: Selected Essays* (Harmondsworth: Viking, 1986), p. 104.

64. Ibid., p. 104.

65. Russian original quoted from Brodsky, *Peremena imperii*, pp. 387–88. The poet's own, not always literal, translation into English is quoted from *To Urania*, pp. 76–77.

66. Ibid., p. 390 (p. 79). In English, Brodsky renders 'скользить' (glide) as numinous 'linking'.

67. Ibid., pp. 389, 390, 392 (pp. 77, 79–81).

68. Georg Wilhelm Friedrich Hegel, *Outlines of the Philosophy of Right* (Oxford: Oxford University Press, 2008), p. 119.

CHAPTER 3

The Furies of Orestes:
Persecutory Agency in the
Narratives of Exile

Given that paranoia has been regarded both as a clinical mental disorder, substantiated by an ever increasing number of textbook cases, and as a metaphoric *maladie du siècle*, the twentieth century's political master-folly, it is hardly surprising that the studies on this disease are numerous and methodologically very diverse. Over the past century, these scholarly approaches have gradually moved from Kraepelin's essentialist and unproblematic definition of paranoia as a distinct form of psychosis, characterized by persecutory delusions and illusions of grandeur, through different hypotheses on its causation and classification, to the more recent idea that paranoia is not at all a firm diagnosis, but a context-specific construct sustained by deep epistemic and logical paradoxes. However, virtually all of these approaches share an underlying assumption. Namely, ever since the nineteenth century, they have been tracing or at least presupposing the histories of 'stationary' patients. Not unlike the archetypal case of Justice Schreber, so eloquently expounded by Freud and Lacan, these individuals had been neatly embedded in their social and geographical milieus until some pathogenic slip set them in irreconcilable opposition to those milieus, and to their earlier selves. In this chapter I will look into the literary coincidence and structural similarity between paranoia and exile. In particular, I will ask how the concealed element of force that accompanies every implied exile relates to the paranoia of the exiles and, also, to what extent the condition is aggravated by the inimical attitudes of their host communities. Rather than taking a psychiatric approach, the discussion will be grounded in the theory of narrative and rhetorical figures. I will explore the paranoid imagination of displaced persons in two literary narratives, Aeschylus' tragedy *Libation Bearers* and Vladimir Nabokov's novel *Pale Fire*. I will argue that in both texts there is a narrative construction of the agency of force which compensates on a rhetorical level for the uncertainty of the persecutors on the level of historical exile. I will then proceed to the autobiographic texts of Jean-Jacques Rousseau to examine a different model of persecution in exile. A paranoid exile arrives to a persecutory community and is eventually compelled to leave it. Finally, I will explore the representation of the legend of the Wandering Jew in Danilo Kiš's novel *Garden, Ashes* and Stefan Heym's novel *The Wandering*

Jew. In these novels, paranoid exiles undergo a catharsis through a real martyrdom at the hands of persecutory communities.

Paranoia, Exile and Narrative Theory

Earlier research on the link between enforced migrancy and psychotic tendencies has suggested that persecutory delusions may arise in individuals who are subject to a severe form of immigrant identity crisis, in particular that resulting from banishment. However, since the most influential approaches to paranoia have been focused on its endogenous causes in personality, the actual mechanisms behind the exogenously determined pathogeny in exile have remained rather elusive. At best, one gets vague pronouncements such as: 'Paranoid anxieties escalate into true panic when the demands the immigrant perceives as overwhelming become too intense, and he becomes unable to face loneliness, ignorance of the language, the search for work and housing, and so on.'[1] Occasionally, cultural historians and biographers note a peculiar 'taste for exile' in philosophers with confirmed paranoid complexes such as Descartes and Rousseau.[2] Still, these hints at a correlation between paranoia and exile have never been taken any further than this germinal form. However, in a number of studies, the prevalent tendency to circumvent or at least underrate the empirical input of geographical mobility in psychoses has been defied by the opposite trend on the rhetorical level, namely the metaphoric use of displacement and its derivative images to describe the paranoia. Therefore, before approaching the rhetoric of paranoia in literary texts of exile, it is apposite to look into the scholarly heuristic tropes through which paranoia and exilic narratives come closer one to another.

To begin with, there appears to be a general analogy between paranoid ideation and narrative fiction in that both depend on an underlying plot. Theoretical and diagnostic studies on paranoia have typically emphasized structural aspects of the patient's *idée fixe* as a determinant feature of the illness, certainly more important than any emotional impairment it may incur. Thus Jacques Lacan stresses that: 'However important for consideration diffuse anxiety might be, the delusion strikes by organization which links its diverse themes.'[3] Lacan's confident definition builds upon earlier attempts to re-articulate the histories of paranoid patients in a way which makes them resemble literary narratives, with immanent structures and themes. Some twenty years before Lacan's study, in his classical psychiatric compendium, Emil Kraepelin described paranoia as 'aus inneren Ursachen erfolgende, schleichende Entwicklung eines dauernden, unerschütterlichen Wahnsystems [...] das mit vollkommener Erhaltung der Klarheit und Ordnung im Denken, Wollen und Handeln einhergeht' [the insidious development of a permanent unshakeable delusional system from inner causes in which clarity and order of thinking, willing, and action, are completely preserved].[4] Kraepelin's stress on the internal coherence and clarity of paranoid thought, as well as on its temporal progression, lends itself to a description of the unravelling of narrative imagination. For in standard narrative texts we come across elaborate plots with clearly delineated agencies and we also expect each of these plots to be structured according to its own internal principle. In his *Poetics*, Aristotle set up the criterion for a well-made plot in which 'the component events should be so structured that if any is displaced or removed, the sense of the whole is disturbed and dislocated'.[5] Some of the more recent developments in narrative theory illustrate the analogy to an even greater degree. For example, building on Propp's seminal study of antagonistic functions in Russian folktales, Greimas and Bremond develop complex inventories of adversarial narrative roles which are conspicuously compatible with the Manichean interpretative pattern in paranoia.[6]

Besides this striking structural analogy, there is another similarity, between the respective ways in which readers question and explode paranoid thought and narrative fiction. Even trained psychiatrists find it extremely difficult to challenge a paranoid person's delusional system, because it is more rigid and at the same time more rationally integrated than the commonsensical worldview, which allows both for flaws and for subsequent modifications. In a different, but uncannily analogous way, it is equally difficult to challenge a literary narrative because it patently substitutes the necessities of art for the contingencies of the empirical world. For in both paranoia and narrative fiction, the flat surface of seemingly accidental occurrences conceals the worlds supported by networks of hidden intentions. To make matters worse, there is no firm ground on which we could base our certainty once we suspend the rules of those worlds, be they narrative or delusional. In the face of these two systems of a higher order of rationality and integration, we have to rely on an implicit, unsteady consensus within the interpretative community on what is the work of folly (delusion) and what is the product of imagination (illusion).

Obviously, stressing the presence of narrative emplotment and universalizing tendencies in paranoia and narrative fiction does not entail a denial of their essential heterogeneity. This distinction is very important because it is not just any coherence that the paranoiac is adamant to maintain. It is not the coherence of a language system, or for that matter of a structured narrative discourse, where the position of each particular sign is defined through a differential relation to all other signs. Instead, in paranoia reality appears to the reflecting consciousness as a web of intricate relations where everything is connected through a dark common centre, the plot. Another substantial difference between the two modes of narrative imagination concerns the nature of the constraints on our recognition of the link between narration and the factual premises of the empirical world. In a piece of narrative fiction, the mimetic function can be adopted, denied, or otherwise subjected to the ambiguous interplay of the forces of genre and individual creativity. In a paranoid system, on the other hand, mimesis is excluded *qua* possibility because this mode does not allow for the simultaneous existence of any two referential frameworks. A paranoid patient would easily grasp the abstract meaning of the concepts of simulation and representation and would even be capable of employing them, as long as they can be made functional within the structures of his or her persecutory thought. However, as soon as the notion of an alternative reality came into play, the most sophisticated persecutory narrative would collapse into a loose set of relativistic sub-plots.

That paranoia and narrative fiction emerge as independent systems with a set of correlating features is not very surprising for a literary theorist. What is less obvious is that there is a similarity between paranoia and a particular class of narrative fiction, namely those narratives that are designated as exilic. The fundamentally disruptive nature of psychotic disorders struck Kraepelin to the point where he differentiated paranoia from other forms of delusional emplotment by arguing that it effects a 'deep-seated change [tiefgreifende Umwandlung] of the overall outlook on life, [...] a "derangement" of standpoint ["Verrückung" des Standpunktes] on the surrounding world'.[7] While Kraepelin framed paranoia through the metaphoric lenses of the inner recesses of home ('deep-seated change') and mobility ('"derangement" of standpoint'), Freud presented a less contradictory view of the illness, one that brings it closer to the experience of exile. Specifically, he incorporated psychotic disorders into his general theory of defence mechanisms and argued that the failure in the dynamics of repression brings about 'the-end-of-the-world' [Weltuntergang] as exemplified by paranoia.[8] By a circuitous turn, this trope links paranoia to the popular perceptions of enforced displacement. For in both paranoid delusion and exile, one encounters an initial trauma, a personal world reduced to rubble through a sudden and overwhelming collapse. This is followed, in both cases, by a reactive move whereby a new world, with its own self-sustained network of meaning, is constructed. This new-found mode of cognition frames persecutors as a foundational agency and it is precisely in this aspect that paranoia is potentially nourished by the experience of expulsion. Moreover, the dismally centrifugal exilic path, where one is more or less forcefully dislodged from the focal point of his or her self, and thrown into a different, fundamentally decentred world, is compounded by a reverse effort, reminiscent of paranoid ideation. Consequently, the immediate, socially sanctioned cognitive framework is cancelled and replaced by a delusion that corresponds to the narcissistic desire to see oneself affiliated to some imaginary centre, or indeed, as the centre itself. Finally, in some studies, paranoia is metaphorically related to exile not through reference to persecutory agency or to megalomania, but through an emphasis on the unshakeably alienated nature of the patient's beliefs. Agassi and Fried thus argue that a paranoid person reveals 'the inflexibility of a stranger who may stick to his home system of thinking and behaviour and feelings'.[9] Other metaphoric construals of paranoia as exile may pass over the spatial aspect of alienation and emphasize dislocation in a temporal sense. Thus, Svetlana Boym sees an underlying link between collective paranoia and exilic nostalgia: 'The conspiratorial world view is fundamentally nostalgic. Its revival in modern times reflects a nostalgia for a transcendental cosmology and a quasi-religious world view dominated by an order of similarities and analogies.'[10]

If anything, these rhetorical transfers raise doubts over the boundaries and disciplinary status of psychiatric and literary critical discourses. While each relies on a set of conceivable statements that may have different extensions (paranoid disorder and exilic narrative), their intensions may come uncomfortably close to one another in that they rely on the metaphoricity of exile and persecution.

Paranoids through Exile: Aeschylus and Nabokov

If paranoia has been described both in terms of narrative *per se* and in terms of the narrative of exile in particular, then it would make sense to approach the trope from the opposite direction in order to seek confirmation of such rhetorical liaison. I will therefore take some exemplary narratives of exile and see whether and how they open up to the convolutions of paranoid thought. Several examples spring to mind. In a bout of foolish suspicion, Shakespeare's King Lear banishes from the court the Earl of Kent and then expels himself from the manor of his unkind daughters, 'contending with the fretful elements'.[11] His case, however, bears a resemblance to what is loosely called paranoid slant, rather than to *paranoia vera*, the delusional disorder. In the Neo-Romantic poetic mode, a memorable image of the self-dethroned king wandering in madness through the woods is found in W. B. Yeats's early poem 'The Madness of King Goll'. In the middle of a raging battle, King Goll is overcome by a strange and piercing feeling of being observed by the stars and by his fellow combatants:

> I stood: keen stars above me shone,
> Around me shone keen eyes of men:
> I laughed aloud and hurried on
> By rocky shore and rushy fen[12]

Upon his sudden sensation, conjured by remarkably resonant rhymes, everything falls into place: the king parts company with other warriors and roams through woods and hills. There, however, he lapses into a vague poeticized madness that captures — and honours, too — Yeats' pantheism rather than any particular clinical condition.

I suggest that what remains incipient in Shakespeare and Yeats is fully developed in two apparently unrelated texts, Aeschylus' tragedy Χοηφόροι (*Libation Bearers*, 458 BCE) and Nabokov's novel *Pale Fire* (1962). Cases of delusional insanity were periodically observed in antiquity just as in the nineteenth and twentieth centuries.[13] However, in each of these periods they are framed in fundamentally different ways. Ancient Greek sources record several uses of the coinage παράνοια, one of which refers to Orestes, but the term seems to have been understood as a metaphoric designator of any insanity with no specific diagnostic content. On the other hand, in the modern age, the diagnostic sense of paranoia was metaphorically inflated to the point where it has become a broad trope circumscribing virtually any form of falsely perceived enmity. Furthermore, it goes without saying that any discussion of resonances between the mythical force of the Greek tragedy and Nabokov's chess-problem poetics is bound to remain speculative rather than directly instructive.[14] It is justified by what it encourages us to say about the narrative rhetorical and integrative principles behind exile and persecutory delusion. Since literary criticism has rarely associated either of the two texts with paranoia, let us firstly bring together those elements in their plots that indicate the vivid interest in how persecutory agency is constructed by the imaginative resources set free in the process of the protagonists' dislocation.

Ancient Greek myth has it that Orestes was instructed by Apollo to return from exile to his native Argos and slay Clytemnestra and Aegisthus in order to take revenge for the horrendous death of Agamemnon. Soon after committing this act, he is subjected to a more severe exile: chased away from the city by the malignant Furies (the Erinyes) he flees firstly to Apollo's temple in Delphi and then to Athena's shrine on the Acropolis where he finally gets reprieve. While in most versions of the myth the ontological status of the Furies seems to have been incontestable, it is Aeschylus who in *Libation Bearers*, the second part of *Oresteia*, makes their existence problematic by allowing for a possibility that they are simply a mental image created by the guilt-ridden Orestes. At the end of the play, after having exacted revenge over his mother and her lover, Orestes senses the approach of these beings, which no one else perceives:

ἆ, ἆ.
δμωαὶ γυναῖκες, αἵδε Γοργόνων δίκην
φαιοχίτωνες καὶ πεπλεκτανημέναι
πυκνοῖς δράκουσιν· οὐκέτ'ἂν μείναιμ' ἐγώ.

[Ah, ah! Ye handmaidens, see them yonder — like Gorgons, stoled in sable garb, entwined with swarming snakes! I can no longer stay.][15]

The vision is immediately dismissed by the chorus as sensory confusion, but Orestes reaffirms that it is genuine and departs from Argos in a state of utter terror:

ὑμεῖς μὲν οὐχ ὁρᾶτε τάσδ', ἐγὼ δ' ὁρῶ·
ἐλαύνομαι δὲ κοὐκέτ' ἂν μείναιμ' ἐγώ.

[You see them not, but I see them. I am pursued. I can no longer stay.][16]

In contrast to the *Iliad*, where a 'temporary clouding or bewildering of normal consciousness' is instrumental to the fulfilment of a divine design, Aeschylus' Orestes is struck by a deep mental perturbation that is an end in itself even if incurred by a daemonic intervention.[17] Although the diagnoses and aetiology that have been ascribed to Orestes' state of mind differ, most commentators agree that his reasoning demonstrates a severe impairment that borders on psychosis.[18] It is important to note that in Εὐμενίδες (*The Kindly Ones*, 458 BCE), the third part of the trilogy about the House of Atreus, Aeschylus apparently reverts to the popular version of the myth as those beings emerge on the stage in the shape of the chorus of the Furies. The obvious reason for this is that — differently from *Agamemnon* and *Libation Bearers*, in which he developed a keen interest in the psychology of the criminal mind and of guilt — in *The Kindly Ones* Aeschylus was primarily concerned with the question of theological justice that could re-establish the shattered moral equilibrium of the city-state. The appearance of the Furies on stage is, therefore, not so much about the denial of Orestes' madness at the end of the earlier play, as about making their transformation into the benevolent Eumenides visually arresting.

As a mythopoeic interpretation of historical violence, Nabokov's *Pale Fire* introduces a different model of persecutory agency in exile. The narrative is embroiled in an elaborate and often absurd critical apparatus imposed by the fictional editor-hero, but the basic narrative line seems to run as follows. Charles Kinbote (anagrammatically linked with Russian émigré scholar Vseslav Botkin), the novel's fictional narrator, is a stymied academic newly arrived at a gloomy college in New Wye, United States. His only compulsion consists in a story which he divulges to his friend, the ageing poet John Shade, for whom he nurtures a homoerotic sentiment. Dr Kinbote nourishes the poet's imagination by retelling him how Charles Xavier II, a dethroned ruler of the country of Zembla, had managed to escape into exile following a revolution in his kingdom. Suspecting that he is chased by the fanatical revolutionary activist Gradus, Dr Kinbote's king has to live incognito, firstly in France and then in the United States. As the king's and Gradus's itineraries finally come critically close to one another, and John Shade perishes as an accidental victim of the assassin's bullet, the reader learns that Dr Kinbote himself is the dethroned king Charles Xavier II and the actual target of the persecution. What does this conventional recognition plot have to do with psychoses? Because it is a work of retrospective prose narration, rather than drama, the clash between madness and its social context cannot be staged in the same way as in *Oresteia*. Yet Nabokov lets slip throughout Kinbote's story a number of details that might indicate that in *Pale Fire* we are not dealing with recollected memories of a real persecution but with the paranoid narrative of a psychotic person who is convinced that he is a king in exile. To begin with, Kinbote bitterly complains that his colleagues from the college treat his behaviour as paranoid, probably in a clinical sense: while some bluntly call him insane in his presence, others take cruel pleasure in sending him anonymous notes.[19] Furthermore, there is a very strong indication that at certain moments of lucidity, Kinbote himself thinks of his persecutory visions as hallucinations: 'At times I thought that only by self-destruction could I hope to cheat the relentlessly advancing assassins who were in me, in my eardrums, in my pulse, in my skull, rather than on that constant highway [...].'[20] As a final signal, at the very end of the novel, he intimates a wish to write a melodrama about 'a lunatic who intends to kill an imaginary king, another lunatic who imagines himself to be that king, and a distinguished old poet who stumbles by chance into the line of fire, and perishes in the clash between the two figments.'[21] Not surprisingly, Kinbote laments what he sees as insufficient importance attached to Zembla in Shade's poem *Pale Fire*, but fails to notice that his own persecutory imagination has found an oblique way into the poem:

> [...] I alone
> Knew nothing and a great conspiracy
> Of books and people hid the truth from me.[22]

Notwithstanding their generic differences and contrasting historical perceptions of madness, what links *Libation Bearers* and *Pale Fire* is the fact that in both texts exile not only concurs with the emergence of persecutory thought but also contributes to the literary shaping of that state. Exile represents, on the one hand, the focal lens for delusion whereby the protagonists construct and integrate their absent persecutors, and, on the other hand, the hall of mirrors where the protagonists' delusion is reflected in fictional illusion. For, what we find in the two texts is a deliberate blurring of the ontological status of the persecutors who stand behind the initial exile, and the only difference consists in the ways in which this agency is blurred. Aeschylus' tragedy hints at a hallucinatory delirium of the visual type but we are uncertain as to whether the advent of the Furies is a consequence of Orestes' derangement, or is it the real though invisible Furies that bring about that derangement as a punishment. In Nabokov's novel, there is a hint at hallucinations but there is also an even stronger emphasis on delusory interpretation of the given components of reality. The reader is left uncertain as to whether the murderer Gradus is conjured up by the sheer force of Kinbote's feverish imagination, or whether Kinbote's awareness of an emergent conspiracy adds up to create a paranoid jigsaw.

Although Orestes and Kinbote perceive themselves as being exposed to unremitting persecution, and although this perception is questioned by others as delusional, we still hesitate to qualify the two heroes as paranoid. Orestes does not have the agonizing urge to constantly redress and expand the malevolent ploy for the simple reason that it is already there, objectified and inscribed into the plot of the myth. Its paramount feature is the vicious conspiracy of powerful transcendental agents who bring particular outstanding mortals to ruin by making use of other humans as tools.[23] The gods of the Pantheon seem to have a firm grip not only on the events that influence Orestes' decisions and actions but also on his consciousness. For, just as he does not have to create an elaborate conspiratorial system, neither does he aggrandize himself, because grandeur is conferred upon him by the virtue of the fact that he stands alone in the centre of the declared ploy of the divinities. In a paradoxical way, the condensed scene at the end of *Libation Bearers* is a *non plus ultra* model of the delusional construct, the ultimate paranoid system which, being embodied on the stage, ceases to be paranoid. By contrast, in *Pale Fire* Kinbote's persecutory thought is at some important moments too cerebral to be described as paranoid. His deliberations demonstrate a level of self-reflexivity that would be unattainable to an ordinary psychotic. This becomes most obvious at the end of the novel, when he anticipates the advent of another assassin ('a bigger, more respectable, more competent Gradus'[24]) who will not bungle the job. Though stretching the role of the persecutor *ad extremis*, this is hardly a paranoid thought. The fact that it is articulated with a sense of humour and at that it comes at the end of the novel makes it look more like an authorial innuendo concerning the fictional nature of both literary and paranoid narratives. Thus, the ambiguity generated by the representation of delusion in exile is only resolved at the second degree, by the reader's transcending the text and applying a template of interpretative conventions — in Aeschylus' case the mythical framework, and in Nabokov's novel the metafictional game.

Therefore, literary theory and criticism cannot give an easy answer to the riddle presented by the rise of persecutory thought in exilic context. Since both paranoia and implied exile are qualified by the absence of persecutors, there is in our interpretative procedures a consequential emphasis on the narrative construction of that persecutory agency. This emphasis makes literary narratives such as *Oresteia* and *Pale Fire* a particularly favourable field of enquiry into the inner rhetoricity of the two phenomena. Nevertheless, any examination of the ways in which literary texts open up to paranoid ideation and encourage the interpretative input from clinical observations necessarily becomes a study of the strategies of ambiguity through which the texts resist such interpretations. What is beyond doubt, however, is that in literary texts that knit exile and paranoia, the former remains a catalyst that enables such ambiguity.

Having discussed how in the scholarly context the exilic narrative was metaphorically applied to fix paranoia and how in literary narratives of exile paranoia condenses and at the same time renders ambiguous the narrative world of the text, I will propose that there is a sense in which exile and paranoia are transformed into social action through a metaphoric turn. More precisely, I will argue that the pattern of Orestes' and Kinbote's delusion is determined by the peculiarly rhetorical nature of their exilic experience.

The social and political circumstances of the two exilic itineraries are not as transparent as they may appear. For Aeschylus, who relied on the archaic Greek nomos to a greater extent than the later tragic poets did, Orestes' crime was dreadful enough to warrant his exclusion from the native community. Such exclusion could have been effected either through his death or through his exile. Neither of these would have been very unusual in Athens: on the one hand, the capital punishment was envisaged for a set of various crimes including the premeditated murders of family members; on the other hand, the law of ostracism, in force since Cleisthenes, provided for a temporary removal of the potential tyrants from the city. Just as importantly, both of these measures were subject to approval by popular vote. However, in *Libation Bearers*, the people of Argos gathered in the chorus do condemn the crime, but remain remarkably reticent in proposing a punishment, and to a certain extent even sympathize with the transgressor. Orestes leaves without any explicit social or legal pressure and yet wants to be remembered as an expellee:

> ἐγὼ δ' ἀλήτης τῆσδε γῆς ἀπόξενος,
> ζῶν καὶ τεθνηκὼς τάσδε κληδόνας λιπών.

[I go forth a wanderer, strangered from this land, leaving behind, in life or death, this report of me.][25]

Charles Xavier II leaves his kingdom in different circumstances which nevertheless leave considerable space for ambiguity. Although he refers to himself as an exile, or a banished person, it transpires through his narration that his departure was a consequence of his own decision rather than of a social action aimed at his exclusion from the polity. Initially, the self-appointed revolutionary regime imprisons him as a royal hostage to ensure the enactment of their plan. However, upon learning that in the next stage he may be put on trial and sentenced to death, the King uses a secret corridor that leads through the royal theatre to escape. Kinbote's wandering through deserted dressing rooms recalls a pervasive poetic topos: the evasion from the grips of death can only be achieved by the transformative agency of art. Thus, rather than being straightforwardly evicted, Charles Xavier II flees through the back door. Kinbote's narrative construction of the persecutory agency is associated with the paradoxical nature of his exile. What remains ambiguous in the political context of his departure is assiduously compensated for by his delusory imagination.

Two significant circumstances link Orestes and Kinbote and determine their persecutory thought: first, their departure is not enforced by any explicit measure of the polity; second, it is perceived as a substitute death penalty. Of course, by emphasizing this parallelism we do not disregard the fact that in Aeschylus' staging of Orestes' expiation there is the overarching mythical thread of the ancient curse which strikes at each successive generation of the House of Atreus. It would certainly be too strong a statement to argue that in *Oresteia* the construction of the agency of force comes as a reactive complement to the fact that Orestes was not banished directly. On the contrary, the trilogy's plot foregrounds the pervasive idea of retributive justice as a predominant framework of motivation. Nevertheless, I will submit a thesis that is logically less committing than the previous hypothesis but one that is much easier to defend: Orestes' construction of the agency of force, under the pressure of retributive justice, is made possible, if not facilitated, by the fact that he was not directly banished by his fellow countrymen. Likewise, in *Pale Fire*, Kinbote's retrospective fixation on the imminent advent of the assassin Gradus would not make narrative sense in the conceivable alternative case in which he were banished by a public decree and chased away from the palace through the main gate.

The one counter-example to test this argument would be Euripides' Ὀρέστης [*Orestes*, 408 BCE]. In this play, the invisible Furies are quoted by Electra as the immediate cause of Orestes' illness and they indeed represent the focal point of his intermittent visual hallucinations.[26] However, they are deprived of their function in structuring the narrative, as Orestes himself perceives them as unreal, and a part of his madness.[27] Instead, there is in *Orestes* a direct social agency in support of punishment. This agency is represented by the people of Argos, who declare a prohibition of fire and shelter and speech (an archaic metonymic formulation of exile), and by Clytemnestra's father Tyndareus, who advocates the punishment of death for both Orestes and Electra.[28] Thus, while Euripides sets Orestes' derangement at the centre of social conflict, and sees temporary exile as a resolution of this conflict, Aeschylus projects the unresolved social conflict into Orestes' persecutory imagination and conceives of exile as a way of externalizing that conflict. In *Libation Bearers*, the Furies act not only as the traditional agency of punishment but also as the agency of social exclusion. This is rhetorically encoded by the Argive community as the action of a transcendental agent only to be rhetorically decoded by Orestes' hallucination. In a paradoxical way, therefore, it is precisely because of the lack of an explicit social action that the delusional process gives Orestes — and Kinbote — a stable point of self-reference.

Uncoerced exile has in this way an *enabling* function in persecution narratives. The question of whether such implied exile triggers paranoia or whether it reinforces it subsequently would definitely shift the discussion to the field of empirical evidence where displacement would have to be considered alongside other contributing factors. From the literary point of view, however, the assumption that uncoerced exile need not directly cause, but still makes probable, in the Aristotelian sense, persecutory narrative has a clear interpretative advantage. It proposes a sensible way of addressing coincidence of exile and persecutory thought in the *Oresteia* and *Pale Fire* while still maintaining the inherent ambiguity and individuality of both texts.

Paranoid Exiles Embattled: The Case of Jean-Jacques Rousseau

After the initially enthusiastic response of the coryphaei of modern psychiatry, Kraepelin, Bleuler and Freud, the second half of the twentieth century brought a significant shift which led to a rather contradictory development in the concept of paranoia. On the one hand, the medical content of the illness had been increasingly brought into question and the very term paranoia was replaced by other, less essentialist, labels such as delusional disorder, or by compound denominators, such as paraphrenia and paranoid schizophrenia. By 1970, this terminological reshuffle had become so manifest that it prompted Aubrey Lewis to claim that 'paranoid' was merely 'a descriptive term carrying no implications about chronicity, permanence, curability, presence of hallucinations, integrity of personality or aetiology'.[29] On the other hand, with its remarkably successful appropriation by political theorists, paranoia has asserted itself as a virtually ubiquitous trope in the social sciences and political life. The new field of rhetorical application was delimited by Richard Hofstadter, who in 1963 coined the concept of 'the paranoid style' to define the recurrent, collectively sustained belief into 'the existence of a vast, insidious, preternaturally effective international conspiratorial network designed to perpetrate acts of the most fiendish character'.[30] In this seminal essay, Hofstadter recognized that there was a distinction to be made between the clinical and the political paranoia and that the latter designator is borrowed from psychiatry for want of a better term in his discipline. In the meantime, however, the idea of collective — as opposed to individual — paranoia had its essential differential premise erased. It became almost like a dead metaphor, one of those figurative expressions that are so common that we stop perceiving them as such.

An alternative approach was articulated by those scholars who, unlike Hofstadter, believed that the confrontational field of politics quite literally represented a magnet for anyone with paranoid tendencies. Thus, Robins and Post roundly argue that there is no substantial break of continuity between the individual and collective paranoid response: 'Paranoia, the most interpersonal of mental illnesses, is also the most political in the broad sense of centering on power relationships. [...] The world of politics has powerful valence for individuals and groups with paranoid features.'[31] In this explanatory framework, paranoid persons have recourse to politics as a part of their coping mechanism. This recourse enables them to substantiate and legitimize their persecutory worldview through the political discourse of danger and pre-emption, and at the same time to alleviate their intense fears by engaging other individuals and groups in it.[32] For one thing, this propitious heuristic merger of clinical and political paranoia opened up a whole range of questions about the interpersonal implications of persecutory imagination. Can paranoid persons take effective control of a polity by stimulating in its members an acute or a chronic sense of persecution and victimization? If groups and their leaders rely on persecutory narratives for cohesion but still have actual political opponents, does this make them less paranoid? Can paranoid anxieties be intentionally appropriated by a totalitarian regime and used as a label against its critically disposed dissidents?

Even so, it is striking that virtually all of these recent studies implicitly rely on the idea of harmony, or at least very smooth passage, between individual and collective paranoia. By rallying around their leaders, groups respond to, and legitimize, individual persecutory narratives. While this type of convergence may represent a run-of-the-mill contact between individual and collective delusion, other, less harmonious situations are both theoretically possible and historically recorded. The case in point is one where an individual's persecutory plot is met by collective conspiratorial narratives that centre precisely upon his or her personality. In view of such cases, one has to allow that the well-known claim, attributed to Golda Meir, that 'even paranoids have enemies' is more than a mere witticism.[33] An additional difficulty is that hardly any of the current studies in collective paranoia discuss the impact of the spatial displacement of the targeted individuals or groups in the evolution of their conspiratorial thinking. It has been suggested that conspiracy theories are 'migrating conspiratorial structures': they cross cultural and administrative borders and spread from one country to another with striking ease.[34] Yet, these migrating structures often quite literally arise from migration, turn upon it and are even meant to lead to further migration, with greater or lesser degree of duress. When individuals with persecutory thoughts and groups that espouse beliefs in a conspiracy narrative get into a direct conflict, singling one another out for mutually hostile narrative projections, some form of exclusion is a likely outcome.

The exilic itinerary of Jean-Jacques Rousseau is bound to occupy a special place in any discussion of paranoid narratives arising from migration and this pre-eminence is due to two main reasons. On the one side, his paranoid thought, ingrained in some aspects of his political philosophy and then stimulated by his consecutive conflicts with the political and intellectual elites of several European countries, was very real and directly informed his autobiographic works in the last decade of his life. Each in its own way, *Confessions*, *Dialogues* (*Rousseau, the Judge of Jean Jacques*) and *Reveries of a Solitary Walker* show how the experience of exile provided him with an opportunity for solitary brooding and, just as importantly, lent his incipient plot a proper narrative structure. The empirical anchorage of Rousseau's construal of force is, thus, much stronger than that of the *Libation Bearers* and *Pale Fire* and enables us better to observe the different rhetorical transfers of force from reality, i.e. a discursive order marked by direct causation, into literature, i.e. a discursive order marked by imagination and polysemy. On the other side, notwithstanding any clinical aspects of Rousseau's adversity, it has been acknowledged that the actual persecution against him was equally real and diverse which makes him a prototype of Meir's 'paranoid with enemies'.[35] The picture that emerges from his correspondence and his posthumous celebrity is that of a misunderstood and distressed Rousseau, a universal *pharmakos*, hounded by personal animosity and religious hatred, and a Jacobin saint, adored by such conspiratorial figures as Robespierre and Bertrand Barère, Anacreon of the Guillotine.[36] In that respect, the dual persecutory narrative emerging from Rousseau's celebrity differs from the single-plot model developed in the *Libation Bearers* and *Pale Fire*. Such a dual plot allows a better insight into the social conflict — and also the interaction — between the individual paranoia and the collective persecutory complex.

Formally, none of Rousseau's successive exiles in 1760s can count as a direct banishment: all were effected by indirect means such as foreclosure, evasion from *prise de corps*, and voluntary departure. In June 1762, following the hostile clerical reactions to the publication of his *Social Contract* and *Émile* earlier that year, and after being advised in confidence that a warrant for his arrest had been issued by the *Parlement* in Paris, Rousseau left his cottage home at Montmorency, in the vicinity of Paris. As he was on the road, bypassing the capital and heading south, copies of his books were burnt in Paris and in his native Geneva. During the next five years he and his mistress, Thérèse Le Vasseur, would keep moving from one state to another, getting rather varied levels of hospitality and very little in the way of a steady legal status. Rousseau's initial plan was to seek asylum in one of the Swiss counties. His Geneva, the citizenship of which he still held, was unlikely because it followed the lead of France and declared a *prise de corps*. The first stay, in the picturesque burgh of Yverdon, was fairly short since the Bernese authorities, to whose jurisdiction the township belonged, declared Rousseau *persona non grata*. Rousseau's next and longest stopover was in the Swiss village of Môtiers, at that time part of the Prussian enclave principality of Neuchâtel, where he spent three relatively calm years under the patronage of its enlightened king, Frederick the Great. In late 1765, however, Rousseau's home was lapidated by a mob and he felt compelled to leave the village. Having decided to try the Bernese territory again, he settled on the island of St Peter (Île de St.-Pierre), on the lake of Bienne, and seems to have found it so agreeable that he planned to spend the rest of his days there. Nevertheless, weeks into his stay on the island he was re-expelled by the Bernese authorities and, after some hesitation, went on to accept the invitation of David Hume to come and settle in England. After an acrimonious quarrel with his host, Rousseau remained confined to Wootton Hall, Staffordshire, which had already been made available to him by another benefactor, Richard Davenport. In 1767, finally, he returned to France under an assumed name and spent the rest of his life in different locales in northern and central parts of the country: at Trie in the Oise valley, in Montquin in the Loire region, in Paris and, in the last six weeks before his death in July 1778, in Ermenonville, again in the Oise area.[37]

There has been a wide consensus amongst both contemporaries and scholars of Rousseau that throughout this period he was prey to recurrent delusions of persecution which alienated all but his most loyal supporters and which only subsided in the last two years of his life. Delusions of observation (spies, walls with ears), reference (uncanny coincidences), interference (poisoning, tempering with manuscripts and correspondence) as well as a progressive belief into a universal conspiracy have all been pinned down in Rousseau's works and confirmed by personal recollections of his ever diminishing circle of friends. To be sure, no biographer of Rousseau has failed to recognize that during the same period he was exposed to a real *ad hominem* campaign by his former friends, the *philosophes*, and by clerical circles who acted with a significant degree of coordination and whose principal accusations — namely hypocrisy (moral leper) and heresy (Antichrist) — chimed with some of Rousseau's darkest obsessions. Whether as a punch bag for intellectual coteries or the mastermind of an arcane conspiracy, Rousseau in his exile took different agential roles in the different persecution narratives and fought them, while at the same time borrowing from them for his own paranoid outlook. Nevertheless, while Rousseau's paranoia and the sundry manoeuvres against him have been thoroughly explored there is still little agreement on the precise mechanisms of their interaction and even less readiness to pinpoint the specific input of exile in that interaction.

To begin with, notwithstanding historical shifts in diagnostic terminology, which have now been resolved in favour of paranoia, the contest over its aetiology and impact on Rousseau's wellbeing and creativity still remains. For some scholars, Rousseau's paranoia is primarily an endogenous phenomenon, arising from his psyche or from his political ideas or from some form of interaction between the two, and it is a mere coincidence that at the same time an actual campaign went on against him. In John Farrell's formulation, 'it was his belief in the conspiracy against him, and not that conspiracy itself, that was cutting him off from his friends and contemporaries'.[38] In other words, the 'infernal affair' — the scholarly term for Rousseau's dispute with the *philosophes* and Hume — was a purely internal affair. For others, Rousseau's paranoia was largely due to a series of adverse exogenous factors, in particular the envy and mistreatment at the hands of different coteries. Eugene Stelzig, for instance, talks of a 'persecution mania, but one originating in and fueled by the actual persecution and misfortunes he experienced as a result of his unprecedented celebrity as a writer and thinker'.[39] In this second approach, all ingredients for a persecutory narrative had already been supplied through the *ad hominem* campaign and the pathological twist only happened when Rousseau identified with his role as a victim to such an extent that he developed a need for villains.

The two aetiological frameworks, namely the psycho-philosophical and the socio-psychological one, have prompted equally polarized interpretations of Rousseau's exile. The first of these interpretations taps the psychoanalytic theory and insists on a repetition mechanism whereby Rousseau would condemn himself to exile and, to quote Starobinski, 'transform the solitude he wanted into a solitude he suffered'.[40] In this case, we would need to assume that a primary paranoid slant would push one into exile. The second interpretation was indicated by Leo Damrosch who argues that Rousseau was 'the only important writer in Europe who had been systematically expelled from one country after another and denounced by former friends and associates as well as by governments and churches'.[41] If this latter approach is correct, it would be exile that leads to paranoia.

Both explanations suffer from the same problem: they do not differentiate between direct and indirect (implied) exile and fail to account for specific ways in which narrative imagination is exercised in both. As it happens, Rousseau's exilic movements were sequential and all of them were implied; actually, they showcase all three forms: evasion, foreclosure, and informal duress. To form the image of a single and direct banishment from such fragmented, implicit exiles required a leap of imagination. While we cannot discuss all of these stages we can still focus on one of them and draw some meaningful conclusions. I propose to look more closely at Rousseau's residence in Môtiers as the one instance where physical force was definitely applied against him and to follow up some representative discursive construals of that force. This focus sets out to achieve two goals. On the one hand, it aims to illustrate an important segment of this chapter's argument on the link between implied exile and paranoia. Namely, it will substantiate the claim that there is, in addition to the single-plot model, another pattern: juxtaposition and interaction of individual and collective persecutory narratives. On the other hand, it is going to contribute to the study of exogenous factors behind Rousseau's paranoia. Scholars have typically framed Rousseau's conflict with the *philosophes* in France (1757–62) and the troubled relationship with Hume in England (1766–67), letting the exile from Môtiers (1765) slip through the net.

To begin with, Rousseau's Môtiers period offers interesting insights in itself. Not only was it Rousseau's steadiest place of residence in exile, it was also a watershed moment in the evolution of his public image. In that distant and autarchic Calvinist parish Rousseau got into the habit of wearing his hallmark Armenian dress, secured the protective attitude if not a wholehearted support of Frederick II, started striking back at the encyclopedists' pamphlets against him and conceived his autobiographic project, *Confessions*. Throughout his stay, the municipal authorities, represented by the castellan Martinet and the governor of Neuchâtel, Lord Marshal George Keith, abided by the King's advice and remained favourably disposed. As a token of civic integration, Rousseau eventually received naturalization papers, a significant improvement because he would be 'à l'abri de toute expulsion légale, même de la part du Prince' [safe from legal expulsion, even at the hands of the Prince], as he would argue in *Confessions*.[42] As the exile of intellectual figures typically adds to their celebrity and brings about some repositioning within both the home and the host community, Rousseau kept receiving numerous visits by friends and admirers from France and made new acquaintances in Switzerland.

Most importantly, the village was the scene of a key episode in his biographic myth, known as the *lapidation de Môtiers*. With his intemperate mindset and unorthodox views on Christianity, Rousseau soon got himself embroiled in a bitter dispute with the local clergy, led by Frederic-Guillaume Montmollin, the recently appointed pastor and a redoubtable rigorist in matters of doctrine. Displeased with Rousseau's *Letters from the Mountain*, Montmollin initially sought to persuade him to refrain from taking Holy Communion — which was tantamount to excommunication — and when the latter refused, a hearing was arranged at the consistory to have him formally excluded. When this, too, failed Montmollin took advantage of his Sunday sermons to stir up parishioners against him. In one of these inflammatory sermons, he quoted a verse from the *Book of Proverbs* (15. 8), 'The sacrifice of the wicked is an abomination to the Lord; but the prayer of the upright is his delight'.[43] Although Rousseau, who attended the service, was not explicitly mentioned there was a tacit agreement that the pastor referred to him. The results of this oratorical campaign were quickly to be seen: Rousseau was mocked as a false prophet, the ambiguous threat 'Kill that dog!' was heard as he passed by with his dog Sultan, a stone was placed on the door frame of his courtyard. After a series of sporadic insults and threats, on the night of 6 September 1765, during a fair in Môtiers, Rousseau's domicile was attacked and lapidated by unknown assailants. Although many stones landed on the veranda and one of them appears to have reached as far as Rousseau's bedroom it was fortunate that no one was injured and that the castellan and the guards quickly came to his rescue. The investigation of the incident was prompt and thorough but since villagers were not willing to cooperate it failed to identify the perpetrators. The local authorities recommended that Rousseau leave the municipality immediately for his own safety, but also in the general interest. The neighbouring community of Couvet was quick to offer him an asylum but Rousseau deemed it too close to the epicentre of the events and eventually left Neuchâtel. Thérèse initially remained in Môtiers to take care of their belongings but joined him soon afterwards.

If anything, this chain of events must have put to the test some of Rousseau's key political ideas. In his *Social Contract*, Rousseau envisaged permanent exile for violators of the compact, a punishment that stands one remove from the death penalty which was to be pronounced on enemies of the state.[44] He stipulated that exile should be enforced after a statutory trial and judgment and somewhat erroneously quoted Cicero as an instance of legitimate banishment. Just as importantly, in the same treatise he stressed that the political subject is only obliged to abide by ordinances of legitimate powers; for example, a brigand with a pistol who asks for one's purse constitutes no such authority.[45] That practically means that exile was allowable only as direct banishment and never as implied exile. As we will see shortly, Rousseau's own exile from Môtiers was rather different from all principles set out in *Social Contract*.

In the first place, the political circumstances differed from Rousseau's model state. While Môtiers was a parochial community within Neuchatel, which itself was a distant enclave of Prussia, it was nonetheless a free community and, as such, riven by several of the lines of divide which typify modern nation states: between officialdom and clergy, between liberals and conservatives, and between men of letters and peasantry. In a system where the social contract is not fully functional, for one fraction to pressurize someone into exile by indirect means is a convenience rather than a convention. Secondly, Rousseau's departure was not enforced by legitimate authority in a statutory procedure. There was no trial, or for that matter a decree of proscription; steps were taken to make him depart of his own volition and, what is more, some of these steps were made by informal groups that are partly opposed to legitimate powers. Firstly, in connection with the right to Holy Communion, Pastor Montmollin wanted Rousseau to give it up, rather than force the consistory to exclude him. Secondly, Montmollin in his sermons made allusions to Rousseau in a cryptic form, which relied on a tacit interpretive consensus, rather than explicitly, in a way that could be challenged. Thirdly, notwithstanding the magistrates' informal encouragements to leave, the final decision was still with Rousseau. Fourthly, he decided not to take asylum in the adjacent village of Couvet because he feared further hostile propaganda from Môtiers, which effectively meant that he felt banished from that area, too.

It might be urged, as against the above argument, that there still is an element of robust force in the lapidation episode. Namely, indirect though all the other slurs and encroachments may appear, at least the stoning of Rousseau's home should be seen as a blatant use of force. At least those stones communicate a peremptory request for the target to leave, i.e. they impart the duress of direct exile. On closer inspection, this claim, too, seems dubious. The perpetrators were never discovered and even if one assumes that they had been instructed or merely inspired by Montmollin — which he vehemently denied — they would have acted as intermediaries on behalf of the clergy, two removes from the secular magistrates. Furthermore, since the culprits were not identified, it is difficult to gauge the actual motives behind the act: was it a message of banishment, or an assassination attempt, or a warning, or perhaps a drunken peasants' charivari for Rousseau and Thérèse?[46] Finally, just as the assailants were hidden from view so too Rousseau remained hidden for them and their stones merely hit different places in the house without ever reaching him, so it is not certain whether bodily harm or material damage was intended. We know for a fact that some stones landed on the veranda of Rousseau's house but this fact is at the same time pretty much everything we do know. For a sovereign's protégé and a naturalized burgher of the county, this cue is hardly enough of an incentive to leave. Thus, in the lack of judicial context, the punitive framework that justifies the departure had to be elicited by imaginative and rhetorical means. And elicited it was, by supporters and opponents, and of course by Rousseau himself.

The contemporaneous recollections and appraisals of the stoning make for interesting reading. Those sympathetic to Rousseau went on to reconstruct the missing elements in the narrative of enforcement and, with the passage of time, tended to portray the event as an act of direct banishment and an attempt at his life. This transfer was significantly aided by a major religious prototype in which stoning and exile went together. Saint Stephen, the first martyr of the early Christian Church, was put to death when the mob 'dragged him out of the city and began to stone him'.[47] The attempt to fill in the narrative gaps in the *lapidation* story by adopting mythical elements is clearly visible in an engraving which started circulating soon after the event and was later included in Pierre Philippe Choffard's collection of *Tableaux de la Suisse* (1777) under the title 'Vue de Môtiers avec le tableau de fermeté du Philosophe de Genêve' ('View of Môtiers with a tableau of the fortitude of the

Philosopher from Geneva').[48] In that engraving, the whole process is transferred into the visual realm; the appropriate adjustments are made in time and setting and the agents are made completely transparent. The event unfolds in plain daylight rather than in the night-time and the scene is displaced from Rousseau's home in the village to a well-lit clearing on the outskirts with a good view of the symbolic landscape: a darkened belfry and the mighty Alps in the background. In the foreground, Rousseau, in his Armenian dress and accompanied by his dog, gives alms to a beggar; on the opposite side, Montmollin instigates peasants gathered around him to throw stones at them. Not only is the force of exile reconstructed in narrative terms, it is also overconstructed in metaphorical terms to reflect Christ's well-known parable from the gospel: 'Which of you, if his son asks for bread, will give him a stone?'[49] In this optic, Rousseau's exile from Môtiers results from the conspiracy of the village's pastor, Montmollin, the unnatural spiritual father who throws stones instead of dispensing the true body of Christ.

This is not, of course, to say that the affair was lacking in doubting Thomases. The opponents of Rousseau, as well as a few friends of suspicious disposition, questioned the veracity of his claims and tried to read in between the lines of the official investigation reports. These sceptics insisted that the stone which allegedly landed in the interior of the house was too large to pass through the window. The point was actually mentioned by one of the witnesses but that line of investigation was curiously dropped. However, once granted, this assumption of necessity points to a conspiracy: somebody must have surreptitiously brought in the stone and then broken the window in order to make Rousseau believe that he was under attack from outside the house. But who would be capable of such a perfidy and why? It was Thérèse, possibly the only person who curried even less favour with the residents of Môtiers than Rousseau, who was made to bear the brunt of this conspiracy narrative. Displeased by Môtiers, where her Catholic confession, lowly origin and gross manners made her a pariah of the community, she was said to have wanted to alienate Rousseau from the village and to make the idea of any further stay repulsive to him. Reminiscing on the event, the publicist Joseph-Michel-Antoine Servan asked with a touch of sanctimony: 'After all, what man would not prefer to have Rousseau's housewife a bit bored to having thousands of Swiss so wicked, enraged and murderous?'[50]

The third conspiracy narrative to emerge in the aftermath of the stoning frames Rousseau as the key adversary and, unsurprisingly, is anonymous, like the attack itself. On the morning of 15 September 1765, just over a week after the event, the guards of Môtiers reported an unusual find on the market square: leaned against the fountain, a large polichinelle puppet observed the traffic. On inspection, the puppet was found to hold a message in one of its pockets and its opening lines read as follows: 'Me Voicy trouvant tout réjouis | en Voyant Motier délivré | de l'Impie qui s'est evader | Sa Servante encore icy | prenez Garde mes amis | et Montrés vous tous Zélés | pour l'aller accompagner' [Here I find all quite pleased | to see Motier saved from the infidel who's fled | His servant being still here | be on the watch my friends | and show your zeal | to see her off.][51] In addition to the arch-foe, Rousseau, and his servant, Thérèse, the composer of the message names several other eminent figures as accomplices. There is, first, chatelaine Martinet, 'le Vieu baboin' [the old ape] who went on to investigate the stoning rather than all the scandals the infamous pair has caused.[52] Then, there is the sovereign himself, King Frederick II, 'le Chatré bavarois' [the Bavarian castrato] who is requested to restrain himself instead of meddling into the local business.[53] And last but not least, the spiteful Covassons, the men from the neighbouring Couvet, who even dared to offer asylum to Rousseau.[54] In this grassroots paranoid microcosmos, the entire political system is reorganized on a conspiratorial basis, as a plot of the powerful of the world against the village: the mastermind has a helper, powerful allies, and local supporters. The fact that the message is articulated by a polichinelle puppet is not coincidental, either. Polichinelle is the French adaptation of *Pulcinella*, a standard character from *commedia dell'arte* whose duty it is inadvertently to communicate the open secret. Polichinelle, thus, has a rather ambiguous role: it is a defiant tenor of popular satire and a dehumanized effigy of the exiled Rousseau.

The three conspiracy narratives arose from the same event, the implied exile of Rousseau, and all of them reconstruct the agency of force *ex ungue leonem* i.e. by starting from the visible elements (stones, departure) and deducing those that are not visible (agents, motives), as well as the whole (a plot). The construction of the network proceeds by metonymic transfers; however, in all three cases there is an element of symbolization. The communicative vacuum of implied exile, thus, stimulates the rise of conspiracy narratives but also provides a convenient framework for their rhetorical interaction.

But what about Rousseau himself? Is the *lapidation de Môtiers* connected to his persecutory imagination and how? Differently from the residents of the divided village, who strived to rationalize the event in terms of the political relations in their community, Rousseau was primarily concerned with integrating it into his nascent autobiographic myth. That narrative self-inscription included several other exiles and ultimately projected horizons much wider than Môtiers and enemies more powerful than Montmollin. Observed in that broader context, it would be erroneous to claim that the episode of Môtiers was a trigger for Rousseau's persecutory imagination. Quite the contrary, its first flare-up is traced to the period preceding exile when he was convinced that Jesuits were planning to destroy the manuscript of *Emile*. It would also be wrong to suggest that the *lapidation* was the catalyst for the final version of Rousseau's conspiracy narrative. Actually, the plot was a long time in coming and the different pieces of the jigsaw only came together in 1770, three years after his return to France. The revelation was occasioned by an unrelated incident, the disappearance of a part of his correspondence (which he assumed was purloined). Finally, it seems fair to stress that the exile from Môtiers does not provide much narrative material for Rousseau's paranoid lucubrations. In addition to the formal deposition to the investigators the day after the event, there are several references in his correspondence, most of them made in the immediate aftermath of his departure from the village, followed by the well-known albeit brief account from Book 12 of his *Les confessions* [*Confessions*, published 1782–89] and, finally, a few passing mentions in his *Dialogues* and the *Reveries of a Solitary Walker*.

Yet, he goes further than that. The last book of *Confessions* begins with the author's agonizing recognition of a sinister rupture in his life that occurred after his flight from France:

> Ici commence l'œuvre de tenebres dans lequel depuis huit ans je me trouve enseveli, sans que de quelque façon que je m'y sois pu prendre il m'ait été possible d'en percer l'effrayante obscurité. Dans l'abyme de maux où je suis submergé, je sens les atteints des coups qui me sont portés, j'en apperçois l'instrument immédiat, mais je ne puis voir ni la main qui le dirige, ni les moyens qu'elle met en œuvre. L'opprobre et les malheurs tombent sur moi comme d'eux-mêmes et sans qu'il y paroisse. Quand mon cœur déchiré laisse échaper des gemissemens, j'ai l'air d'un homme qui se plaint sans sujet, et les auteurs de ma ruine ont trouvé l'art inconcevable de rendre le public complice de leur complot sans qu'il s'en doute lui-même et sans qu'il en apperçoive l'effet.

> [Here begins the work of darkness in which I have been entombed for eight years past, without ever having been able, try as I might, to pierce its hideous obscurity. In the abyss of evil in which I am sunk I feel the weight of blows struck at me; I perceive the immediate instrument; but I can neither see the hand which directs it nor the means by which it works. Disgrace and misfortune fall upon me as if of themselves and unseen. When my grief-stricken heart utters groans, I seem like a man complaining for no reason. The authors of my ruin have discovered the unimaginable art of turning the public into the unsuspecting accomplice of their plot, who does not even see its results.][55]

The gloomy setting of this famous overture has been usually related to entombment but it is fair to say that it is also uncannily reminiscent of Môtiers. It is dark and foes are all around; blows keep falling upon the victim who nonetheless cannot discern any hands and therefore cannot name perpetrators. Yet, the arrangement of imagery is in stark contrast to other recollections of the *lapidation*. Not only is force condensed and amplified but also transposed into a timeless void where it can be applied with no cessation. While in all earlier accounts conspiracy lead by way of metonymy to exile and exile to conspiracy in this vision conspiracy itself is represented metaphorically as exile. That exile is anomalous: it is neither enforced ('a man complaining for no reason') nor voluntary ('grief-stricken heart'); the target of the persecution is extraneous ('the abyss of evil into which I am sunk') and at the same time available ('blows struck at me').

This idea of conspiracy as exile and, following on from that, exile as continued exposure to conspiracy is further developed in *Dialogues* (*Rousseau, the Judge of Jean-Jacques*, published in 1782), that extravagant and, to some scholars at least, disingenuous text. Unlike Rousseau's other autobiographic works, this text is cast in the form of a Platonic dialogue — one thinks of *Apology* — in which a fictional character named 'François' (the Frenchman) tries to convince his collocutor, named 'Rousseau', of an alleged conspiracy hatched up by a third, absent personality, Jean-Jacques, or 'J. J.' The persecutory narrative of the *Confessions* is, thus, taken a step further and comes to engulf the very narrative situation: Rousseau yearns to be at the same time the victim of and privy to the universal conspiracy. Throughout the protracted and often tedious discussion, 'François' relates with barely concealed smugness the sundry methods of surveillance applied against 'J. J.', the enemy of the polity, whereas 'Rousseau' goes out of his way to exculpate him and, after much persuasion, manages to do so. In the process, François's account of Jean-Jacques's assumed conspiracy is revealed as the actual conspiracy of the society against Jean-Jacques:

> des dépenses immenses qu'ils font, pour l'entourer de tant de piéges, pour le livrer à tant de mains, pour l'enlacer de tant de façons qu'au milieu de cette liberté feinte il ne puisse ni dire un mot, ni faire un pas, ni mouvoir un doigt qu'ils ne le sachent et ne le veuillent. [...] on l'a fait décreter à Paris; quel mal lui a-t-on fait? Il falloit, par la même raison, l'empêcher de s'établir à Genève; on l'y a fait decreter aussi; quel mal lui a-t-on fait? On l'a fait lapider à Môtiers ; mais les cailloux qui cassoient ses fenêtres et ses portes ne l'ont point atteint; quel mal donc lui ont-ils fait? On l'a fait chasser à l'entrée de l'hiver de l'Isle solitaire où il s'étoit réfugié et de toute la Suisse; mais c'étoit pour le forcer charitablement d'aller en Angleterre chercher l'azyle qu'on lui préparoit à son insçu depuis longtems.

> [the huge expenses they make, to surround him with so many traps, to deliver him into so many hands, to ensnare him in so many ways that in the midst of this feigned freedom, he can neither say a word, nor take a step, nor lift a finger unless they know it and want it. [...] A warrant against him was issued in Paris. What harm did that do to him? For the same reason, it was necessary to prevent him from settling in Geneva. A warrant was issued there too. What harm did that do to him? He was stoned in Môtiers, but the rocks that broke his windows and doors did not strike him. So what harm did they do him? He was evicted at the beginning of winter from the solitary Island where he sought refuge, and from all of Switzerland. But it was in order to force him charitably to go to England in search of the asylum long prepared for him without his knowledge.][56]

Two seemingly incongruous images emerge from the above account: encirclement, where the subject is captured and enclosed, and ejection, where he is expelled and prevented from coming back. Whereas in the earlier case he is exiled to the society's imagined geometrical centre and exposed to a never-ending row of silent gazes which surround him as an animate wall made of eyes, in the latter case he is driven away from that centre and across the boundaries of the society, a trajectory that coincides with his actual itinerary from France to Switzerland, then to England, and then back to France. These two patterns of persecution are actually consistent with each other: Rousseau argues that he is forced to leave his home and go to specific places which are conjured up for him as deceptive safe havens. Wherever he sets foot, his persecutors are already there ahead of him and treat him to an ignominious welcome.

The whole description seems curiously anticipative of one of the political theories that have already been discussed in connection with Cicero, namely Agamben's notion of the sovereign capture of bare life. It is worth reminding ourselves that in *Homo Sacer* and *State of Exception* Agamben argued for exile — in particular *aquae et ignis interdictio* — as an instance of *sacratio*. In antiquity, so Agamben's argument runs, the expellee is excluded from both *ius publicum* and *ius divinum* and exposed to sovereign power as a constitutive exception that legitimizes the order. However, our analysis of the historical practices of *aquae et ignis interdictio* indicates that extraneous exile, typical of the Roman Republic and modern nation states, represents the sovereign power's wilful surrender of life to another jurisdiction rather than its capture. It has also been stressed that in most cases that surrender happens on a bilateral basis rather than through a unilateral exclusion. Nevertheless, the prospect of one's being excluded from the order and at the same time remaining captured by it — unrealistic as it is in the realm of international law — still haunts imagination and stimulates paranoid or dystopian construals. Rousseau sees himself excluded from the political system, by being repeatedly evicted, and from the religious order, by being denied access to Holy Communion. Furthermore, Agamben talks of a 'sphere' which captures the sacred life: '*The sovereign sphere [sfera] is the sphere in which it is permitted to kill without committing homicide and without celebrating a sacrifice and sacred life — that is, life that may be killed but not sacrificed — is the life that has been captured in that sphere.*'[57] This 'sphere' — signifying both a domain and a circle — appears to match Rousseau's vision: in each new round, his exclusion is paralleled by an act of capture whereby he is enlaced to such an extent that he cannot even move his finger. Thus, while the ethico-political status of implied exile is different from *homo sacer*, it still prompts a paranoid projection of that notion as part of the compensatory elicitation of force.

The above point is a major milestone in this book's argument. The authors writing in response to implied exile do not elicit force only as individual metaphoric images—lyrical, as seen in the imagery of fire in Dante, Brecht and Brodsky, or narrative, as in the persecutory agency in Aeschylus and Nabokov. They also rethink the entire political systems in which to embed their recollections and generate new imaginative metaphors of the polity. Whether these compensatory construals of force are 'normal' or 'pathological' should be of secondary importance here. Not only is the relevant information unavailable, because the authors are dead, or ambiguous, because evidence is merely textual and genre-specific, but, as we know from Foucault, the boundaries between what is subclinical and clinical are a function of the template political systems. It is those political matrices that generate implied exile and the entire rhetorical process of imaginative litigation as well as clinical diagnoses with which to assess and classify the outcomes of that process.

As we have seen, the *lapidation* episode in Môtiers represents one of the standard scenarios of implied exile: force is communicated by anonymous proxies, with ambiguous intentions and without reaching the body of the person concerned. The event prompted Rousseau to depart from the village where he was formally entitled to stay and protected by the sovereign even before the investigation was carried out fully. Following his departure, the narrative lacunae were reconstructed *ex ungue leonem* (i.e. metonymically): collective conspiracy plots suggested that stoning amounts to direct banishment by Pastor Montmollin, or insinuated that everything had been organized by Rousseau's mistress, or claimed that Rousseau himself is the key villain who controls local authorities and even the King. Rousseau, however, did not elicit force metonymically but made it a metaphoric template of his captivity in the society, a cruel, repetitive rhythm of capture and eviction. Thereby, his persecutory thought availed itself of exile to create a nightmarish political vision which dwarfs some of the bleakest theories of the contemporary world.

Paranoid Exiles Redeemed: The Wandering Jew in Danilo Kiš and Stefan Heym

Paranoids, real and literary, like to think of themselves in terms of great mythical precursors, often to the point of a complete self-identification, and, vice versa, many conspiratorial narratives are redeemed as myths in broader, collectively sustained cultural discourses. That the itinerary of Jean-Jacques Rousseau is reminiscent of the story of Ahasuerus, or the Wandering Jew, may have been obvious to his contemporaries, some of whom recalled his leaving a note 'J.-J. Rousseau — proscribed, wandering, sick'.[58] Some others preferred to think of him as a *voyageur perpétuel*, and even claimed that he signed some of his letters by this sobriquet, which Rousseau vehemently denied.[59] To be sure, perpetuity is not something which Rousseau the philosopher would embrace. In his treatise on education, *Emile* (1762), published shortly before his departure from France, he suggested that eternal existence in and of itself would be an ultimate damnation as a life which cannot be lost would cease to have any value for the holder.[60] Perpetuity is, thus, part of the *auto-sacratio* which Rousseau the exile performs upon himself.

There are, however, some substantive analogies with Ahasuerus which pertain to deeper strata of Rousseau's persecutory thought. The Wandering Jew is at the same time an eternal migrant, whose destiny it is never to remain at the same place, and the subject of encirclement, provoking suspicion, vigilance and resistance wherever he appears. The legend of the perpetual exile seems to provide an excellent framework for bifocal persecutory narratives. On the one hand, Ahasuerus is bound to appear vaguely paranoid to whatever community hosts him because he will have to explain his wanderings with reference to a transcendental agency and to a moment in distant past.[61] On the other hand, those host communities are very likely to appear to Ahasuerus as paranoid because the notion of someone who offended their Lord will stir up bigotry and xenophobia.

The story of the Wandering Jew has a significant pedigree and diverse offspring. Variants and cognates are encountered both in the Western and in the Eastern legendry from antiquity to the present day. George Anderson, the author of a magisterial study on the Wandering Jew, lists six thematically related narratives about accursed wanderers: the jealous Cain, who expiates the murder of his brother Abel by vagabondage on the earth; the all too resourceful al Sameri of the Koran, who creates a golden calf and suffers the curse of Moses to wander without ever receiving the comfort of a human touch; the Indian sage Pindola, condemned to immortality for daring to fly in front of the Buddha himself; the Frankish legend of the Wild Huntsman, the ghost of a sinful nobleman who haunts the Black Forest in a mad chase; the Flying Dutchman, whose blasphemous attempt to sail around the Cape of Good Hope, even if he has to try until eternity, led to his ship actually having to sail until the Doomsday; Peter Rugg, the impetuous Missing Man of Boston, who disappeared in a thunderstorm and always reappears with a thunderstorm, all over the United States.[62] This list includes only the Wandering Jew's close relatives, those who appeared in religious myths and folk legends; the literary variations with various Ancient Mariners, Peter Schlemihls, Akakiys Akakieviches, and Gerontions are too numerous to be listed here.

From the vantage point of European modernity, the legend of the Wandering Jew seems to take precedence before all of these narratives even if that precedence has to do with a colonial disregard of other cultures' paradigms. The central character is implicated in the main event of the divine history, the Passion of Christ, and the legend itself plays out one of the most intractable conflicts in human history, that between Christians and Jews. In the context of this enquiry, however, the priority of the Wandering Jew does not only have to do with cultural valence and political leverage; it is equally important that it is the only version of the myth where exile (that of Jesus) was countered by another exile (that of the Jew).

The germinal version of the story of the Wandering Jew appeared in 1242, in the chronicles of the Abbey of St Albans, edited by Matthew of Paris. The narrative was conveyed by a chain of narrators, which would later become a hallmark feature of this legend, and related how a man, known as Joseph, appeared to prelates in Armenia and claimed that a long time previously he had been known by a different name, Cartaphilus, that he had worked as a porter in Pilate's palace and that he had offended Christ after the trial by telling him not to drag his feet but hurry up to Golgotha. Jesus had responded that he would indeed go but that the porter would have to wait till he returned. The second, more influential version of the legend emerged after three hundred years of desuetude, this time in the German principalities. The Bishop of Schleswig, Paul von Eitzen, confided to a friend how during a stay in Hamburg back in his youth he chanced to meet in the cathedral an unusual, poorly clad man who sat motionless and only moved at the mention of Christ's name, beating his chest and releasing deep, agonized sighs. When interrogated, the man, whose name was Ahasverus, claimed to have witnessed the Passion of Christ and, what is more, to have been implicated in it. When Christ, exhausted by the weight of the cross, wanted to lean for a moment against the wall of Ahasverus's cobbler's workshop he told him to move away from his door-step and hurry up to Calvary. Christ told him that he would still make stops later on but that Ahasverus would have to wander restless until the Second Coming.[63] The story was circulated as the *Volksbuch*, the German term for the popular chapbook, and, boosted by print technology, gained both in popularity and geographic outreach. Further sightings of the Wandering Jew were reported in Madrid (1575), in Vienna (1599), and in Lübeck (1601), after which he assumedly repaired to Cracow and Moscow and then to Paris (1604). In the late seventeenth and throughout the eighteenth century the legend was well known but the new cases seem to be increasingly dubious and the narrative itself underwent substantial transformations. In everyday life there appeared various Jewish and Christian impostors who saw it as an opportunity to obtain alms, while in pamphlets the story about the Wandering Jew himself seems to lose its interest and it morphs into the Wanderer's story about different realms and events including royal genealogies and various natural phenomena.

Three broader historical points are to be made in connection with this brief survey. Firstly, the legend of Ahasuerus was supposed to display a lurid and resonant image of the Jew to the Christian community. In particular, the story accounted for the discontinuous presence and the ambiguous status of the Jewish Diaspora in the wake of the expulsions in the early modern period and, therefore, informs the early period of anti-Semitism. In that sense, the historian of anti-Semitism Paul Lawrence Rose rightly observed that 'a living, Wandering Jew was a far more pregnant emblem of enduring Jewish wickedness than a dead Judas Iscariot'.[64] The legend also included several socio-political spheres and established metaphorical and allusive links between them. The Jew rebuffed Christ from the threshold of his house and this breach of hospitality in the private realm stood for the denial of hospitality both in the religious sphere, in that Jews turned a deaf ear to Christ's teaching and effectively excommunicated him, and also in the political sphere, in that the early apostles were banished or persecuted in all lands they came. Secondly, Ahasuerus was meant to provide a living example of Christian faith, for the instruction of Jews. Ahasuerus was not only a sinful Jew but also a penitent and, consequently, reformed Jew, who should provide the role model for other members of his race. In broader terms, the story tallied with the religious sensibility of the time and its rendition of humility could have appealed to Christians, too. Thirdly, Protestantism stressed the need for a true witness of the passion as a token of continuity between the present day and the early, uncorrupted period, and for poignant examples of how one's ways can be amended by the sheer power of inner repentance, without recourse to the institutionalized faith. The legend of the Wandering Jew clearly fitted the bill on both accounts.

The persecuted persecutor in the early modern Europe, Ahasuerus is even more of an unsettling figure for some of the modern political theorists. He is not merely an extraterritorial in the sense of transnationality but a paradoxical double exile: from the divine monarchy, the passport of which he holds but cannot use, and from the earthly states, the territories of which he enters and leaves by curse. As already remarked, each Leviathan (theorist of sovereignty) has his Behemoth (the dodger of the system). Take for instance the theories of the German jurist and political philosopher Carl Schmitt. Hypothetically, he could have met Ahasuerus in the 1930s, while teaching on the 'total state' at the University of Berlin, and one could speculate what they would have had to say to each other. Notwithstanding this possibility, Ahasuerus also poses a purely speculative risk for his argument. The main claim of the Schmittian political theology of the Weimar period was that 'all significant concepts of the modern theory of the state are secularized theological concepts'.[65] In particular, the concept of the miracle, God's prerogative to suspend the laws of the nature, is said to have morphed into the state of exception, the sovereign's right to decide on suspending the legal system. Yet, Ahasuerus seems to operate on both regimes: state of exception because of miracle and the other way round, miracle because of an ongoing state of exception. In a different way, Ahasuerus also challenges the key point of Schmitt's post-war thought, expressed in *The Nomos of the Earth* (1950). Precisely at the period when Europe is said to have started its drive for coherent and comprehensive hegemony of the land and the sea Ahasuerus is spotted traversing the continent on foot.[66]

One is also tempted to think of Ahasuerus as a mythical correlate of Agamben's *homo sacer* where even more serious difficulties emerge. Like Schmitt, Agamben never mentions Ahasuerus but his status does bear some resemblance to the mechanism of exclusive inclusion: he is denied recourse to the law (as part of its constitutive abandonment) and a place at the altar, while at the same time being exposed to the sovereign power. Yet, his eternity is a rather ambiguous point. On the one hand, it can be interpreted as the perpetualization of the bare life. In his essay on the image of Ahasuerus in the work of Serbian writer Radomir Konstantinović, Stijn Vervaet makes an important general point about the legend: 'Therefore, the executioner does not kill Ahasver because he needs him as the "čivutin" i.e. as the Jew reduced to the meaning of a pejorative signifier, as a subject who is completely desubjectivized but not dead.'[67] In other words, Ahasuerus would be the *non plus ultra* of the sovereign power's capture of bare life: the mythical projection of his dream of perpetual capture, as it were. However, one could put forward a different argument and suggest that his eternal wandering means that he is not the holder of bare life. Following Agamben's model, he would stand at the sovereign power's disposal to be killed with impunity if he could only be killed in the first place. If, however, the sovereign power knows that Ahasuerus's life cannot be taken then its act of constitutive exception turns into mere posturing. Thus, if the figure of *homo sacer* was compared to Rousseau's persecutory nightmare, the Wandering Jew could be seen as the sovereign's nightmare: an instance of capture gone terribly wrong or, even worse, perpetual resistance to that capture. Therefore, the Wandering Jew can be both the realization and the subversion of sovereignty and there is no way of predicting what he will actually do. If Agamben's *homo sacer* is the constitutive ambiguity of the sovereign power, Ahasuerus is the constitutive ambiguity of the *homo sacer* i.e. the ambiguity of ambiguity.

This controversy cannot be resolved at the level of the legend — there will always be two ways of explaining it — but rather at its confluence with history. The cataclysmic events of the twentieth century changed the evolution of the legend and led to its retrospective reappraisal. The story of the impious Jew Ahasuerus who awaits the Second Coming on the road while generations and generations of Gentiles die peacefully in bed had to be revised in a situation where some of those Gentiles set out to exterminate the entire Jewish population of Europe in the Holocaust. After the Second World War, Ahasuerus no longer shows up at public places as an alien somnambulist that haunts the collective imaginary of the rational Europe; rather, he is summoned by writers' creative imagination as a sober witness of the human woes and ethical rigours of the time. I propose to examine how exile and conspiracy narratives are interlinked in two modern novels, *Bašta, pepeo* (*Garden, Ashes*, 1965) by Yugoslav writer Danilo Kiš and *Ahasver* (*The Wandering Jew*, 1981) by German writer Stefan Heym. The two novels are far from being the only literary renditions of the theme after the Second World War; nevertheless, by the sheer scale of their intervention into the legend, they mark its ethico-political amplitudes. Namely, whereas in Kiš's novel the Eternal Jew's travels through space and time are brought to an abrupt end as he dies in the Holocaust, in Heym's novel he perseveres and, what is more, he is found to be quite literally eternal, i.e. attendant on the creation and the destruction of the world.

Before looking at Kiš's and Heym's interpretation of the Wandering Jew, it is worth noting some biographical analogies. Both Kiš and Heym are of Jewish ancestry and for both of them the problem of descent was an occasion for dissent as well as the cause of a prolonged exile. Kiš was born in 1935 to a Hungarian Jewish father and a Montenegrin mother and spent his early childhood in the northern Yugoslav towns of Subotica and Novi Sad. In 1939, he was baptized into the Serbian Orthodox Church, his mother's confession, but also one that his parents thought would protect him against anti-Semitism which was on the rise throughout Europe. Yugoslavia was occupied by the Axis powers in 1941 and after a Hungarian-organized massacre in Novi Sad in early 1942, which claimed lives of hundreds of local Jews and Serbs, the family was forced to fly for safety to his father's birthplace in Western Hungary (village of Kerkabarabás, county Zala), where anti-Semitic laws were applied less strictly. In 1944, after two relatively peaceful years, Kiš was to witness the final clampdown on Hungarian Jews, organized by Adolf Eichmann, and the transportation of his father and a number of other relatives to Auschwitz, where nearly all of them perished. After the end of the war, Kiš was repatriated to Yugoslavia with his mother and sister and stayed with his maternal relatives in Cetinje, Montenegro. A life-long admirer of French literature, he would later spend his career in Belgrade and as a Serbo-Croat *lecteur* in different cities in France (Strasbourg, Bordeaux, Lilles, Paris).[68] Heym was born in 1913, in Chemnitz, to Jewish parents, and in his youth espoused Marxism which led to his eviction from the local gymnasium under the pressure from the local Nazi organization and to relocation to the more cosmopolitan Berlin. After Hitler's capture of power in 1933, Heym left Germany with the first wave of anti-Nazi emigration and settled first in Prague and then in the United States, where he eventually joined the US forces in the Second World War. In the wake of McCarthy's persecution of the leftist intelligentsia, he returned to Europe and settled in the East German part of Berlin where he would spend his literary career and witness the fall of the Berlin Wall. For both writers, then, exile was indirect, prolonged and sequential, which may have predisposed them to conceive of their itinerary in terms of Ahasuerus's wanderings.[69]

If Kiš's and Heym's biographical circumstances show some broad analogies, their novelistic approaches to Ahasuerus are largely opposed. To be sure, they start from the same narrative premises but then proceed to turn the legend on its head in different ways. As usual, the two novels develop, *qua* novels, various other thematic lines, but for the purposes of this argument it will suffice to focus on the inter-section of exile and persecution.

Kiš's novel *Garden, Ashes*, the first part of an autobiographic trilogy which also includes the collection of short stories *Rani jadi* (*Early Sorrows*, 1970) and the novel *Peščanik* (*Hourglass*, 1972), is a lyrical and playful reconstruction of his family's wanderings in an attempt to conjure back the father who vanished along the way. The stages of the itinerary — the halcyon days in Novi Sad, the precarious arcadia in Western Hungary, the gloomy post-apocalyptic existence in Cetinje — are related mainly chronologically, as a string of memories by the mature narrator called Andreas Scham. At the centre of the narrator's world, both as the boy and as the mature person, is the mercurial figure of the father, Eduard Scham, a retired railway inspector, a confirmed alcoholic with a paranoid slant and an impassioned fantast. The whimsical father develops the idea of himself as a latter-day incarnation of Ahasuerus and, years after his death in Auschwitz, the cue is enthusiastically taken up by his son who articulates it in a series of metaphoric allusions. These references are not continuous but rather sporadic and seem to mimic the periodical sightings of Ahasuerus in different towns. In the first part of the novel, before the family's evasion to Hungary, Eduard Scham spends his days in shabby rented rooms and mental hospital wards dreaming of a magnum opus, the comprehensive *Bus, Ship, Railway and Travel Guide* which makes the narrator think of Ahasuerus's wanderings.[70] In the second part, after the family has settled in Hungary, the legend takes a more sinister turn: as Eduard Scham's mental health deteriorates, he falls prey to delusions of persecution and grandeur, and the narrator recalls him as an embattled Ahasuerus confined to his home place.[71] Finally, in the third part, many years after his disappearance (and presumed death), Eduard Scham re-appears in his son's dreams as a grotesque mixture of a German tourist and Ahasuerus, an unappeased apparition that torments the survivor.[72]

Heym's approach to Ahasuerus in *The Wandering Jew* is more direct and at the same time more detailed. The plot traces the vagaries of the actual Ahasuerus, rather than his latter-day impersonator, and spans three key historical periods, moving from one to another in an alternating rhythm. In the first and formative period, Ahasuerus is introduced as a rebellious angel who was expelled from heaven along with Lucifer and who, having later met the Son of the Lord, becomes completely disillusioned by what he sees as his resignation at the injustice of the world. As a gesture of protest, he chases him away from his door in Jerusalem. In the second plot, which unfolds in the sixteenth century, Ahasuerus and Lucifer, the latter assuming the German calque-name Leuchtentrager, meet Bishop Paul von Eitzen at the time when he was still a young lacklustre theologian and goad him into a deal which would help his ambition grow but his faith and moral consciousness would diminish. In the third plot, finally, Ahasuerus's and Lucifer's clandestine journey through history ends in the 1980s with Leuchtentrager appearing in the unlikely guise of an academic from Jerusalem who exchanges letters with his East German colleague Siegfried Beifuss, from a fictional Institute for Scientific Atheism, to convince him that Ahasuerus exists and is actually his very good friend. The subversive camaraderie of Lucifer and Ahasuerus is based on complementary political strategies: whereas the earlier believes God's creation to be beyond redemption and tries to cause it to collapse, the latter recognizes good intentions behind the act of creation and believes the world only needs to be reformed to repair the damage done by negligence and ambition. Eventually, Lucifer and Ahasuerus reveal their identities and, in a *tour de force* which links back to Marlowe and Goethe, take the souls of both von Eitzen and Beifuss: the earlier departs routinely through a chimney and the latter flies spectacularly over the Berlin Wall, as a transcendental *Mauerspringer*.[73]

Before proceeding to look at what connects *Garden, Ashes* and *The Wandering Jew*, let us note some differences. Whereas in *Garden, Ashes* the Ahasuerus theme is part of the complex imaginative transfers between the father and the son, and is envisioned by both, in *The Wandering Jew* there is a gliding narrative focus: from Ahasuerus himself to his persecutor Paul von Eitzen to the epistolary mode. Not only do Kiš's and Heym's novels have different narrative structures; they also have different emotional hues. Inspired by the bitter-sweet evocation of the Jewish provincial community in the prose of Bruno Schulz, Kiš has the father-Ahasuerus as the tenor of what Vuletić rightly calls 'protective irony'. He plunges into the mundane in order to achieve its lyrical transformation.[74] Heym, obviously incited by the complementary myths of Prometheus and Faustus, sees Ahasuerus as the purveyor of, in Hutchinson's words, a 'pessimistic theme [...] cynical view of man'.[75] To this metaphysical and historical rebel, everything mundane appears submissive, conceited and, ultimately, prone to evil. Nevertheless, these differences do not obfuscate the fundamentally important fact that Kiš and Heym trace the figure of the Wandering Jew in the post-Holocaust context.

In the popular imaginary of the early modern Europe as well as in the recent theories of sovereignty, Ahasuerus is, as we have seen, a deeply ambiguous figure: at the same time the expeller and the expellee, the persecutor and the sufferer, the *homo sacer* and the subversive. Kiš's and Heym's interpretations of the legend of the Wandering Jew cancel its intrinsic ambiguity and pursue it to its furthest ethico-political and narrative possibilities. In Heym's version, there is an actual conspiracy on the part of Ahasuerus: he ceases to be a solitary wanderer and acquires a mighty ally, Lucifer (Leuchtentrager), with whom he works together to undermine the order in a genuine belief that it is corrupt. With this dangerous partner, the image of the exile is geared towards that of the arch-conspirator. In Kiš's novel, Ahasuerus changes persona several times. He starts as a mental traveller 'consumed [izgara] by the fire of creative imagination' and daydreams about maps and timetables; he subsequently emerges as a clinical paranoid, 'obsessed with the idea [fiksnom idejom] that he was destined to expiate the sins of his family, the sins of all mankind'; finally he masquerades as 'a West German tourist in riding breeches [s rajthoznama]', a painfully ironic apparition of someone who was incarcerated, obliterated and released back into the nature as a smoke from a crematorium chimney.[76] With this last appearance, the eternal exile is eventually transformed into a pure victim, resigned not only to his mortality but also to anonymity, barely recognizable to his own son. In the fictional world of the two novels, Ahasuerus, thus, changes his uncanny biopolitical status: in Heym, he is coeval with the world and becomes a dauntless challenger of heavenly and earthly orders; in Kiš, he is the epitome of a *homo sacer*.

Yet, there is more to this: as Ahasuerus is in the centre of the conspiratorial narrative by his hosts he becomes the immediate target of persecution.[77] Both *Garden, Ashes* and *The Wandering Jew* feature dramatic scenes of an abortive lynching by the enraged populace. Much like in Rousseau's imagining of capture, Ahasuerus is surrounded by unknown people and an attempt is made upon his life which he eventually survives. The only major difference between the two novels is in the religious affiliation of the populace: while in *Garden, Ashes* Eduard Scham is assaulted by devout Catholics, in *The Wandering Jew* Ahasuerus confronts zealous Protestants.

The encounter which nearly cost Eduard Scham his life happens near the Hungarian village where his family found a safe-haven, in a wood which he uses as a secondary, natural asylum in the style of Rousseau's *Reveries of a Solitary Walker*. The villagers, who have been suspicious about his solitary ramblings, begin 'to dog his tracks, to eavesdrop on his soliloquies, and to file reports',[78] and eventually hatch up a plan to kill him. A bunch of angry peasants surround him as he sleeps, 'arms spread wide as if crucified [razapet]', and try to lynch him on the spot.[79] Facing the threat, Eduard Scham assumes the guise of a Messiah who is about to be nailed to a cross and addresses the assailants as sinful Jews who are about to perpetrate a primal crime: 'I only preach in my temple, in the woods, my religion which unfortunately has no followers yet but which will someday be revived. Its temple will be erected here. [...] My tormented and helpless body is at your disposal, my spirit is ready in philosophical terms for crucifixion [raspeće].'[80] After some hesitation at seeing an unlikely Messiah, the peasants recoil and release him. Eduard Scham's posturing as Christ in order to save his life is paradoxical and can be explained in several ways: psychologically, it is part of the hero's distinctive taste for travesty, a sort of method in his madness; socially, it is a satirical view on the peasants' bigotry that easily mistakes blasphemy for a true aura. Crucially, however, the episode indicates Ahasuerus's readiness to assume the burden of Christ and undergo martyrdom.

The reversal of roles, signalled by the parody of lynching in *Garden, Ashes*, becomes a tragic reality in Heym's novel. In one of the episodes from the early modern section of the plot, Ahasuerus is captured, charged with heresy and sentenced to run the gauntlet no less than eight times and be whipped all along. In accordance with the Protestant custom, the ordeal is administered by the secular authority but pastoral support is provided by *Doctor theologiae* Paul von Eitzen who by that time has advanced to the position of the Superintendent at the court of the Schleswig prince and turned into a veritable monster of ambition and anti-Semite zeal. Here again, we see Ahasuerus exposed to the 'bloody violence' (Benjamin) by Christians who surround him from all sides: soldiers with whips, officers and rows of curious bystanders. From the vantage point of the victim, the paranoid fantasy of animate walls is made real: 'Ahasver sieht die endlose Gasse vor sich, rechts Gestalten, links Gestalten, Augen, Augen, Augen, zwei Mauern von Augen, sämtlich auf ihn gerichtet' [Ahasuerus sees before him the lane, the lines of men stretching along its sides, eyes, eyes, eyes, two endless walls of eyes, each pair of them glaring at him].[81] The horizon of the eternal exile's wandering is, thus, reduced to running the gauntlet: fleeing one blow only to be greeted by another. As Ahasuerus reaches pastor Paul von Eitzen he does not ask for blessing but, just like Christ on the road to Golgotha, merely for a moment of rest: 'Laßt mich ausruhen ein wenig bei Euch, denn ich bin wund und zum Sterben matt.' [Let me rest a little with you, for they have beaten me sorely and I am weary to death.][82] The request is rejected, with an ill-tempered reminder of the Passion, and before returning to the gauntlet Ahasuerus curses von Eitzen with eternal punishment by the devil. Eventually, he succumbs to his wounds and is declared dead but will soon be resuscitated to join his more radical half, Lucifer. The loop is fully closed: the archetypal exile, Ahasuerus, turns into the victorious victim, Christ, and the adherent of Christ into Ahasuerus or, more precisely, into Ahasuerus's former, uncharitable self.

Writing in the post-Holocaust world, Kiš and Heym have, thus, boldly rearticulated the old legend about paranoid exile: in their novels, almost everyone turns out to be paranoid except him. Rather than nourishing delusion, exile produces a tragic insight and actual martyrdom. On the one side, Ahasuerus comes to realize what it feels to suffer as Christ; on the other side, Christians step into Jews' shoes to find out what it feels to persecute the Son of Man. In addition to this reversal, the two novels also mark the ethico-political *limes* of Ahasuerus. That the Eternal Jew should die in the Holocaust, as he does in *Garden, Ashes*, is a scandal of the first order of magnitude in the modern political theology and that he should team up with Lucifer to challenge God's jurisdiction for ethic failings, as he does in *The Wandering Jew*, is no less of a paradox.

To summarize, literary texts, which have often been theorized in terms of pseudo-paranoid plots, play out the different possibilities of the *in situ* link between exile and paranoia. In particular, three narrative patterns have been explored which at the same time represent distinct political constellations. Aeschylus' *Libation Bearers* and Nabokov's *Pale Fire* focus on the individual persecutory narratives which arise from implied exile. The heroes appear to compensate for the lack of force in departure by creating their own persecutors, which no one but they can see. Rousseau's exilic itinerary, especially the episode in Môtiers, illustrates a different scenario: paranoids are assimilated into a suspicious community which initially shuns them and eventually develops its own conspiracy narrative about them. This leads to a new act of exile which further corroborates the individual's paranoid plot. Kiš's *Garden, Ashes* and Heym's *The Wandering Jew* present different yet correspondent versions of the legend of the cursed wanderer Ahasuerus: the exile, whose story initially appears paranoid, reaches to a higher insight and actual martyrdom whereas his hosts turn to conspiratorial thinking and real persecution. Above and beyond these three psycho-socio-political scenarios of implied exile, the literary texts discussed in this chapter show diverse strategies of eluding unilateral determination: instead of the sovereign power's capture of bare life we see the imaginative capture of the sovereign power.

Notes to Chapter 3

1. León Grinberg and Rebeca Grinberg, *Psychoanalytic Perspectives on Migration and Exile* (New Haven, CT, and London: Yale University Press, 1989), p. 87. See also Karl Jaspers, *Heimweh und Verbrechen* (Munich: Belleville Verlag, 1996), p. 51.

2. John Farrell, *Paranoia and Modernity: Cervantes to Rousseau* (Ithaca, NY, and London: Cornell University Press, 2006), p. 2.

3. Jacques Lacan, *De la psychose paranoïaque dans ses rapports avec la personnalité* (Paris: Éditions du Seuil, 1975), p. 199.

4. Emil Kraepelin, *Psychiatrie: Ein Lehrbuch für Studierende und Ärzte*, vol. IV (Leipzig: Barth, 1915), p. 1713 (my translation).

5. *Peri poetikes* VIII. 32–34, in *Aristotle, Poetics, Longinus, On the Sublime; Demetrius, On Style* (Cambridge, MA, and London: Harvard University Press, 1995), p. 59.

6. See Vladimir Propp, *Morphology of the Folktale* (Austin: University of Texas Press, 1968), A.-J. Greimas, *Sémantique structurale: recherche de méthode* (Paris: Librairie Larousse, 1966), pp. 172–221 and Claude Bremond, *Logique du récit* (Paris: Éditions du Seuil, 1973).

7. Kraepelin, *Psychiatrie: Ein Lehrbuch*, p. 1713 (my translation).

8. See Sigmund Freud, 'Psychoanalytic notes upon an autobiographical account of a case of

paranoia (dementia paranoides)', in *The Standard Edition of the Complete Psychological Works of Sigmund Freud*, ed. by James Strachey, vol. XII (London: The Hogarth Press and the Institute for Psychoanalysis, 1958), pp. 68–71. For the the original see Sigmund Freud, *Gesammelte Werke*, vol. VIII (Frankfurt am Main: Fischer Taschenbuch Verlag, 1999), pp. 304–08.

9. Joseph Agassi and Yehuda Fried, *Paranoia: A Study in Diagnosis*, Boston Studies in Philosophy of Science, 50 (Dodrecht: D. Reidel, 1976), p. 66.

10. Svetlana Boym, 'Conspiracy Theories and Literary Ethics: Umberto Eco, Danilo Kiš and *The Protocols of Zion*', *Comparative Literature*, 51.2 (Spring 1999), 97–122 (p. 98).

11. *King Lear*, III. 1. 4, in *The Library Shakespeare*, vol. II (Quarry Bay: Midpoint Press, 2005), p. 236.

12. William Butler Yeats, 'The Madness of King Goll', in *The Collected Poems of W. B. Yeats*, ed. by Richard J. Finneran (New York: Macmillan, 1993), pp. 16–17.

13. For the case of Menecrates, the physician who identified himself with Zeus, see Otto Weinreich, *Menekrates, Zeus und Salmoneus* (Stuttgart: Kohlhammer, 1933).

14. Nabokov's tantalizing games and ironies in *Pale Fire* are most thoroughly explored by Brian Boyd in his *Nabokov's Pale Fire: The Magic of Artistic Discovery* (Princeton, NJ: Princeton University Press, 1999).

15. *Choephoroi*, v. 1048–50, in Aeschylus, *Agamemnon, Libation Bearers, Eumenides, Fragments* (Cambridge, MA: Harvard University Press; London: William Heinemann, 1971), pp. 262–63.

16. Ibid., v. 1061–62, pp. 264–65.

17. On the genesis of madness in Homeric epics, see the classical study of E. R. Dodds, *The Greeks and the Irrational* (Berkeley and Los Angeles: University of California Press, 1956), pp. 1–27.

18. For a critical overview of some of these studies, see John R. Porter, 'Madness and ΣΥΝΕΣΙΣ in *Orestes*', in John R. Porter, *Studies in Euripides' Orestes* (Leiden, New York and Köln: E. J. Brill, 1994), pp. 298–313. Peter Toohey in his book *Melancholy, Love and Time* traces a different tradition of representation of Orestes' madness, one that tends towards melancholia ('as an agitated form of melancholy, as an agitated depression') rather than towards psychotic delusion. See Peter Toohey, *Melancholy, Love and Time: Boundaries of the Self in Ancient Literature* (Ann Arbor: University of Michigan Press, 2004), pp. 15–58.

19. Vladimir Nabokov, *Pale Fire* (London: Weidenfeld and Nicolson, 1962), pp. 25, 98.

20. Ibid., p. 97.

21. Ibid., p. 301.

22. Ibid., p. 39.

23. See *Agamemnon*, v. 1481–88, in Aeschylus, *Agamemnon, Libation Bearers, Eumenides, Fragments*, pp. 132–33.

24. Nabokov, *Pale Fire*, p. 301.

25. *Choephoroi* v. 1041–42, in Aeschylus, *Agamemnon, Libation Bearers, Eumenides, Fragments*, pp. 260–61.

26. Euripides, *Orestes*, v. 34–38, 255–57, 260–61, in *Euripides in Four Volumes*, vol. II (Cambridge, MA: Harvard University Press; London: William Heinemann Ltd, 1988), pp. 128–29, 146–47.

27. Ibid., v. 270, pp. 148–49 and v. 400–12, pp. 158–59.

28. Ibid., v. 46–48, pp. 128–29 and v. 607–29, pp. 174–77.

29. Aubrey Lewis, 'Paranoia and Paranoid: A Historical Perspective', *Psychological Medicine*, 1.1 (1970), 2–12 (p. 11).

30. Richard Hofstadter, 'The Paranoid Style in American Politics', in Hofstadter, *The Paranoid Style in American Politics and Other Essays* (London: Jonathan Cape, 1966), p. 14.

31. Robert S. Robins and Jerrold M. Post, *Political Paranoia: The Psychopolitics of Hatred* (New Haven, CT, and London: Yale University Press, 1997), pp. 17–18.

32. Ibid., pp. 18–19.

33. Quoted from: Joseph H. Berke et al., *Even Paranoids Have Enemies: New Perspectives on Paranoia and Persecution* (London and New York: Routledge, 2001), p. 1. During the Sinai talks, in November 1973, when Henry Kissinger had been pressing Golda Meir for further Israeli concessions and she hesitated, he called her 'paranoid'. To this she is said to have responded: 'Even paranoids have enemies.'

34. Boym, 'Conspiracy Theories and Literary Ethics: Umberto Eco, Danilo Kiš and *The Protocols of the Zion*', p. 99.

35. Henri Guillemin, *Cette affaire infernale* (Paris: Librairie Plon, 1942), Maurice Cranston, *The Solitary Self: Jean-Jacques Rousseau in Exile and Diversity* (London: Penguin and Chicago: Chicago University Press, 1997), pp. 9–10, 102–05, Leo Damrosch, *Jean-Jacques Rousseau: Restless Genius* (Boston, MA: Houghton Mifflin, 2005), pp. 231, 418.

36. See Reginald Somerset Ward, *Maximilien Robespierre: A Study in Deterioration* (London: Macmillan, 1934), pp. 35–40, Bertrand Barère, 'Éloge de J. J. Rousseau, Citoyen de Genève', in Barère, *Éloges académiques* (Paris: Renouard, 1806), pp. 223–81.

37. See Cranston, *Solitary Self: Jean-Jacques Rousseau in Exile and Adversity* and Guéhenno, *Jean Jacques Rousseau*, vol. II (London: Routledge and Kegan Paul and New York: Columbia University Press, 1966).

38. John Farrell, *Paranoia and Modernity: Cervantes to Rousseau* (Ithaca, NY and London: Cornell University Press, 2006), p. 301.

39. Eugene L. Stelzig, *The Romantic Subject in Autobiography: Rousseau and Goethe* (Charlottesville, VA and London: University Press of Virginia, 2000), p. 115.

40. Jean Starobinski, *Jean-Jacques Rousseau: la transparence et l'obstacle suivi de Sept essais sur Rousseau* (Paris: Gallimard, 1971), p. 243 (my translation).

41. Damrosch, *Jean-Jacques Rousseau: Restless Genius*, p. 418.

42. Jean-Jacques Rousseau, *The Confessions* (London: Penguin Books 1978), p. 573, the original quoted from Jean Jacques Rousseau, *Œuvres complètes I: Les Confessions, autres textes autobiographiques* (Paris: Gallimard, 1959), p. 621. The quotations from this and other works by Rousseau follow the orthography of the original edition.

43. See the outline of de Montmollin's sermon, Appendix 383 in *Correspondance complète de Jean Jacques Rousseau*, vol. XXVI (Oxford: The Voltaire Foundation, 1976), pp. 325–26.

44. Jean-Jacques Rousseau, *Discourse on Political Economy and Social Contract* (Oxford: Oxford University Press, 1999), p. 72.

45. Ibid., p. 49.

46. See Damrosch, *Restless Genius*, p. 396.

47. Acts 7. 58, in *Holy Bible: New International Version* (London: Hodder and Stoughton, 2000), p. 1114.

48. See Appendix 408 in *Correspondance complète de Jean Jacques Rousseau*, vol. XXVI, Fig. 107.

49. Matthew 7. 9, Luke 11. 11, in *Holy Bible*, pp. 983, 1055.

50. See Appendix 408 in *Correspondance complète de Jean Jacques Rousseau*, vol. XXVI, p. 361. For other articulations of this plot, as well as for those who suggested that stones were actually pebbles, and therefore too small to make fuss about, see ibid., pp. 357–65.

51. Appendix 393 in *Correspondance complète de Jean Jacques Rousseau*, vol. XXVI, p. 342.

52. Ibid., p. 343.

53. Ibid., p. 343. The 'castrato' is an allusion to Frederick II's alleged homosexuality but the insinuation about his Bavarian origin remains obscure.

54. Ibid., p. 343.

55. Rousseau, *The Confessions*, p. 543 (*Œuvres complètes*, p. 589).

56. Rousseau, *Œuvres completes I (Les Confessions, autres textes autobiographiques)*, p. 710. English translation in *Rousseau Judge of Jean-Jacques: Dialogues*, in Roger D. Masters and Christopher Kelly (eds), *The Collected Writings of Rousseau*, vol. I (Hanover, NH, and London: University Press of New England, 1990), pp. 39–40.

57. Giorgio Agamben, *Homo Sacer* (Stanford, CA: Stanford University Press, 1998), p. 83.

58. Matthew Josephson, *Jean-Jacques Rousseau* (London: Victor Gollancz, 1932), p. 443.

59. Letters no. 6398, 6399, 6434 in *Correspondance complète de Jean Jacques Rousseau*, vol. XXXVI (Oxford: The Voltaire Foundation, 1980), pp. 44–49, 98–108.

60. Jean-Jacques Rousseau, *Emile; or, On Education* ([New York]: Basic Books, 1979), p. 54.

61. The psychiatrists of Charcot's circle were inclined to see the Wandering Jew's peregrinations as an archetypal example of a neurotic disorder that made many Jews visit the Salpêtrière clinic. Charcot is quoted to have introduced one of his patients in the following way: 'I introduce him to you as *a true descendant of Ahasverus or Cartophilus*, as you would say. The fact is that, like the compulsive (neurotic) travelers [...] he is constantly driven by an irresistible need to move on, to travel, without being able to set down anywhere.' Quoted from Henry Meige, *Le Juif-errant à la Salpêtrière* (Paris: [n. pub.], 1893), p. 5 (my translation).

62. George K. Anderson, *The Legend of the Wandering Jew* (Providence, RI: Brown University Press, 1965), pp. 2–10.

63. See Anonymous, *Kurtze Beschreibung und Erzehlung von einem Juden mit Namen Ahasuerus*, Volksbuch, 1602.

64. Paul Lawrence Rose, *Revolutionary Antisemitism in Germany from Kant to Wagner* (Princeton, NJ: Princeton University Press, 1990), p. 24.

65. Carl Schmitt, *Political Theology: Four Chapters on the Concept of Sovereignty* (Chicago, IL, and London: University of Chicago Press, 2005), p. 36.

66. Carl Schmitt, *The Nomos of the Earth* (New York: Telos Press, 2003), p. 49.

67. Stijn Vervaet, 'Pisati subjekat nakon Holokausta: Konstantinovićev *Ahasver, ili traktat o pivskoj Flaši*', *Sarajevske sveske* 41–42 (June 2013), 94–104 (p. 97). In Serbian, 'Čivutin' is a pejorative, anti-Semitic term for a local Jew.

68. For more details, see Mark Thompson's biography of Danilo Kiš, *Birth Certificate: The Story of Danilo Kiš* (Ithaca, NY, and London: Cornell University Press, 2013), pp. 1–105.

69. See Stefan Heym's memoir, *Nachruf* (Munich: C. Bertelsmann, 1988). A condensed autobiographic account is given in Wolfgang Homering (ed.), *Stefan Heym: Im Gespräch mit Dirk Sager* (Berlin: Ullstein, 1999).

70. Danilo Kiš, *Garden, Ashes* (London: Faber and Faber, 1985), pp. 16–17.

71. Ibid., p. 50.

72. Ibid., p. 120. Occasional references to the legend are found in the other parts of the autobiographic trilogy. In one of the short stories from the collection *Early Sorrows*, the father eavesdrops on his son's innocent game in which he sells feathers from pillows to an imaginary fair lady; the scene reminds him of his own father, a goose feather trader called Max Ahasuerus. In the novel, *Hourglass*, the hero is locked in a mental asylum where he outlines the plot of a novel in which the hero masquerades as Cartaphilus, Buttadeus, Joao d'Espera em Dios and Isaac Laquedem, all documented as regional cryptonyms for the Wandering Jew. It is quite clear from these cues that Kiš appropriated the legend as a profound symbolic template for reflection on his own past and as a token of an insouciant, even superficial erudition: in his biographic legend, both postures were important. See Danilo Kiš, 'Game', in Kiš, *Early Sorrows* (New York: New Directions, 1998), pp. 21–28 and Kiš, *Hourglass* (London: Faber and Faber, 1990), p. 208.

73. See Stefan Heym, *Ahasver* (Munich: btb Verlag, 2005).

74. Ivana Vuletić, *The Prose Fiction of Danilo Kiš: Serbian-Jewish Writer: Childhood and the Holocaust* (Lewiston, NY: The Edwin Mellen Press, 2003), p. 82.

75. Peter Hutchinson, *Stefan Heym: The Perpetual Dissident* (Cambridge: Cambridge University Press, 1992), p. 194.

76. Kiš, *Garden, Ashes*, pp. 17, 50, 118. Original in Danilo Kiš, *Porodični cirkus* (Beograd: Srpska književna zadruga, 1993), pp. 103, 136, 203.

77. Franz Hippler's infamous documentary *Der Ewige Jude* [*The Eternal Jew*, 1940] portrays the centennial Jewish diaspora across the world as a brazen conquest of territory: the Wandering Jew becomes a pregnant image of the invader and the parasite. As the images of hapless, shabby people cramped in various Polish ghettos unroll, the voice-over declares that 'their faces bear the age-old features of the perpetual sponger: the Eternal Jew who in the course of time and worldwide wanderings has always been the same.' These frames are then replaced by ominous maps with spider webs which establish a parallel between the expansion of the Jews and that of rats. The film is indirectly referenced in Kiš's *Garden, Ashes*, in the description of Eduard Scham's harmless atlas of routes for the *Bus, Ship, Railway and Travel Guide*, as well as in Heym's *The Wandering Jew*, where one of the episodes unfolds during the rebellion in the Warsaw Ghetto and the leadership of Ahasuerus is 'more than merely a poetic necessity'.

78. Kiš, *Garden, Ashes*, p. 88.

79. Ibid., p. 92; *Porodični cirkus*, p. 176.

80. Ibid., pp. 95–96; *Porodični cirkus*, p. 180.

81. Heym, *Ahasver*, p. 221. Heym's translation in Stefan Heym, *The Wandering Jew* (Evanston, IL: Northwestern University Press, 1999), p. 252.

82. *Ahasver*, p. 222; *The Wandering Jew*, p. 253.

CHAPTER 4

The Burden of Aeneas:
Paternity and Patrimony in Family Exile

Amongst the steadiest semiotic patterns of exile, one easily recognizes the habit of thinking of displacement with reference to origins, as if one's past attachments formed the bedrock of all narrative possibilities. By severing ties with one's land of origin one disrupts the whole maze of human relationships ranging from family and friends to preceptors and public figures. In view of this associative disposition, it would be justifiable to ask whether one could possibly imagine an exilic situation with the emotional and intellectual bequest brought by other people completely preserved. It has been a less frequent venture to ask what patterns of political and literary imagination attend the exodus of larger groups of people. It is particularly the cases which involve the displacement of entire families, rather than that of isolated individuals, that provide the most apposite field for the observation of the changing forms of imagining patrimony. The force that resides in the familial organization in conjunction with the one that attends exile as a political event shapes the text as a literary discourse. The text becomes a projection screen for the political tropes that marked its author in the conflictual stage of exile. This chapter will propose that the fundamental equation of political theology, that between the magistrate (representing the state) and the father (representing family), cannot hold in the practices and narratives of implied exile. Rather, it is replaced by another, more appropriate analogy: between exile and the father. In particular, I will show how in two modernist autobiographies of exile, *Speak, Memory* by Vladimir Nabokov and, once again, *Garden, Ashes* by Danilo Kiš, fathers appear metonymically, as drivers and victims of exilic movement, and at the same time metaphorically, as uncanny visitors and as timeless symbols, to mend the gap between homeland and host country.

Families in Exile: Between the State and *patria potestas*

The phenomenon of implied exile, which occupied us in the previous chapters, is ambiguous but its empirical instances have been fairly clear-cut. These cases happened in relatively settled polities with functional legal systems; the Roman Republic is, of course, the prototypical example but analogies are encountered in the early modern period as well as in the authoritarian regimes of the twentieth century. To sum up the process, in implied exile, as distinct from banishment, one would depart from a country to avoid a legal process or would be compelled to leave it through informal duress, or otherwise would depart and subsequently find oneself locked out of it. Also, the cases explored were typically those involving solitary exile. One would either leave on one's own or as part of a larger outflow of political opponents but without bringing family dependants. The family, which either stayed behind, as in the case of Cicero and Brodsky, or was disowned, as in Rousseau's, has hitherto remained unaccounted for in the exiles' rhetorical contest with the state and in our analysis of those discourses.

Nevertheless, there are some cases that are not so clear-cut and they become increasingly frequent as we get into the twentieth century. For instance, one might depart from an occupied territory, where laws upheld previously are no longer in force and are replaced by various exceptional clauses or by a martial law. In such unsettled circumstances, if an early return appears unlikely one can also take family members along or, even if one is not directly involved, one can decide to join those family members who are already about to depart. This complicates the picture considerably because the force of law appears to be not merely displaced but actually *dispersed*. This dispersal appears to affect both its political source, since it is articulated from diverse centres of power in an interregnum, and its human targets, since it strikes not only immediate opponents but also their next of kin. Therefore, one has to acknowledge that implied exile, originally conceived as a blurred zone between compulsory eviction and voluntary departure, has its own borderline cases which need to be explored. In what follows, I will be looking at several narratives in which family has the role of a mediator in the redistribution of political force.

The argument is predicated upon some historical premises. The family and the state, which are kept apart in contemporary political theories, have historically interacted with each other in several ways. One cluster of metaphors converges around the notion of matrimony whereby the state is seen as a marriage, between Christ and the Church, between the spiritual sacerdotium and the secular regnum, between elected princes and their republic.[1] The second major cluster of metaphors is based on the notion of parenthood which is thought to inform the relations between the fathers of the church and clergy as well as between the sovereign and subjects.[2] As we will see, the narratives of exile typically exploit the second of these clusters, in which spousedom gives way to origination.

The homeland is usually associated not with both parents but with the masculine progenitor only. Symbolically and linguistically, the connection is epitomized in the form of the metaphor of the fatherland as the land associated with the father (and forefathers). This concept illustrates one of those remarkable changes that affected the transfer of Roman jurisprudence and political theology in the modern era. In the Roman Republic, *patria* primarily meant the interest of the selected few among the fathers — patricians — and only by extension the rest of the lot — the people. In the Middle Ages, the notion was part of the ladder of being and involved the triple hierarchy: the Lord (the universal father of everything visible and invisible), the sovereign (the father of the monarchy) and the father of the family. In the popular etymology of the modern period, however, the father-land metaphor became secularized and democratized, so that every member of the state is referred to the one and general model of the father and children, the ethos neatly captured in the encyclopedists' explanation of the concept of *patrie*.[3] This symbolic association is in no way restricted to Latin and appears as a semantic universal. Most modern European languages uphold the etymological link (French 'patrie', English 'fatherland', German 'Vaterland', Serbian 'otadžbina') and in the lexical store of Russian language the standard word 'отечество' is also semiotically linked up with another word which denotes homeland, 'родина', which stems from the words 'родить' (to give birth) and 'родитель' (parent).

The link between fatherhood and fatherland has also been inscribed in political myth. In Book II of Virgil's *Aeneid*, Aeneas, one of the few Trojan heroes to survive the fall of the city, is prompted by divine portents to set on a journey and start a new lineage in another land. During the evasion, the hero's little son Ascanius walks beside him grasping his hand, his wife Creusa follows the group at a distance, and his old father, Anchises, too frail for a long march, has to be carried upon the hero's shoulder: 'ergo age, care pater, cervici imponere nostrae | ipse subibo umeris, nec me labor iste gravabit' [Come then, dear father, mount upon my neck; on my own shoulders I will stay thee, nor will such task o'erburden me].[4] For Virgil's contemporaries, there could hardly be any doubt about Aeneas' priorities. The act of carrying his father on his shoulder was a plastic example of the filial piety, as was the transport of Penates and Lares into the new land. However, the family's escape from the Troy is primarily about the son, Ascanius, and the new empire, Rome. Nevertheless, the dramatic image of Anchises on Aeneas's shoulder has called for more liberal interpretations of the scene, whereby the father takes over as the most precious possession. This patrimonial turn in the interpretation of *Aeneid* is epitomized by the famous sculpture by Gian Lorenzo Bernini, *Aeneas, Anchises and Ascanius* (1618–19). Confidently placed in the foreground is Anchises, a stately, muscular figure carrying the household Penates on his shoulder, his gaze fixed on something in the distant future. He is carried in his turn by Aeneas who appears in the mid-ground, somewhat struggling under the burden, and looking towards the ground. In the background, finally, Ascanius, represented as a tender *putto*, toddles behind them. Reflecting on this myth, the Italian psychoanalyst Luigi Zoja enthusiastically claimed that 'the image of Aeneas in flight with his father and his son is the central link in the chain of fathers that held society together'.[5]

Finally, the father-land has been enshrined in the legal discourse and popular perceptions thereof. On the one side, the notion of family as a blood tie has been firmly embedded in citizenship laws ever since the Roman Republic. While one of the possible principles, *ius soli* ('the law of soil'), derives one's right to a nationality from the fact of being born within a territory under a particular jurisdiction, another principle, more ancient and more widely accepted, is *ius sanguinis* ('the law of blood tie') that bases the right to citizenship on the fact that one has been born to parents who — at least one of them — already hold the citizenship of that country. To be sure, the principle of *ius sanguinis* has never been absolute and has some exceptions as well as other coextensive principles (bestowal by territorial conquest or by individual merit). However, the sheer continuity of that principle means that

Gian Lorenzo Bernini, *Aeneas, Anchises and Ascanius* (1618–19)

familial bonds are enshrined in the very foundations of one's civic status. On the other side, the principle of the sovereign power has been firmly integrated into the very foundations of family organization, starting with the Roman institution of *patria potestas*, the father's uncontested power of life and death over his children. In reality, this feature had numerous practical limitations and eventually became obsolete in the imperial period. Nonetheless, the notion of an unlimited power over progeny bore obvious resemblances to the magistrates' power over subjects and triggered different evolutionary myths and critical theories. For Gian Batista Vico, *patria potestas* was very real and effective: in the earliest families, the fathers 'exercised monarchic power subject only to God over persons and property of their children' and only agreed to join into a state as a lesser evil, when they felt threatened by *famuli*, domesticated servants who initially sought refuge in their areas but in the meantime swelled in numbers.[6] For Hegel, the early father's authority is primarily moral and, alloyed by emotions, prepares the family for a more advanced form of alliance, the state: 'by its means the State obtains as its members individuals who are already moral'.[7]

As we have seen, from the early modern period onwards, the ambiguities in the Latin language, Roman myth and law have been consistently simplified to generate a straightforward identification between the powerful father and the powerful state. Taking his cue from Aquinas, who portrayed families as historical prototypes for monarchies and republics, Giorgio Agamben argued for their consubstantiality at the synchronic level, within the structures of the state. According to him, the paternal prerogative is both a 'genealogical myth of sovereign power' and the structural zone of indistinction, 'the limit of both the *domus* and the city', where bare life is constituted.[8] My concern in this chapter is deceptively simple: what happens in the case of exile when the father himself is reduced to the holder of bare life and together with his family forced to flee from the fatherland? Following such a centrifugal thrust, an irreparable rift occurs in the Agambenian model. The sovereign power — if one exists under the circumstances — can no longer be perceived as the father of the people and at the same time the father's role as the magistrate of the family is discredited by his being driven away from the state. In cases of enforced displacement, where the politico-theological equation between *patria potestas* and the sovereign power does not apply, a wholly new trope of force emerges which links the father to exile. Rather than providing an image of the force of law, this trope becomes one of memory: exile will be remembered through the structural metaphor of the father and, conversely, the father will be remembered through the violent narrative of exile.

Father as Exilarch and Victim: The Exodus of Nabokov and Kiš

In 1986, Kiš claimed, in an extraordinary, almost emphatic praise of artistic autonomy, that Nabokov saw through both the splendour and the misery of exile:

> On je video, u Berlinu i Parizu podjednako, silu talenata koji su izgoreli u vatri političkih strasti i nostalgije, u rasprama, svađama, u bedi i ludilu, bežeći u mesijanizam, u panslavizam, u zapadnjaštvo, u spiritističko dozivanje ruske prošlosti, u pravoslavlje, u nacionalizam, u antisemitizam, u izdajstvo, u špiju-

nažu, u hiromantiju i nirvanu, ili su se, gonjeni nostalgijom, stavivši znak jednakosti između boljševizma i narodnjaštva, vraćali u 'Rusiju,' u duhovno sužanjstvo ili pravo pod nož ili u samoubistvo.

[In both Berlin and Paris he had seen countless talents burn themselves out in the flames of political passion and nostalgia, in polemics, feuds, poverty, and madness, escape into messianism, Pan-Slavism, Occidentalism, spiritist evocations of the Russian past, Orthodoxy, nationalism, anti-Semitism, betrayal, espionage, palmistry and Nirvana, or else, driven by homesickness and equating Bolshevism with populism, return to Russia and spiritual servitude, the firing squad, or suicide.][9]

This sweeping denunciation of émigré literati is based on Kiš's all-out refusal of politics. Nabokov himself was less harsh about his fellow émigrés. For, despite his fierce individualism, which, as Charles Nicol argues, 'prevented Nabokov from joining any group — especially one of a political nature',[10] he had a definite set of political beliefs which were anti-Marxist to the same extent as liberal and which prompted him to attach a comparative aesthetic value to precisely those émigrés whom Kiš thought he had denounced:

In serene retrospect, however, and judged by artistic and scholarly standards alone, the books produced *in vacuo* by émigré writers seem today, *whatever their individual faults*, more permanent and more suitable for human consumption than the slavish, singularly provincial and conventional streams of political consciousness that came during those same years from the pens of young Soviet authors whom a fatherly state provided with ink, pipes and pull-overs.[11]

It appears that Nabokov's and Kiš's views fit well into the poetic myth of Brodsky's poem 'The Fifth Anniversary': the writer faces a Gorgon of dismal political ideologies, each represented by a snake on its head, engendered by the totalitarian excrescences of the sovereign power or by desperation over the loss of native land. This Gorgon could only be defeated by the hero not looking into it, by him refusing to engage in a dialogue with it. The writer, wherever he might find himself, has his inner assignment to complete: it is solely up to his maturity to transform the uprooting experience of exile from a setback to the paramount catalyst to this activity.

The itineraries of Nabokov and Kiš illustrate how two very different sociopolitical contexts of exile can converge and produce broadly similar rhetorical responses. On the one hand, the twentieth century witnessed the exile from St Petersburg of a distinguished family of courtiers and jurists, rich in wealth and political influence but forced to wander from one European capital to another because of a class revolution. On the other hand, the same brutal era of totalitarian regimes set the scene for the exile from a completely different place, Novi Sad, of a middle-class family who, running away from racial persecution, found refuge in a rural region of West Hungary. What, if anything, can there be in common between these cases?

To begin with, the families of both Nabokov and Kiš left their homelands on account of a certain, more or less explicit, duress visited upon their fathers. Nabokov's father, Vladimir Dmitrievich Nabokov, was a prominent legal expert in imperial Russia with distinctly liberal reformist views. His constant appeals for peaceful and gradual reforms of society became inapplicable and plainly culpable after the violent overturn brought by the October Revolution. In the eyes of Lenin's supporters, Nabokov's participation as a secretary in the provisional government of Alexander Kerensky only added to the basic culpability of his bourgeois origin and wealth. After a brief and dangerous period of arrest, Nabokov decided to leave St Petersburg with his family and settle in the White Army's stronghold of the Crimea where he served as the minister of justice in the Crimean Regional Government. After the government was dissolved, he left Russia for Western Europe, to save the lives of his family and himself. Thus, the revolution, which he thought could and should have been avoided, left his family pauperized and exiled.

A quarter of a century later, Eduard Kiš, the father of the author of *Garden, Ashes*, was forced into exile not as a prominent member of a particular social class but as an anonymous member of a persecuted race. By birth a Hungarian Jew, Eduard Kiš conceptualized his Judaic origin in the rather formal terms of certain rabbinic rites which he had witnessed in his childhood, and which had eventually become a distant memory disconnected from his spiritual development as a mature person. However, the annexation of Novi Sad and Bačka by Hungarian forces brought him closer to the Holocaust and, paradoxically, to his ancestry. Eduard Kiš's elusive Judaic provenance suddenly gained in importance and became a force that influenced not only his fortune, but also the lives of his wife and two children. After being exposed to the escalating anti-Semitic measures of the Hungarian authorities, in January 1942 he survived by chance the notorious 'cold days of Novi Sad'.[12] The event triggered the hasty departure of the family, penniless and in a rented sleigh, to Eduard Kiš's native village of Kerkabarabás, in a remote province of Western Hungary, where the Jews were still protected, partially at least, by virtue of their Hungarian citizenship and their role in commerce.[13]

It is important here to observe a distinctly metonymic nature of these displacements. The exodus of the families of Nabokov and Kiš started as escape to safety, which in all likelihood was seen as temporary. However, it eventually turned into a prolonged exile as what emerged as a state of exception solidified into a persecutory system within which threats to their lives persisted. As soon as the last Whites left the Crimea, the nascent institutions of the Soviet state passed measures to ensure their emigration was permanent. In November 1921, for example, the Soviet Government proclaimed an amnesty for all opponents of the revolution who returned to the homeland; however, another decree, dated December 1921, declared that those who had not returned by July of the next year would be deprived of their citizenship, affecting the overwhelming majority of the emigrants.[14] In Kiš's case, unlike the rest of the country, Novi Sad, from which the family fled, was under a special military regime and, once left, they were not in a position to contemplate resettlement. From the perspective of Eduard Kiš, this exile may not have looked like a lot to write home about: after all, he took refuge in the place where he was born rather than in an unknown, foreign land. Nevertheless, from the vantage point of his family, who had never gone there before, it was exile at its harshest, representing political, spatial, social and linguistic alienation. In important ways, thus, both families were in an implied exile.

Let us now follow these families on their exilic path. In both cases, the safe haven was precarious and exile proved to be fatal for those who assumed the leadership. In 1922 Vladimir Dmitrievich Nabokov was shot dead in the Berlin Philharmonic Hall by political assassins whose views were opposed to those of the Bolsheviks. Ironically enough, in retrospect, the whole event appears to be one of those horribly absurd mistakes that none of the dialectics of history can ever redeem. During a ceremonial dinner that took place in the Berlin Philharmonic Hall and which was presided over by Nabokov, the publicist and former politician Pavel Milyukov gave a speech. Two fanatic rightists from the audience targeted the speaker but ended up shooting the chairman of the session, Nabokov.[15] The impact of the event upon the young Nabokov was such that instead of succumbing to a revengeful passion he surrounded the death of his father by a wall of silence and never made any public pronouncement, either on the event itself or on his attitude to it.[16] Nabokov's father was buried in the Russian cemetery in Tegel, Berlin. Hitler's anti-Semite policies prompted Nabokov to leave the city for good in 1937 and the construction of the Berlin Wall in 1961 meant that he would never wish to visit it again. The father's grave, trapped in the perilous border zone of West Berlin, was consigned to exilic memory.

The temporary relief which Kiš's father obtained by moving with his family to Hungary was irreversibly over by the spring of 1944. At that point, the Nazi regime directly interfered in Hungarian internal policy by sending a delegation of the Gestapo, headed by Adolf Eichmann, to organize the railway transfer of the whole of the country's Jewish community to extermination camps in the Third Reich. In a matter of weeks, the bulk of Jewish population, up to a million people, had been killed in gas chambers.[17] Among those who never returned were Eduard Kiš and the majority of his relatives from Kerkabarabás. His children were spared, on the grounds of their mother's Christian faith and the Orthodox baptism which Danilo Kiš received in 1939. The fact that no grave was accorded to his father would haunt Kiš throughout his life and find a poetic outlet in almost all his narrative works: Orpheus in *The Mansard* (1962), Ahasuerus in the family trilogy, the cenotaph in *A Tomb for Boris Davidovich* (1976) and the secret archive of the dead in *The Encyclopaedia of the Dead* (1983).

The political background and the method of these murders have important implications for our argument. In addition to the retroactive reasoning of implied exile which we have already mentioned, three additional forms of displaced force were brought to bear on Vladimir Nabokov and Danilo Kiš. In the first place, they had to internalize the coded political message that their exile was not because of them but displaced on them because of their fathers. Secondly, the fathers were not assassinated by those political agents who caused their exile, namely Soviet and Hungarian authorities, but, ironically, by different perpetrators: a right-wing extremist and the German forces of the SS. Thirdly, and probably crucially, neither Nabokov nor Kiš was there when their fathers were murdered: in their personal remembrance, as well as in their autobiographic texts, they were bound to feel displaced from that ultimate act of violence, as well as from their fathers' resting places.

Notwithstanding these broad analogies, the two itineraries show some contextual differences. In their respective homelands, Nabokov and Kiš were born into different social classes and by the nature of things were received into different classes in their host countries. When the Nabokovs reached Western Europe, they initially contemplated settling in England, a natural destination on account of Nabokov's father's anglophile outlook. However, very soon the family split into two: while the parents and the three younger children left London for Berlin, Vladimir Nabokov and his brother Sergey went to study at Cambridge, a high-brow environment which matched their aristocratic status but remained unresponsive to their inner concerns. In their rural haven, the family of Kiš were greeted to a more grudging welcome from their relatives. Accused of using cutlery and fire without paying a fee, they are promptly banished from the kitchen, more notably from the hearth, that symbol of homely security.[18] Thus, while Nabokov's family headed towards dispersal, the members of Kiš's family were forcefully brought together and concentrated in their experience of exile. Furthermore, the prism through which Nabokov and Kiš perceived these traumatic events was largely determined by the cognitive, intellectual and emotional capacities that qualified their respective ages. In 1917, when he moved from St Petersburg to the as yet unoccupied Crimea, Nabokov was eighteen, and two years later, when he left the Crimea for good, he was an adult. Kiš, however, was only seven years old at the time of his exile and blissfully ignorant of the secret reasons that stood behind the family's abrupt change of dwelling place.

Nevertheless, these differences, important though they may be to a historian, cease to carry weight from the vantage point of the modernist poetics to which both Nabokov and Kiš subscribed. Their principal autobiographic works, *Speak, Memory: An Autobiography Revisited* (1966) and *Garden, Ashes* (1965), were written after a significant period of inner reflection and foreground a mature narrator, who conjures memories with a palette of verbal devices, from synaesthesia to transcendental vision.[19] The modernist poetics, with its stylistic sleights of hand, levels out the differences in age between the authors' earlier selves. In a like manner, it also cancels class differences between them. Both authors were aiming for the quintessentially modernist 'biographic legend' which would remain impervious to such empirical accidents as social status.[20] Regardless of whether one was sinking from aristocracy to vagabondage, as was the case with Nabokov, or from petty bourgeoisie to peasantry, as in Kiš's case, the life writing was to be suffused with 'rich nostalgia' and coated with unmistakable patina of irony.

Two Explanatory Models: Structuralism and Psychoanalysis

As we have seen, Nabokov's and Kiš's retrospective narratives of the years of exile are driven by the same *spiritus movens* but they differ in contexts. It is important to stress that they also differ somewhat in their compositional logic. In *Speak, Memory*, the overall majority of the recollected scenes, distributed in chapters 1–11, are set in Russia, in the family's sylvan period before the Revolution; the Revolution itself as well as the ensuing exile are related in Chapters 12–15, which include a cursory overview of the author's life in the Crimea, Cambridge, Berlin and Paris, from 1917 and 1940. In *Garden, Ashes*, only the initial three chapters are concerned with the narrator's life in Novi Sad before the city was occupied by the Hungarian forces; the rest of the book relates the family's winter journey to Kerkabarabás (Chapter 4) and their life in exile until their repatriation to Yugoslavia in 1947 (Chapters 5–12). In *Speak, Memory*, thus, we have, predominantly, a recollection of homeland from the point of view of the narrator in exile; in *Garden, Ashes*, however, there is, predominantly, a recollection of exile from the point of view of the narrator who is in his homeland.

Central to both writers' endeavour was the discovery of a symbol, or a network of symbols, that would guarantee the continuity of their lived experience between home and exile and, at the same time, the aesthetic autonomy of their autobiographic works. In her important theoretical essay on Nabokov's memoir, Maria Louise Ascher described this modernist strategy in terms of metonymic and metaphoric transfers that take place within the text but also sketched something like a general tropology of autobiography as a genre. Since Ascher's argument is the first and to my knowledge the only application of the metonymico-metaphoric paradigm to exile it needs to be sketched out in more detail.

The theoretical basis of Ascher's text is Roman Jakobson's paper 'Two Aspects of Language and Two Types of Aphasic Disorders'. In this landmark text of Structuralism, Jakobson takes up De Saussure's distinction between two fundamental operations of language: on the one hand, the selection axis, which structures the vocabulary of a language with relations of synonymy and antonymy, and, on the other, the combination axis, which structures the syntax of that language with relations of subordination.[21] While in De Saussure's *Course in General Linguistics* these axes define language at its most general, systemic level, Jakobson elaborates their broader implications. Selection and combination command everyday communication; they are, also, associated with two types of aphasia, the incapacity to begin speaking and the incapacity to recall the right word; furthermore, they are the pivots of two key rhetorical figures, metaphor and metonymy; finally, they command different styles in literary history, symbolism and realism. If selection (metaphor) and combination (metonymy) are important not only to language but also to rhetoric and literary history, the way is open for their exploration within specific literary genres and even topoi.[22] It is precisely this possibility which Ascher explores.

Ascher's argument is strikingly consistent. On the one hand, all autobiographic writing takes place in what she calls the 'exilic mode': the narration of one's previous self involves a metaphysical banishment from a halcyon childhood, an ontological eviction from the lived past into memory and a narrative expulsion of living memory into the script. On the other hand, the relationship asserts itself the other way round, too: political exile, with its spatio-temporal discontinuities and psychological rifts, naturally calls for autobiographic writing. In view of these reciprocal tropaic affinities, the autobiographies of exile represent the key nexus and the most fertile ground for the exploration of the exilic mode of life writing. The second element of Ascher's argument is that autobiographic texts arising from exile epitomize the Jakobsonian model of paradigmatic and syntagmatic relations. On the one hand, the exile (and the autobiographer in general) needs to present a linear chronological account of his or her life, which unfolds from homeland to exile (and from the past to the present). This outbound, narrative motion is embedded on the syntagmatic axis, 'the axis of sequence, combination, metonymy'. On the other hand, in order to present that account, the exile (and by extension the autobiographer) needs to perform a homecoming in memory — because the actual return is impossible — and hence resorts to timeless symbols that bridge the gap between exile and homeland (and between the present and the past). This inbound, mnemonic motion happens on the paradigmatic axis, 'the axis of simultaneity, substitution, metaphor'.[23]

A lucid re-articulation of the Structuralist paradigm, Ascher's model also provides an apt interpretive tool to describe the condensation that takes place in the typical modernist work, 'highly wrought, self-conscious in its narrative and rhetorical strategies'.[24] What is more, Ascher's interpretive application of the model to her chosen example, *Speak, Memory*, also convinces: it accounts not only for the sundry homecoming metaphors within the text but also for the history of Nabokov's revisions of that text, effectively a series of interlingual returns.[25] We now need to draw a difference between the model adopted in this study and Ascher's application of the Jakobsonian paradigm. In both models, metonymy and metaphor are connected into a chronological sequence, a significant difference from the Jakobson's theory where they unroll simultaneously. Likewise, in both models they are involved in a sort of conflict, reacting to each other. This study argues that the metonymico-metaphoric transfers take place between two different discursive fields (or structures, to use the correlate term of the Structuralist theory): force is metonymically displaced in implied exile and then metaphorically condensed in the literature of exile. In Ascher's framework, metonymies and metaphors are integrated within a single discursive field (or structure), namely the autobiographic text of exile, and designate its two constitutive functions: syntagmatic linear narration which is overdetermined — at least in such master rhetoricians as Nabokov — by paradigmatic nexuses of remembrance.

The unusual thing about Ascher's essay is that, although drawing upon a wide selection of Nabokov's tropes, she never mentions the figure of the father, who can be described as *agnus in fabula*. The father's metonymico-metaphoric role within *Speak, Memory* is quite clear: he is the exilarch, and therefore intrinsically connected with the linear (metonymic) narrative sequence from home to exile; at the same time, he is the ancestor, and hence the repository of the circular (metaphoric) memory loop from exile to home. Here is an exquisite example of the paternal metaphor combined with metonymy: 'Annoyance changed to distress, when after making a precise little cross over the face of each of us, my father rather casually added that very possibly, *ves'ma vozmozhno*, he would never see us again; whereupon, in trench coat and khaki cap, with his briefcase under his arm, he strode away into the steamy fog.'[26] The disappearance of the father, who is metonymically framed by his tailor-made coat and cap, and by the homey fog, becomes emblematic for exile. It heralds the loss of the childhood world embedded in the native landscapes, a precarious *in illo tempore* swiftly receding into the mist of memory. In view of such rhetorical configuration, the father could actually provide the master example for Ascher's argument.

However, I will go a step further and suggest that Ascher's intratextual model does not account for the rhetorical drivers in the political practice of exile. To be sure, she states that the work of the exiled writer 'bears the unmistakable imprint of those experiences'.[27] Imprint is a very convenient metaphor: political duress does not produce merely a fleeting image on the surface of the work by way of reflection but rather a deep and indelible mark through pressure. Yet, Ascher does not explain how exactly the political field makes such an imprint in the work; her metonymico-metaphoric model allows merely for surface reflections and intratextual simulacra of political pressure. The father in *Speak, Memory* — as well as the one in *Garden, Ashes* — is the exilarch, and the autobiographer receives and internalizes political pressure through him. In addition to being the exilarchs, the fathers in *Speak, Memory* and *Garden, Ashes* are also the victims of bloody violence whose demise has been agonizingly hidden and displaced from the eyes of both autobiographers. This means that we need not only better examples for but also a substantive expansion of Ascher's model.

If Ascher's model informs us about exile but does not explain the psycho-political duress communicated through the figure of the father, perhaps the psychoanalytic model, which is all about constructing the father, could be of help. To be sure, both Nabokov and Kiš expressed some very negative views about psychoanalysis. Nabokov, whose resentment against Freudianism was famous, denounced its interpretative methods as 'one of the vilest deceits practised by people on themselves and on others' and even as a residuum of medievalism that is 'still adored by the ignorant, the conventional, or the very sick'.[28] In his interviews, Kiš was flexible on all theories and interpretative methods except psychoanalysis, which he considered guilty of vulgar psychological reductionism: 'please do not explore me from the Freudian perspective, it just drives me mad...'[29] Latter-day inquisition or annoying quackery, Nabokov and Kiš insist that psychoanalysis had no place in literature. Yet, such emphatic attempts to expel psychoanalysis from the realm of modernity need not constrain a critic; actually, to a psychoanalyst they may appear as a coded invitation to perform precisely that reading. Indeed, an alternative, non-Structuralist model has been proposed in connection with Kiš and it gives the family drama more psychological depth. I will proceed to explain it in more detail because its main theoretical claim, like Ascher's, applies to other autobiographies of exile.

In their fine analyses of Kiš's *Garden, Ashes*, Daniel Ross and Ivana Vuletić suggest a psychoanalytic explanation of why the narrator of *Garden, Ashes* is so fascinated with the trivia of his father's life. As the core text for this interpretation, they rediscover one of the less frequently used texts by Sigmund Freud, 'Der Familienroman der Neurotiker' [Family Romances, 1908–09]. In this astute and imaginative paper, Freud suggests that as part of the normal psychological development children master intra-family relations and at the same time internalize behavioural models and salient figures in the society at large. The outcome of this maturation process is social dexterity, in that they learn how to play one against the other, and at the same time, psychic gratification, in that they find substitutes for their libidinal urges. For example, if a child feels slighted or deprived of the due amount of affection by parents, he or she will promptly find alternative ones in imagination which are typically 'sozial höher stehende' [of better birth].[30] The models for this identification will be found in 'any opportune coincidences [das zufällige Zusammentreffen] from his actual experience, such as his becoming acquainted with the Lord of the Manor or some landed proprietor if he lives in the country or with some member of the aristocracy if he lives in town.'[31] Failing to find appropriate models of nobility in immediate surrounding, the child will have recourse to various imaginative stories, either literary or concocted by him-/herself. In the second part of the romance, which is sexual, the child gets punished for 'sexuelle Unarte' [sexual naughtiness] or otherwise learns about 'die geschlechtlichen Vorgänge' [sexual processes] between parents. As revenge, the child invents various erotic scenarios involving the mother, whose identity will remain firmly fixed (who is 'certissima'), in order to cast doubt on the identity of the father (who remains 'incertus').[32]

At the end of his essay, Freud made an important suggestion that the family romance is not limited to the vicissitudes of a child's coming of age but that it also has a deferred effect on adults, especially in their dreams. The dream-work, as Freud specified in *Traumdeutung* [*The Interpretation of Dreams*, 1900], proceeds on two complementary principles which broadly chime in with Jakobson's metaphor and metonymy: condensation [Verdichtung], which selects some unconscious dream-thoughts and discards others, and displacement [Verschiebung], which displaces unconscious dream-thoughts onto different loci in actual dreams.[33] In dreams, thus, the father may be displaced onto a different, often imaginary person who still has some tell-tale features of the prototype. Since in Freud's theory dreams are sublimated in the works of art, the way is open for exploring this paradigm in the works of accomplished writers. The only difference from the Jakobsonian paradigm is that selection and combination would not negotiate within one textual system but between two systems, namely dream-thoughts and dream-contents.

How was this model applied to Kiš? In his essay on *Garden, Ashes*, Daniel Ross suggested that the entire novel may be read as the narrator's spinning of the family romance with an unconscious goal of replacing his ordinary, lacklustre parents with more admirable prototypes.[34] According to that argument, the boy's precocious literary fantasy, his secret fascination with the sundry figures of authority, and even references to the Wandering Jew, would be part of his imaginative thrust of the father. Thus, to reinterpret Ross's claim in terms of the rhetoric of force, the author, Kiš, tells the story of a boy, Andreas Scham, who displaces the libidinal energy from the father and condenses it in alternative figures of authority, real and fantastic. Following Ross's cue, Vuletić proposes a more liberal interpretation of Freud's paper and goes on to suggest that Kiš's narrative does not literally replace the hateful father with a more dignified progenitor. As befits an adult person, it proceeds with more sophistication and seeks to 'reinvent' him in the first place and transfer him in another area, that of a fictional biography. On the one hand, Eduard Scham appears as 'a figure larger than life whose every statement and gesture [...] seem somehow admirable and uniquely significant' and, on the other, as the repository of 'hostility and frustration' of an oversensitive son.[35] In rhetorical terms, Vuletić's argument suggests that the author firstly condenses the father into a personal hero, one with the distinctly mythical mixture of good and evil, and then displaces him to another realm, literary prose.

Both versions of the family romance explanation provide valuable insights into Kiš's prose and, what is more, have broader implications for the understanding of the autobiographic genre. Following Freud's two-system narrative they articulate the crucial nexus between reality and imagination which remained beyond the reach of Ascher's one-system model. The sphere of the social practice, permeated with frustration, blights and duress, provides an impulse and the sphere of imagination responds with a compensatory construal of force, picking up elements of social reality and combining them into a new whole. This imaginative elicitation of force brings the Freudian interpretative model very close to the framework developed in this study. Like family romance, the mechanism of implied exile negotiates between the two rhetorical drivers: political imagination which displaces force and literary imagination which reconstructs it.

Nevertheless, there are some important differences between the two frameworks. In order to understand those counter-analogies, we need to bear in mind that the Freudian theory is predicated on the notion of a certain stable amount of libidinal energy which in real life can change vectors (from admiration to fear) which can then be brought to bear on different outlets (from the self to other people to objects and mental ideas) by psychic rhetorical transfers, which Freud defines as condensation and displacement. It is an essentially ambiguous and versatile kind of energy and the force which this energy elicits may consequently appear as good (protective) but also as bad (threatening). On the one hand, a new father can express the child's nostalgia, a 'longing [Sehnsucht] for the happy, vanished days when his father seemed to him the noblest and strongest of men',[36] but also his trauma, 'the dreaded father [den gefürchteten Vater] at whose hands castration is expected'.[37] The political force of implied exile, however, is always a threatening one and the threat it encodes is existential — exile as a substitute capital punishment and literal civic death — rather than sexual.

This difference in type of forces involved is probably the main reason why psychoanalysis was slow to pick up on political exile, irrespective of whether it affected individuals or families. Characteristically, Freud treated a number of displaced neurotics, many of them dispirited members of the Russian landowning elite like Sergey Pankeev (the Wolf-Man),[38] but did not consider geographical displacement a significant factor in the habitual process of the emancipation of personality. Being himself a tourist with a 'Reisefieber'[39] and a keen cultural archaeologist, he tended to attribute his patients' nostalgic bouts, somewhat disparagingly, to a relapse of their primary neurotic symptoms. Likewise, in his interpretations of the ancient myths, geographic elements, such as those inherent in Oedipus's displacement, were regularly glossed over. By a similar token, in their psychoanalytic readings of *Garden, Ashes* Vuletić and Ross did not think of Kiš's enforced geographic displacement as particularly important. In fact, Vuletić cautions against decontextualized projections of Freud's family romance but only mentions 'persecution and death',[40] while Ross does not even consider the political background of the story.[41]

However, it is clear that exile has a significant bearing on Kiš's literary commemoration of his father. To provide but one example from *Garden, Ashes*: reflecting on his family's flight from Novi Sad, the narrator recalls almost romantically how their sleigh glided for days through the snow and how his father sat next to the rider, 'kao svrgnuti ruski knez, odjednom nekako čudno lucidan, patetično svestan da ispunjava svoju sudbinu ispisanu u genealogiji njegove krvi, u proročkim knjigama' [like a deposed Russian prince, suddenly strangely lucid, pathetically aware of his destiny as inscribed in his genealogy, in the books of the prophets].[42] Sure, it is very much in line with the Freudian family romance to imagine the father as a prince and that prince may well be Russian. However, to recall him as a 'deposed' Russian prince and simultaneously as the modern upshot of the Jewish Exile from Jerusalem (the Babylonian Captivity, sixth century BCE) introduces a whole new aspect of political imagination that cannot be explained away by the Freudian paradigm. The father emerges not as a settled aristocrat, the lord of the manor or a prince, but as the exilarch, one who has been dislodged both from his political state and from his family status. His sudden feeling of power, as a prince and as an archetypal Jewish expellee, compensates for the lacklustre nature of his departure. In the narrator's imagination, an anonymous refugee, who is not important enough to be banished and whose life or death would not be noticed in the books, turns into an aristocrat of exile. He becomes the archetypal banished man, who has faced direct force and who responds by eliciting that force in imagination. Therefore, we must assume that in this important reference the political mechanism of implied exile overdetermines any psychological mechanism of family romance.

Let us sum up the key points of this survey of the two interpretative methods. It is clear that Ascher's Structuralist paradigm can inform us about exile as the intrinsic memory trope of the autobiographic genre and thereby highlight the two authors' modernist poetics. However, being limited to one system, memory *qua* narration, it cannot account for the political role of the father as both the leader in exile and its victim. Conversely, Ross's and Vuletić's model of family romance can inform us about how the father subliminally determines the patterns of imagination of his son, both as the precocious child and traumatized narrator. However, since it assumes an essentially static family, it cannot adequately explain the experience of exile and, consequently, the political role of the father as the exilarch and the victim remains beyond its reach.

Unsettling Father: Estrangement as Repression

In the cases of impasse with theory, it is always helpful to return to literary examples because some of these dilemmas are much more effectively articulated through paradox and irony. In his memoir *Les Mots* [*Words*, 1963], Jean-Paul Sartre reflects upon the loss of his father, who died of Cochin-China fever when he was a toddler, and concludes that his early death was a gesture of favour. His peers with living fathers appear to him as 'Énées qui portent sur les dos leurs Anchises [...]

ces géniteurs invisibles à cheval sur leurs fils pour toute la vie' [the Aeneases each carrying his Anchises on his shoulders [...] those invisible fathers who ride piggy-back on their sons throughout their lives].[43] This is, obviously, a very sardonic point which does not exclude the possibility that the denial of burden may be what Robert Harvey described as 'an implicit desire to vicariously experience the very suffering of "Aeneas and his cohorts"'.[44]

In fact, although Sartre himself was not an exile, his ironic counter-Aeneid illustrates two concepts which could be far more valuable to the study of paternity and patrimony in exile than the Jakobsonian metonymico-metaphoric transfer and family romance. The concepts I have in mind, namely Shklovsky's *остранение* [translated variously as estrangement and defamiliarization] and Freud's *Verdrängung* [repression], have already been proven to work well together, in particular in connection with Hoffmann's story 'Der Sandmann' [The Sandman, 1816]. Sartre's parody of the Virgilian narrative only confirms this affinity: making the father more difficult to bear makes the reader's perception more difficult (Shklovsky) and elicits subliminal anxieties (Freud). On the one hand, thinking of Aeneas as a comic character, a hero manqué, who struggles under his smug, self-righteous progenitor is an excellent example of defamiliarizing not only a worn-out myth in literature but also a worn-out family discourse in the society at large. On the other hand, Aeneas's submitting wilfully to the burden of the father as a holy load is an emblem of the compensatory glorification of what has been locked out of the conscious as dangerous. Therefore, each of the two concepts has a literary and a psychological aspect. Defamiliarization as a literary device may arise from repression and, vice versa, defamiliarization can trigger the release of repressed contents in the psyche.

However, I will go a step further and suggest that in addition to the shared psychological and literary orientation they showcase a distinctly political reasoning which makes them particularly useful in approaching narratives of exile. For one thing, in Freud's theory exile represents the fundamental psychological matrix from which all energies spring up and branch into external reality and conscious life.[45] What is more, that internal psycho-trope is intrinsically connected to the father. In the first place, the father comes across as something of a concealed, implied exile. The psychic life rests on the steady work of *Verdrängung* [repression] whereby the father who is already in the unconscious has to be kept at bay, by 'Abweisung und Fernhaltung vom Bewußten' [turning something away, and keeping it at a distance from the conscious].[46] It is crucial for the psychological well-being of the individual that this process does not turn into conscious expulsion: as soon as one attempts to banish an undesirable psychic content consciously, one receives backlash which causes pain. However, in another area of Freud's theory, the father also comes across as the expeller, the one who drives the others into exile. In the famous genealogical myth about the primal horde from *Totem und Tabu* [*Totem and Taboo*, 1913], the father enjoys full psychological supremacy over his sons, taking all women for himself and banishing all contenders as soon as they reach sexual maturity. The unchecked reign of the father's libido ends when the number of 'exiles' on the other side of the border swells enough to enable an alliance and a brutal counterstrike: 'Eines Tages taten sich die ausgetriebenen Brüder zusammen, erschlugen und verzehrten den Vater und machten so der Vaterhorde ein Ende' [One day the brothers who had been driven out came together, killed and devoured their father and so made an end of the patriarchal horde].[47] Yet again, Freud himself is a man and just like other men has an unconscious. It would not be difficult to see how this and other narratives of the father's direct banishment of the son arise from the son's indirect expulsion of the father.

The political aspect of Shklovsky's estrangement is not as obvious as that of Freud's *Verdrängung* but it is still there. In the first place, with a bit of linguistic imagination, one could follow Svetlana Boym's suggestion that *остранение* comes from both *странное* (strange) and *страна* (country) and that, consequently, 'ostranenie means more than distancing and making strange; it is also dislocation, *dépaysement*'.[48] Then, given that what slows down perception may also cause annoyance, literary estrangement can be part of a broader political strategy to dislocate political practices; as Shklovsky himself points out, 'Tolstoy described the dogmas and rituals he attacked as if they were unfamiliar'.[49] Estrangement has been adopted as the literary style and ethos in the Russian emigration. Greta Slobin hinted that the Russian émigrés, '*estranged* from home and *strangers* abroad' experienced a form of cultural identity crisis which they resolved by conservative clinging to an olden Russian language and by tapping its estrangement potential for both the host community and the Soviet audiences.[50] Finally, in the dissident circles in the Soviet period, techniques of estrangement became a token of resistance to the Marxist concept of alienation and in fact were a prelude to the actual exile of some of those dissidents, such as Brodsky.[51]

Let us now see how this latent political vector in Freud's repression and Shklovsky's estrangement may work in a literary text of exile. In our discussion of the legend of Ahasuerus in *Garden, Ashes*, we have already mentioned that well into his mature years the narrator is haunted by a cynically disguised apparition of his dead father. It is now time to look at this passage in more detail:

> Jer da je moj otac pristao da se lepo povuče iz sveta, da se pomiri sa smrću i da se konačno opredeli za jedan od svetova, za jednu od država i za jednu porodicu, ja od svega toga ne bih pravio problem. No on je jednako terao svoj prkos prema svetu, nije hteo da se pomiri sa starošću i sa smrću, nego je uzeo na sebe oblik Ahašveroša i, odeven najčešće u nemačkog turistu, dolazio je da provocira moju radoznalost, da me muči u snovima, da me opominje na svoje prisustvo.
>
> [If my father had agreed to withdraw nicely from the world, to reconcile himself to death, to commit himself definitely to one world, one country, one family, I would not have created a problem for him. But he continued to vent his spite toward the world, to reject reconciliation with old age and death, to assume the visage of the Wandering Jew and descend upon me — usually dressed as a German tourist — to provoke me, to torment me in my dreams, to remind me of his presence.][52]

There is in this passage something genuinely uncanny and unsettling, which goes beyond the reference to the legend of the Wandering Jew. By this point the reader has learnt that the narrator perceives his father not in the basic unity of his personality, but in the multiplicity of the imaginary roles he was forced to play or that he himself preferred to play. This passage is, however, a turning point at which it becomes clear that mimicry is not only about the father himself, but also about the narrator's imaginative projection of force. It is clear how Shklovsky's and Freud's concept come together: Ahasuerus is made unfamiliar as a carefree tourist, and at the same time *unheimlich*, as the persecuting agent. However, in this process, defamiliarization and repression turn political: the father haunts him in the guise of a German tourist. By 1965, when *Garden, Ashes* appeared, tourists from West Germany had started to spend their summer holidays on the Adriatic Coast, bringing hard currency to Yugoslavia's socialist economy and haunting memories to the local population, who recalled the occupation of the country during the Second World War. Thus, the dead father's homecoming as Ahasuerus *and* as a German tourist is linked to three forms of political displacement. It reminds the narrator of his native land but also of the land of his exile and, particularly, of the mentally inaccessible and rationally incomprehensible place where the father disappeared.

It is significant to note that in his own autobiographic writing Nabokov evolved the idea of an uncanny correlate who remains behind, in Russia, and with whom he has some spiritual connection. Here, one can observe the growth of force from one version of the memoir to the other. In the first book-length version of the memoir, *Conclusive Evidence* (1951), he envisions an imaginary double:

> Very lovely, very lonesome. But what am I doing there in that stereoscopic dreamland? Somehow, those two sleighs have slipped away; they have left my imaginary double behind on the blue-white road. No, even the vibration in my ears is not their receding bells, but my own blood singing. All is still, spellbound, enthralled by that great heavenly O shining above the Russian wilderness of my past. The snow is real, though, and as I bend to it and scoop up a handful, forty-five years crumble to glittering frost-dust between my fingers.[53]

In Nabokov's self-translation into Russian, *Другие берега* [*Other Shores*, 1954], which followed suit, the ontological designator 'imaginary' is removed and the double, consequently, becomes very real:

> Совершенно прелестно, совершенно безлюдно. Но что же я-то тут делаю, посреди стереоскопической феерии? Как попал я сюда? Точно в дурном сне, удалились сани, оставив стоящего на страшном русском снегу моего двойника в американском пальто на викуньевом меху. Саней нет как нет; бубенчики их—лишь раковинный звон крови у меня в ушах. Домой—за спасительный океан! Однако двойник медлит.[54]

In *Speak, Memory: An Autobiography Revisited* (1966), finally, a curious transformation takes place. The double cedes place to a passportless spy, a mental traveller with invalid papers:

> Very lovely, very lonesome. But what am I doing in this stereoscopic dreamland? How did I get here? Somehow, the two sleighs have slipped away, leaving behind a passportless spy, standing on the blue-white road in his New England snowboots and stormcoat. The vibration in my ears is no longer their receding bells, but only my old blood singing. All is still, spellbound, enthralled by the moon, fancy's rear-vision mirror. The snow is real, though, and as I bend to it

and scoop a handful, sixty years crumble to glittering frost-dust between my fingers.[55]

It might be seen as ironic that an author as much opposed to psychoanalysis as Nabokov would articulate one of the most striking metaphorical inscriptions of repression and its return. The author finds himself in a dreamland, a realm that brings together oneiric and literary imagination. In that land, just like in a dream, a Russian sleigh becomes a New England car with the moon as rear-view mirror; and receding bells turn into heartbeat. The boundaries of this land are traversed by a double, or a spy, who has no passport and in fact does not need it. This uncanny idea of the exilic *Doppelgänger*, the self's silent observer from the past, creates an admirable loop connecting literary estrangement and political alienage. On the one hand, the spy is immersed in the snowy blizzards of St Petersburg in Dostoevsky's *The Double*; on the other hand, his shady, illicit movement negotiates the territorial divides imposed by the Cold War.

Paternity Settled: *Mise-en-abyme* and the Abyss of Exile

Another way of addressing the eminently political role of the father as the mediator of implied duress of exile and the target of 'bloody violence' would be to trace his appearance as a macro-metaphor of textual coherence, also known as *mise-en-abyme*. If we disregard its ostentatious and largely abstract use in the French *nouveau roman* of the 1960s, the term has a distinctly political lineage and is linked to the idea of family. To be sure, in literary criticism *mise-en-abyme* has been domesticated since the late nineteenth century and is now treated as an almost autochthonous term, but the concept and the basic visual template come from heraldry.[56] In a coat-of-arms, the key emblem is placed in the middle of the visual field and *commands* other, lateral elements thus throwing into relief the family's political idea, its structure and hierarchy. In a literary work, an emblematic image may be placed anywhere in the text and its key function is to act as its microcosmos, i.e. to *reflect* on the small scale the structure of the entire text. In literature of exile, however, these structural archetypes are subverted as both family and the text become discontinuous. One could say that there is in exile something of a literal *mise-en-abyme*, in that a member of the state is consigned to the abyss of civic death, which is then followed by the construal of a literary *mise-en-abyme*, where political force is elicited and then consolidated as the commanding principle and reflection of the entire text.

Hence, we need to explore the different emblems of textual coherence in *Speak, Memory* and *Garden, Ashes* and probe their different forms and degrees of force. I propose to compare three pairs of such macro-metaphors. We will start with two instances of the typically modernist *mise-en-abyme* which are not linked to paternity. Then, we will move on to two examples of the more forceful figure of narrative ellipse which involves the account of the fathers' death. Finally, we will end with two condensed metaphors where the fathers disappear and then emerge as symbols of continuity and cohesion.

'A coloured spiral in a small ball of glass'; this is how Nabokov metaphorically described the development of his personality over the course of his life.[57] Captivatingly nostalgic, the metaphor of the marble, spiral in the circle, reveals the essential structural logic of *Speak, Memory* and its authorial persona. The perceptive reader will notice that his life story displays a plethora of experiences but also an underlying unity as these units usually come into a limited number of distinct patterns, marked by coincidental repetitions which Nabokov calls 'small' and 'large' convolutions of the spiral. In *Speak, Memory*, the author traces these thematic patterns in his life that both impress upon his persona a mark of individuality and raise his self-awareness to ever higher stages. We encounter the author in a large variety of situations — hunting butterflies, talking to his uncle Ruka, playing chess with his father, writing poetry, seeing his 'first dead man', 'suffering the pangs of exile' at Yalta — and each of these situations bears a special and inalienable meaning in his own self-perception. For, throughout his memoir, Nabokov constantly leaps forward to find an echo of one or another scene from his childhood in some of the events which arrived later and these repetitions appear to him as emergent patterns of the spiral. The same goes for the reader's understanding of Nabokov's personality: the psychological and intellectual qualities of the authorial persona transpire through every successive incident he relates. In the beginning, he is just a cajoled child, though with some exceptional faculties (hallucinations, coloured hearing, mathematical skill); gradually, however, the reader gets to know about his obsession with nature and the first causes of his later political liberalism, learns about his haughty behaviour towards his tutors and his elitist attitudes towards his classmates, and, finally, about his highly individualistic metaphysical and aesthetic concerns. Therefore, the metaphor of the marble, a spiral enclosed in a transparent circle, is a *mise-en-abyme* of the biographic legend articulated in the memoir: it is impervious to external influence and yet transparent; it conjures the halcyon childhood and at the same time exalts the growth of the mature writer.

The opening of *Garden, Ashes*, presents a different form of the sealed glass which is, nevertheless, also metaphoric. The narrator recalls how in his early childhood his mother used to come softly to the kids' bedroom to wake up him and his sister. On a big tray, she used to bring jars of honey and little bottles of cod-liver oil, which would suddenly come aglow as the curtain was pulled to let the daylight in: 'Majka je [...] donosila ćilibarske boje sunčanih dana, guste koncentrate pune opojnih mirisa. Te su teglice i čaše bile samo uzorci, specimeni onih novih zemalja pri kojima bi izjutra pristao ludi šlep naših dana' [my mother carried to us the amber hues of sunny days, thick concentrates full of intoxicating aromas. The little jars and glasses were just samples, specimens of the new lands at which the foolish barge of our days would be putting ashore on those summer mornings].[58] What we have in Kiš, thus, is not a coloured spiral in a marble but amber and dense oil and honey in jars. Indeed, *Garden, Ashes* can be seen as a prolonged, voluptuous surrender to the plenitude of day's sensations which are then celebrated in the night's oneiric journey on the foolish barge, the Rimbaldien *bateau ivre*. In *Garden, Ashes*, exile itself is toned down and there is a sense of a smooth slippage from place to place, with a dream-like easiness. Consequently, there is very little psychological evolution, be it linear or spiral, in the child protagonist of *Garden, Ashes*. In the tranquillity of lyrical reflection and with occasional flashes of protective irony, the narrator simply reports what happened to him and his family and how these events affected him and his dreams at the time. Thus the amber jars gratify the palate, tease the eye, and spur the imagination to new mental journeys: all of these sensations stand for the plenitude of life and its lyrical transformation in *Garden, Ashes*.

As we have seen, the metaphors of the marble in Nabokov and of amber jars in Kiš, similar though they may appear, indicate some important differences between their autobiographic projects. In *Speak, Memory*, the author's elusive personality is gradually made clear through the events he relates; in *Garden, Ashes*, we deal with precisely the opposite case: it is the events which are made clear by a candid glance from within. In other words, and paraphrasing Lejeune's definition of autobiography, in the former case there is a history of personality whereas in the latter case there is more of a history around personality.[59] These metaphors, based on the tight and round glass form symbolize a life contained within the sealed poetic work and identify its pattern and substance. In another, equally important sense, they showcase the resistance which each globular form shows to external force: like a marble, Modernist literary text appears impervious to political pressure.

Nevertheless, in the two autobiographic texts we are also confronted with some more forceful forms of *mise-en-abyme*. For one thing, one can be 'placed into abyss' by being literally displaced from the text at the critical moment of the plot in a forceful thrust of imagination. A case in point is the moment of imagining and telling how their fathers died. Not only were they traumatized by the loss, they were also displaced from their displaced fathers' death which adds an additional element of psychological duress. It is striking that Nabokov and Kiš came up with essentially the same solution for the trauma of displaced force: the narrative ellipse. They convey the unique horror of the event not by relating it *in extenso* but, conversely, by the displacement of force from the narrative sequence.

The tragic end of Nabokov's father, which we know had made an enormous impact on him, is reported in the following way:

> On the night of March 28, 1922, around ten o'clock, in the living room where as usual my mother was reclining on the red-plush corner couch, I happened to be reading to her Blok's verse on Italy — had just got to the end of the little poem about Florence, which Blok compares to the delicate, smoky bloom of an iris, and she was saying over her knitting, 'Yes, yes, Florence does look like a *dimniy iris*, how true! I remember — ' when the telephone rang.[60]

The telephone rang, bringing the bleak news that his father was not coming back home because he had been assassinated in the Berlin Philharmonic Hall. Despite the obvious narrative suspense created by the end of the paragraph, this is almost all the reader is ever to learn about the father's death in *Speak, Memory*.[61] The next sentence shifts abruptly from the sombre innuendo and opens a new paragraph which is entirely about Nabokov's relationship with his mother: 'After 1923, when she moved to Prague, and I lived in Germany and France, I was unable to visit her frequently; nor was I with her at her death, which occurred on the eve of World War Two.'[62] Thus, the only reference to the shot which claimed his father's life is vested in the image of Florence as a 'smoky iris'.

Kiš also had a reason to displace the death of his father from the syntagmatic axis of narration. For, despite the enormous personal toll his family paid during the Holocaust, when it came to direct knowledge about the most gruesome part of the extermination process, Kiš's viewpoint was one of a contemporary of the Holocaust, rather than that of a direct witness. It seems only a sensible choice that he resisted the challenge of representing it directly at the time when the Holocaust survivors were coming to terms with their memories in the first reports, as Jean Améry elevated in the following way: 'while the Holocaust is truly the existential reference point for all Jews, only we, the sacrificed, are able to spiritually relive the catastrophic event as it was or fully picture it as it could be again.'[63] Kiš understood this statement both in its ethical and in its aesthetic significance: all we discover in *Garden, Ashes* about Eduard Scham's last days is that he spent some time in a ghetto, where he was visited by his family, and was later transported by train in an unknown direction, the two key words, 'geto' [ghetto] and 'zapečaćeni furgon' [sealed cattle car], being mentioned only once and without much emphasis.[64] Kiš's circumspection is probably one of the reasons that accounts for his displacement of lived experience into the novel genre, with a fictional narrator and protagonists, instead of the straightforward autobiographic approach.

Imaginative writers though they were, Nabokov and Kiš considered it a bitter irony that they were also forced to imagine the final moments in the life of their fathers because they were displaced from the scene of their death. The stakes were high: in addition to conjuring up the fathers, the imagining of force had to avoid the pitfalls of *poshlost'*, Nabokov's term for complacent mediocrity and irresponsible confabulation, which Kiš also shunned. In responding to that displacement from force, Nabokov and Kiš form a lacuna in the narrative which then becomes a form of enacted *mise-en-abyme*. Let us now proceed to the third pair of *myse-en-abyme* images which does not elide the force visited upon the father but actually condenses it into a metaphor of authority.

As it happens, instead of suppressing the trauma, the intentional silence makes the father figure omnipresent, and it is precisely that presence that opens the field for a transcendent vision. In *Speak, Memory* the most important of these visions is the one that closes the first chapter. At this point Nabokov recalls how his father was thrown up into the air in the arms of peasants at Vyra, in a traditional sign of reverence and gratitude:

> Thrice, to the mighty heave-ho of his invisible tossers, he would fly up in this fashion, and the second time he would go higher than the first and then there he would be, on his last and loftiest flight, reclining, as if for good, against the cobalt blue of the summer noon, like one of those paradisiac personages who comfortably soar, with such a wealth of folds in their garments, on the vaulted ceiling of a church while below, one by one, the wax tapers in mortal hands light up to make a swarm of minute flames in the mist of incense, and the priest chants of eternal repose, and funeral lilies conceal the face of whoever lies there, among the swimming lights, in the open coffin.[65]

At the beginning of this hauntingly long sentence, Nabokov has his father alive, admired by the peasants in his homeland; at the end of the sentence, he lies dead in his coffin, in exile. Thus, if read as the linear sequence, the paragraph condenses in two concise images the whole narrative of the father's — and the family's — fall, from the height and splendour of life in their native land downward to the underworld

El Greco, *Burial of the Count of Orgaz* (1586–88), in the Church of Santo Tome, Toledo

of exile, where the long hand of ideological hatred has finally reached him. Just as the distant revolver shot in the Berlin Philharmonic Hall was incorporated into the text in the metaphoric guise of a deadly, smoking iris, so too the father's body, overwhelmed by gravity and death, remains concealed by ominous lilies. On the other hand, if understood not consecutively, but synoptically, the paragraph suggests a very different reading, one that involves religious connotations. Taking into account the church setting, and the fact that the father's figure remains invisible — hidden and displaced — beneath the funeral lilies, we comprehend the essential unity of a baroque painting behind the seemingly linear sequence. Nabokov's sentence proposes the inverse reading similar to that displayed in El Greco's famous painting, *Burial of the Count of Orgaz*, in the Church of Santo Tome, Toledo. In that painting, the body of the deceased count is laid into sepulchre whereas his soul in the form of a child rises to the heavenly ranks. By the same token, the death of Nabokov's father in exile is immediately followed by his ascension into the paradisiac regions of the native land where his soul is rejoicing with his faithful peasants in an eternalized moment of the felicitous past.

At the end of *Garden, Ashes*, after the father has been taken to the extermination camp, the narrator becomes aware of the sway which he had over his story and laments his disappearance with a Dionysian metaphor:

> Njegova moćna pojava, njegov autoritet, pa čak i njegovo ime, njegovi slavni rekviziti, bili su dovoljni da drže potku priče u čvrstim okvirima, tu priču koja vri kao grožđe u bačvama, tu priču u kojoj voće polako gnjije, izgaženo nogama, smrvljeno presom uspomena, opterećeno svojim sokovima i suncem. Sada su pak naprsli obruči, istočilo se vino priče, duša voća, i nema tog boga koji će ga vratiti u mešinu, koji će ga sabiti u priču, saliti u kristalnu čašu.

> [His mighty figure, his authority, even his very name, were sufficient to hold the plot within fixed limits, the story that ferments like grapes in barrels, the story in which fruit slowly rots, trampled underfoot, crushed by the press of memories, weighted down by its own juices and by the sun. And now that the barrel has burst, the wine of the story has spilled out, the soul of the grape, and no divine skill can put it back inside the wineskin, compress it into a short tale, mold it into a glass of crystal.][66]

The image of the barrel conceals a rich irony at both literal and metaphoric level. Eduard Scham, a notorious alcoholic in life, is entrusted with fermenting the wine of the story after death. He, whose every sentence was a pretext for somnambulistic divagation, becomes the backstop of coherence in the post-rational era ushered in by the Holocaust. Thus, in his last disguise the mercurial father, the unrecognized Diogenes, is transformed into the poetic metaphor of the tightly sealed work. Once the story has reached to his transport to Auschwitz, the wine has gone out and the autobiographer's project has outlived itself. And it is precisely this departure from the story that conceals a more sinister version of the barrel. That in *Garden, Ashes* the story is trampled, crushed and weighed down by the father's overbearing and yet indispensable presence is a haunting inversion of the pressure in the sealed cattle cars of the Holocaust. In those cars, he and so many thousands of other Jews were cramped, squeezed and crushed by the sovereign power, before they would be cramped again in the gas chambers of the extermination camps.

Therefore, Aeneas's burden comes to mean different things for Nabokov and Kiš. Nabokov overcomes the force of exile by creating a transcendental image of the father who dies in a foreign land and is resuscitated in homeland as a memory land. Kiš compresses that force in the metapoetic trope of the father as the textual authority whose disappearance ushers the dissipation of the story. To be sure, the metaphors of levitation in Nabokov, and the opposite image of the barrel (press) in Kiš, are aesthetic tropes — instances of *mise-en-abyme* — that encapsulate aspects of the authors' modernist poetics. However, it is equally important to bear in mind that these tropes are enabled by, and permeated with, the political duress that drove them into exile and caused the death of their fathers. Importantly, this force is not elicited merely as a general and vague feeling of duress but as a very specific configuration of violence brought to bear on the fathers. In both authors, the literary *mise-en-abyme* is based on a literal one: in Nabokov, levitation comes after entombment; in Kiš, the broken barrel of the story points to the sealed cattle cars and gas chambers of the Holocaust.

Thus, to conclude, despite obvious differences in the socio-historical backgrounds, the implied exile which Nabokov and Kiš experienced in their formative years confronted them with multiple forms of political duress. Central to this duress was the figure of the father who in changed circumstances is stripped of the symbolic insignia of paternal power: in exile, he cannot remain the magistrate of the family just as the state can no longer be the family's father-land. Rather, he comes across as the family's leader in exile, and thereby conveys political pressure to its members, but is also killed in exile, and therefore becomes its victim. This displacement of force is the key fact in the implied exile of Nabokov and Kiš and it confronts them with the same challenge: reconstructing the father as a figure of force and subject to that force. The forceful images in the memoirs of Nabokov and Kiš may be a function of their modernist poetics, master metaphors of the impregnable biographic legend and of the coherent literary work. They could also be seen as versions of family romance, a retrospective imaginative reconstruction of the father as something more than an anonymous *homo sacer*. However, these metaphors are also much more than that: their estrangement and repression are insidiously political and their *mise-en-abyme* is not only literary but also quite literal. The imagined fathers bear uncanny stigmata of the force placed upon them in the political field. In other words, while shunning the dispersive field of politics in their essays, interviews and other aesthetic pronouncements the two autobiographers eventually capture political force in the metaphoric net — or, more precisely, abyss — of their memoirs of exile.

Notes to Chapter 4

1. See Ernst H. Kantorowicz, *The King's Two Bodies: A Study in Medieval Political Theology* (Princeton, NJ: Princeton University Press, 1987), pp. 207–32.
2. Ibid., pp. 232–72.
3. See *Encyclopédie ou dictionnaire raisonné des sciences, des arts et des métiers*, vol. XXII (Stuttgart‡Bad Cannstatt: Friedrich Frommann Verlag [Günther Holzboog], 1967), p. 178 (my translation).
4. *Aeneid* II v. 707–08, in *Virgil in Two Volumes*, vol. I (Cambridge, MA: Harvard University Press; London: William Heinemann, 1978), pp. 340–43. For a discussion of the ethical implications of

such a grouping, see Winfried Schleiner, 'Aeneas's Flight from Troy', *Comparative Literature*, 27.2 (Spring 1975), 97–112.

5. Luigi Zoja, *The Father: Historical, Psychological and Cultural Perspectives*, ebook (London: Routledge, 2003), p. 142.

6. Giambattista Vico, *The New Science* (Ithaca, NY, and London: Cornell University Press, 1984), p. 180.

7. Georg Wilhelm Friedrich Hegel, *The Philosophy of History*, ebook (Kitchener: Batoche, 2001), p. 56.

8. Giorgio Agamben, *Homo Sacer: Sovereign Power and Bare Life* (Stanford, CA: Stanford University Press, 1998), pp. 89–90.

9. Danilo Kiš, 'Nabokov ili: Nostalgija', in Danilo Kiš, *Život, literatura* (Sarajevo: Svjetlost, 1990), pp. 59–60; translation in Danilo Kiš, 'Nabokov, or Nostalgia', in Kiš, *Homo Poeticus: Essays and Interviews* (Manchester: Carcanet, 1996), pp. 149–50. It is interesting to note that such stereotypes about widespread individual or collective folly among Russian emigration circulated as early as the middle of the nineteenth century, when Alexander Herzen declared that in London 'there are men, actuated by secret, ill-concealed ambition, for whom the revolution meant office, *position sociale*, and who scuttled into exile when they failed to attain a position. Then there were all kinds of fanatics, monomaniacs with every sort of monomania, madmen with every variety of madness. It was due to this nervous, strained, irritable condition that table-turning numbered so many victims among the exiles.' See Alexander Herzen, *My Past and Thoughts* (Berkeley, Los Angeles and London: University of California Press 1982), p. 449.

10. Charles Nicol, 'Politics'. in Vladimir E. Alexandrov (ed.), *The Garland Companion to Vladimir Nabokov* (New York and London: Garland Publishing, 1995), p. 625.

11. Vladimir Nabokov, *Speak, Memory: An Autobiography Revisited* (London: Weidenfeld and Nicolson, 1967), pp. 280–81.

12. See Danilo Kiš, 'Life, Literature', in *Homo Poeticus: Essays and Interviews* (Manchester: Carcanet, 1996), pp. 235–38.

13. Under strong pressure from Nazi Germany, the Hungarian parliament adopted three consecutive and increasingly rigid pieces of legislation (in 1938, 1939 and 1941) which came to be known as 'Jewish laws'. These laws defined who was to be considered a Jew in racial terms and made a set *numerus clausus* for the allowed Jewish share in particular professions. Despite this, argues Carlile A. Macartney in his book *October Fifteenth*, 'the business went on as before, all the real work being done by the Jews', and the level of strictness in applying the laws seems to have depended on the pragmatic attitude of local authorities. See C. A. Macartney, *October Fifteenth: A History of Modern Hungary, 1929–1945*, vol. I (Edinburgh: Edinburgh University Press, 1961), p. 350. Quoted from Ezra Mendelsohn, *The Jews of East Central Europe between the World Wars* (Bloomington: Indiana University Press, 1987), p. 122.

14. See *Dokumenty vneshneĭ politiki SSSR*, vol. IV (Moskva: Gosudarstvennoe izdatel'stvo politicheskoĭ literatury, 1960), pp. 475–76.

15. See Andrew Field, *VN. The Life and Art of Vladimir Nabokov* (London: Queen Anne Press, 1987), pp. 73–76.

16. He did, however, compose several poems on his father's murder ('Easter' and 'In Memory of V. D. Nabokov'), and it is now widely accepted that the mistaken murder of John Shade in *Pale Fire* is a fictional replica of the gruesome event in the Berlin Philharmonic Hall. See Field, pp. 77, 81.

17. For a comprehensive account of the extermination process, see Randolph Braham, *The Politics of Genocide* (New York: Columbia University Press, 1981). Braham gathers available information on the ghetto at Zalaegerszeg, the concentration centre where Kiš's father was summoned before his transportation to the camp, and traces the itinerary of the deportation trains from Hungary to Auschwitz. See Braham, pp. 670–71, 674–76.

18. Danilo Kiš, *Hourglass* (London: Faber and Faber, 1990), pp. 268, 271.

19. Unlike Kiš's novel, Nabokov's memoir has a complex genesis and publication history. Although from the beginning of his career in exile Nabokov used to lend some of his Russian experiences to his fictional heroes, it appears that by the late 1930s he intuited that the biographical circumstances of his life had obtained an inherent *Gestalt* that warranted an autobiographic

project. It is acknowledged today that the initial step towards what was to become his memoir was a short story 'Mademoiselle O', written in French and published in the periodical *Mesures*, which evolves around the narrator's memory of a person who is recognizable as his Swiss governess. Throughout the 1940s this memoirist nucleus was continually complemented by further narrative *tableaux*, composed in English and published in various periodicals, to be finally extended into a full-scale autobiographic narrative which appeared in print in 1951 under the title *Conclusive Evidence* (*Speak, Memory* in the United Kingdom). With the bulk of the autobiographical scenes already elaborated, Nabokov proceeded with the next stage which comprised the preparation of the Russian edition of the text that was published in 1954 under the title *Другие берега* [*Other Shores*]. The final point in the evolution of the autobiography was *Speak, Memory: An Autobiography Revisited* — actually the English rendition of the previous Russian text — and it is this text that gained the widest distribution since 1966, when it was published. See Vladimir Nabokov, 'Mademoiselle O.', *Mesures* 2.2 (April 1936), 145–72, *Conclusive Evidence* (New York: Harper & Brothers Publishers, 1951), *Drugie berega* (Ann Arbor, MI: Ardis, 1954).

20. On the versatile concept of 'biographic legend', see Boris Tomashevsky, 'Literature and Biography', in Ladislav Matejka and Krystyna Pomorska (eds.), *Readings in Russian Poetics: Formalist and Structuralist Views* (Ann Arbor, MI: University of Michigan Press 1978), pp. 47–55.

21. See Ferdinand De Saussure, *Course in General Linguistics* (London: Peter Owen, 1960) and Roman Jakobson, 'Two Aspects of Language and Two Types of Aphasic Disturbances', in Jakobson, *Language in Literature* (Cambridge, MA, and London: The Belknap Press of Harvard University Press, 1987), pp. 95–114.

22. It is important to note that Jakobson explored this field well before his essay on aphasia, in the context of Russian Formalist school. For instance, his fellow Formalist, Yuri Tynjanov, differentiates between 'auto-function' which corresponds to selection and 'syn-function' which refers to combination and traces their synchronic and diachronic intertwinements across different genres in literary history. See Yuri Tynjanov, 'On Literary Evolution', in Ladislav Matejka and Krystyna Pomorska (eds.), *Readings in Russian Poetics: Formalist and Structuralist Views*, p. 68.

23. Maria Louise Ascher, 'The Exile as Autobiographer: Nabokov's Homecoming', in Domnica Radulescu (ed.), *Realms of Exile: Nomadism, Diasporas and Eastern European Voices* (Lanham, MD: Lexington Books, 2002), pp. 67–68.

24. Ibid., p. 69.

25. Ibid., pp. 72–73.

26. Nabokov, *Speak, Memory*, p. 242.

27. Ascher, 'The Exile as Autobiographer: Nabokov's Homecoming', p. 70.

28. Vladimir Nabokov, *Strong Opinions* (London: Weidenfeld and Nicolson, 1974), pp. 23–24.

29. Lily Halpert Zamir, *Danilo Kiš: jedna bolna, mračna odiseja* (Beograd: Ateneum, 2000), p. 23.

30. Sigmund Freud, 'Family Romances', in *The Standard Edition of the Complete Psychological Works of Sigmund Freud*, vol. IX (London: The Hogarth Press and the Institute of Psychoanalysis, 1959), p. 239. German original in Sigmund Freud, 'Der Familienroman der Neurotiker', in Freud, *Gesammelte Werke*, vol. VII (Frankfurt am Main: Fischer Taschenbuch Verlag 1999), p. 229.

31. Ibid., p. 239 (p. 229).

32. Ibid. pp. 239–40 (pp. 229–30).

33. See Sigmund Freud, *The Interpretation of Dreams*, in *The Standard Edition of the Complete Psychological Works of Sigmund Freud*, vol. IV (London: The Hogarth Press and the Institute of Psychoanalysis, 1958), pp. 279–309. The original German terms are quoted from Sigmund Freud, *Die Traumdeutung; Über den Traum* in Freud, *Gesammelte Werke*, vol. II–III (Frankfurt am Main: Fischer Taschenbuch Verlag, 1999), pp. 283–315.

34. Daniel Ross, 'The Text You Read (and Write) May Be Your Own: The Family Romance in Danilo Kiš' *Garden, Ashes*', *The Review of Contemporary Fiction*, 14.1 (1994), pp. 136–43.

35. Ivana Vuletić, *The Prose Fiction of Danilo Kiš, Serbian Jewish Writer: Childhood and Holocaust* (Lewiston, NY: The Edwin Mellen Press, 2003), pp. 99–100.

36. Freud, 'Family Romances', p. 241; 'Der Familienroman der Neurotiker', p. 231.

37. Sigmund Freud, 'The "Uncanny"', in *The Standard Edition of the Complete Psychological Works of*

Sigmund Freud vol. XVII (London: The Hogarth Press and the Institute of Psychoanalysis, 1957), p. 232. German original in Sigmund Freud, 'Das Unheimliche', in Freud, *Gesammelte Werke*, vol. XII (Munich: Taschenbuch Verlag 1999), p. 244.

38. Ernest Jones, *The Life and Work of Sigmund Freud* (Harmondsworth: Penguin, 1964), p. 317. For a comprehensive analysis of the case of the Wolf-Man, see Alexander Etkind, *Eros of the Impossible: The History of Psychoanalysis in Russia* (Boulder, CO: Westview, 1997), pp. 80–107.

39. Jones, *The Life and Work of Sigmund Freud*, p. 171.

40. Vuletić, *The Prose Fiction of Danilo Kiš, Serbian Jewish Writer*, p. 103.

41. To be sure, it is always possible to argue for an extension of the family romance from human agents onto political entities. León Grinberg and Rebeca Grinberg argued that a displaced person is likely to project the parental functions onto his homeland and his country of exile: 'At times, migration sets up a triangular Oedipal situation between the two countries, as if each country symbolically represented one of the parents, in relation to whom ambivalence and conflicting loyalties reappear. The emigrant experiences this as if his parents were divorced, and he engages in fantasies of forming an alliance with one against the other.' Yet, this avenue might be far-fetched and ultimately simplistic in such self-conscious writers as Kiš and Nabokov which probably explains why Ross and Vuletić did not take it into consideration. See León Grinberg and Rebeca Grinberg, *Psychoanalytic Perspectives on Migration and Exile* (New Haven, CT, and London: Yale University Press 1989), pp. 87–88.

42. Kiš, *Garden, Ashes*, p. 48; *Porodični cirkus*, p. 135. The reference to the 'deposed Russian prince' is oddly missing in the translation.

43. Jean-Paul Sartre, *Les Mots* (Paris: Gallimard, 1964), p. 19. English translation in Jean-Paul Sartre, *Words* (Harmondsworth: Penguin Books, 1971), pp. 14–15.

44. Robert Harvey, *Search for a Father: Sartre, Paternity, and the Question of Ethics* (Ann Arbor: University of Michigan Press, 1991), p. 30.

45. Throughout his career, Freud used three major tropological matrices. The best known is the topographical one, in which psychic life is split into two (or three) zones, Conscious and Unconscious (and Pre-Conscious); then, there is the functional matrix, in which certain instincts cathect (libidinize) certain ideas and these ideas are then assigned different roles in the conscious sphere; finally, there is the economic matrix in which libidinal energy undergoes transformation (for instance, from admiration to fear) but never gets dissipated. Although these matrices are different and largely autonomous, in the second decade of the twentieth century Freud uses them together, adjusting the terms slightly from one paper to another. Nevertheless, the fundamental layer remained a topographical one: personalizing and mapping various instinctual urges, which grow in isolation or form alliances, and thinking of the conscious self's borders as a defence system swayed Freud's model towards political tropology. It is precisely that topographical layer — the tense relations between the conscious and the unconscious — that is conceived in terms of a sequence of exile.

46. Sigmund Freud, 'Die Verdrängung', in Freud, *Gesammelte Werke* vol. X (Frankfurt am Main: Fischer Taschenbuch Verlag, 1999), p. 250. Translation in Sigmund Freud, 'Repression', in *The Standard Edition of the Complete Psychological Works of Sigmund Freud*, vol. XIV (London: The Hogarth Press and the Institute for Psychoanalysis, 1957), p. 147.

47. Sigmund Freud, *Totem und Tabu*, in Freud, *Gesammelte Werke*, vol. IX (Frankfurt am Main: Fischer Taschenbuch Verlag 1999), p. 171. Translation in Sigmund Freud, *Totem and Taboo*, in *The Standard Edition of the Complete Psychological Works of Sigmund Freud*, vol. XIII (London: The Hogarth Press and the Institute for Psychoanalysis, 1957), p. 141.

48. Svetlana Boym, 'Estrangement as Lifestyle: Shklovsky and Brodsky', in Susan Rubin Suleiman (ed.), *Exile and Creativity: Signposts, Travelers, Outsiders, Backward Glances* (Durham, NC, and London: Duke University Press, 1998), p. 245.

49. Viktor Shklovsky, 'Art as Technique', in Lee T. Lemon and Marion J. Reis (eds), *Russian Formalist Criticism: Four Essays* (Lincoln, NE and London: University of Nebraska Press, 1965), p. 17.

50. Greta Slobin, 'Why the First-Wave Russian Literary Diaspora Embraced Shklovskian Estrangement', *Poetics Today*, 26.4 (Winter 2005), 697–718 (p. 708).

51. Boym, 'Estrangement as Lifestyle: Shklovsky and Brodsky', p. 254.

52. Kiš, *Garden, Ashes*, p. 120; *Porodični cirkus*, pp. 204–05.

53. Vladimir Nabokov, *Conclusive Evidence* (New York: Harper & Brothers Publishers, 1951), p. 61.

54. Vladimir Nabokov, *Drugie berega*, p. 88.

55. Nabokov, *Speak, Memory*, pp. 99–100. For a lucid and imaginative interpretation of this shift in the context of Nabokov's fictional works, which feature instances of a real return to Soviet Union (esp. the early novella *Mashenka*, and the novels *Glory* and *Look at the Harlequins*), see Svetlana Boym, *The Future of Nostalgia*, pp. 259–83.

56. See Lucien Dällenbach, *Le récit spéculaire* (Paris: Seuil, 1977), p. 4.

57. Nabokov, *Speak, Memory*, p. 275.

58. Kiš, *Garden, Ashes*, p. 4; *Porodični cirkus*, pp. 91–92.

59. Philippe Lejeune, *Le pacte autobiographique* (Paris: Editions du Seuil, 1975).

60. Nabokov, *Speak, Memory*, p. 49.

61. On three occasions in Chapter 9, Nabokov briefly informs the reader that his father was assassinated but does not go into details. See Ibid., pp. 173, 177, 193.

62. Ibid., p. 49.

63. Jean Améry, 'On the Necessity and Impossibility of Being a Jew', in Michael L. Morgan (ed.), *A Holocaust Reader: Responses to the Nazi Extermination* (Oxford and New York: Oxford University Press, 2001), p. 35.

64. Kiš, *Garden, Ashes*, pp. 116, 118; *Porodični cirkus*, pp. 201, 202.

65. Nabokov, *Speak, Memory*, pp. 31–32.

66. Kiš, *Garden, Ashes*, p. 147; *Porodični cirkus*, p. 231.

CHAPTER 5

Polyglot Monsters:
Metalingual Tropes of Force
in the Poetry of Exile

There is in modern poetry a distinct class of interlingual poems that are qualified by the textual presence of lexical units from more than one language. Most of these poems have been associated with some form of exilic displacement of their authors and thematically they dwell upon that experience. Though often considered as an exceptional case of poetic discourse, interlingual poems of exile raise important challenges to conventional views on the relationship between language and poetry. Firstly, they question the underlying assumption about poetic language as an essentially monolingual idiom independent of social and historical developments. Second, they present a problem for existing literary theoretical models which usually deal with such highly atypical texts by bracketing of at least one of the constituent features: exile or poetry. Would it be possible to construct a form of poetic discourse that accommodates diverse linguistic codes in a way that would fully reflect the duress of the exilic context while still presenting a verbally coherent and aesthetically relevant response to that context? In order to address this question, in the first part of the chapter I revisit some of the main theories of poetic language to assess their explanatory value in interlingual poetic sequences. Specifically, I claim that Roman Jakobson's theory of equational relations, if applied with some readjustments, may show how any interlingual sequence projects a derivative metalanguage with different codes united in an overarching metaphoric nexus. The second part asks whether this enforced code switching leads to images that are specific to this metalingual situation. While the core text in my analysis is Miloš Crnjanski's poem 'Lament nad Beogradom' [Lament over Belgrade], I also examine other instances of exilic interlinguality, such as Ovid, Tsvetaeva, Brodsky and Milosz. I argue that the apparent rhythmic and syntactic disparity of 'Lament over Belgrade' and other code switching poems is countervailed by a set of metaphors of outsideness which, on the one hand, project an imagined metalanguage and, on the other hand, reflect the human trauma of enforced displacement.

Interlinguality and the Language(s) of Poetry: Jakobson's Theory Revisited

The problem of interlinguality reaches to the very core of modernist poetics. In an early review essay on T. S. Eliot, Conrad Aiken excludes from his otherwise favourable appraisal of *The Waste Land* all verses written in languages other than English: 'We could dispense with the French, Italian, Latin, and Hindu phrases — they are irritating. But when our reservations have all been made, we accept *The Waste Land* as one of the most moving and original poems of our time.'[1] In Aiken's view, the expatriate poet's shifts from one language to another do not contribute in any sense to the overarching impression of the fragmentariness of modern life and of classical tradition. These shifts are, therefore, hardly more than irrelevant and idiosyncratic clutter in Eliot's poetic texture. However, depending on the interpretative standpoint, Eliot's linguistic medley may have different implications. For the striking thing about Aiken's statement is that in dismissing interlinguality he denounces the very same 'kaleidoscopic confusion' which he praises on the level of the poem as a whole.[2]

That Aiken found polyglot verses in Eliot's poem so irksome is all the more surprising in that the overriding poetical and intellectual programmes of the twentieth century were decisively in favour of linguistic diversity. In her essay 'A New Type of Intellectual: The Dissident', Julia Kristeva argues for the emancipating value of exile and specifies language as one of the key symbolic fields that have to be estranged: 'How can one avoid sinking into the mire of common sense, if not by becoming a stranger to one's own country, language, sex and identity? Writing is impossible without some kind of exile.'[3] There is in this exuberant quotation an unexpected echo of Joyce's *Portrait of the Artist as a Young Man*, in which Stephen Daedalus claims that he will try to 'fly by' the nets of nationality, language, and religion and express himself by means of silence, exile, and cunning.[4] Like Joyce, Kristeva conceives of exile in the archetypal modernist way — as a prerequisite for whatever there is of value in human verbal creativity.[5] There is, meanwhile, another trope of unhomeliness in modernist perceptions of language, one according to which the very process of signification represents a trespass in a foreign land. The world we once duly tried to objectify through the use of symbolic substitutes has changed aspect — it cannot house us anymore. Rilke acknowledged in 'Duineser Elegien' [The Duino Elegies] that 'wir nicht sehr verläßlich zu Haus sind | in der gedeuteten Welt' [we don't feel very securely at home | in this interpreted world].[6] Therefore, the metaphoric idea of some form of spatial outsideness remains central to understanding the relationship between language and poetry. If this is so, then the interlingual switches in poetry, such as those epitomized by Eliot's *The Waste Land*, would not represent an aberrance from the norm but a most apposite field for the observation of the inner dynamism of language in poetry. By a similar token, the poetry of historical exile, rather than the poetry of imaginary displacement, would represent the most likely context in which such interlingual switches are generated.

Although a forbidding prospect in the interpretation of individual poems, multilinguality has been endorsed as a metaphor by literary theory. If we dismiss the view expressed by a few critics that foreign words are mere rhetorical ornament or an irritating supplement to this or that poem, there seem to have been two types of arguments with which literary theorists addressed the problem. It is unsurprising that both rely upon — or more precisely, intentionally embed — outsideness as a heuristic trope.

The first argument dwells on the alienating and at the same time cohesive role of foreign words in poetic discourse. The main catalyst for such an approach was the early Formalist concept of *остранение*. Etymologically derived from both the adjective *странное* [unfamiliar] and the substantive *страна* [country], it suggests that poetic language incurs some form of existential displacement that is reflected in both the perception of the object represented and the means of its representation.[7] In his seminal paper 'Art as Technique' Viktor Shklovsky listed the poetic interlinguality of Classical and medieval literary texts side by side with the stylistic intricacies of more recent poems by Pushkin and Khlebnikov, in order to show that a wilfully tortuous, difficult poetic speech inevitably accompanies deautomatized artistic perception: 'According to Aristotle, poetic language must appear strange and wonderful; and, in fact, it is often actually foreign: the Sumerian used by the Assyrians, the Latin of Europe during the Middle Ages, the Arabisms of the Persians, the Old Bulgarian of Russian Literature.'[8] Although Shklovsky's argument regarding multilingualism did not exercise a direct influence on literary criticism in the West, there is an important sequel to his view in George Steiner's discussion of modern poetry in his book *After Babel*. Steiner argues that interlingual transfers have partly taken over the role once fulfilled by metre and rhyme. Thus, what distinguishes such texts as T. S. Eliot's *The Waste Land* from earlier forms of poetry is the emphasis on the processes of translation as a new cohesive force in poetic diction.[9] As exemplified (albeit somewhat differently) by Shklovsky and Steiner, this first theoretical approach to interlinguality thus ambiguously involves both fissure and bond. On the one hand, the poetic word is irreversibly divorced from the word in everyday use; on the other hand, owing to analogies in semantic systems, the word belonging to one language is conceived of as related to components, as well as to the whole, of another language. The very same interlinguality that secures a distinctively rough, defamiliarized perception of the text also generates a coherent poetic diction.

Those who have recourse to the second type of argument stress the disaggregating potential of the foreign word, its precious role in transcending any immanent and coherent 'meaning' in a text. This view is epitomized by Mikhail Bakhtin and his circle, for whom the concept of *вненаходимость* defines the outsideness that is irreducible to any singular position in space, time and culture.[10] In his essay 'From the Prehistory of Novelistic Discourse' Bakhtin distinguishes between *heteroglossia*, the general disposition of language to break along ideological lines into mutually opposed formations, and *polyglossia*, the coexistence and interanimation of different languages in the specific historical conditions of the contact and clash of cultures. Polyglossia, as practised in Hellenism, in Ancient Rome, and in the Orient, is understood to be historically prior and preparatory to the heteroglot demise of a unitary language that paved the way for the modern novel: 'But this speech diversity achieves its full creative consciousness only under conditions of an active polyglossia. Two myths perish simultaneously: the myth of a language that presumes to be the only language, and the myth of a language that presumes to be completely unified'.[11] In such an agonistic optic, not all genres fare equally and poetry, with its peculiar focus on private and uniform verbal idioms, becomes a major force of monoglossia. Even if some poems allow a limited degree of ideological and interlingual otherness, Bakhtin tells us in 'Discourse in the Novel', it is not because they bring the inner possibilities of poetic language to fruition. In fact, it is precisely the opposite: they strike us as heteroglot because their authors wisely give up pursuit of the most extreme stylistic aspirations of poetic language.[12] Ironically, these authors are redeemable because they are not poets enough. The polyglossia that for both Shklovsky and Steiner functions as a remarkable and distinctive feature of poetic language becomes for Bakhtin the vehicle for dismantling that very category.

To be sure, both approaches remain emphatically affirmative to interlingual concatenations. However, it is equally obvious that both are premised on certain unbending restrictions when evaluating various contexts in which interlinguality may arise. On the one hand, in his focus on the differential fabric of poetry, Shklovsky completely excludes the incidental everyday template he calls *быт*. As a result, if we follow his line of reasoning, we will fail to observe that it is precisely this crude social reality — individual exile and collective migrations — that gives rise, firstly, to language interaction and, consequently, to at least some of the periodic shifts in verbal idiom. On the other hand, when stressing the sociohistorical mediation in heteroglossia Bakhtin excludes poetry, as an artificially enclosed verbal microcosm, from that realm. This exclusion is surprising in that it does not follow from the premises of Bakhtin's theory as strictly as Shklovsky's elimination of *быт* follows from the early Formalist views on art as a peculiar mode of cognition and expression. It is likely that Bakhtin chose to consider poetry in a rather narrow sense — that is, as a utopian project of poetic language that is torn between neoclassicist and neoromantic stylistic modes. The last, though not the least, difficulty pertains to both arguments equally. Namely, Shklovsky's and Bakhtin's self-confident inclusiveness has led to a certain abstractness in their conclusions. The problem is not just that Shklovsky and Bakhtin have not raised the question of how the difficulties in the poets' acquisition of a second language are reflected in their poetic texts. At a more fundamental level, the two theorists failed to take into account the fact that when exposed to languages other than their own, poets develop verbal strategies unique to their own experience rather than follow a predictable pattern of creativity.

Other approaches that for various reasons do not consider poetic interlinguality may nevertheless offer valuable insights into this literary phenomenon. This is certainly the case with the crosscutting axes of selection and combination of the Structuralist linguistic model, as put forward by De Saussure and applied by Jakobson.[13] For the sake of clarity, let us consider only Jakobson's set of concepts. At the surface level, his model seems to have little to do with social contexts or, for that matter, exile. However, in his book *О чешском стихе* [*On Czech Verse*, 1923] he employs, somewhat surprisingly, a human analogy as an explanatory metaphor that captures the way in which poetic language is independent of external context: verse is an 'organised violence of poetic form over language'.[14] In the later articulations of his position, Jakobson never excludes contexts and functions, including the referential one; he simply hierarchizes them according to the dominant principle of organization.[15] How, then, do Jakobson's categories accommodate interlingual poetry in its double capacity as both a consequence of spatial displacement and a form of hermeneutic displacement?

First, there is in any interlingual poetic practice a mental component that is observable through the paradigmatic (selection) axis as defined by Jakobson. Through a conscious mediation between, and the unconscious interference of, two or more codes, the poet's selection of words negotiates the relations of equivalence and opposition between the elements of these codes. In Keats's ballad 'La Belle Dame Sans Merci', for instance, the eerie lady from faraway is euphemistically referred to by her French appellation, but her own words, though experienced as foreign, are reported as if they were pronounced in a genuine English utterance: 'And sure in language strange she said — | "I love thee true." '[16] Instead of the possible line in French 'Je t'aime vraiment', the code is displaced and the message is communicated in English. It is of course true that the displacement in Keats's ballad is an oneiric one, but it is representative of the hermeneutic processes of substitution and transference by which authors constitute their discourse. In the interlingual lexical store, words and their semantic and auditive templates commute, in two senses of the word: they travel from one unstable context to another and they are mutually interchangeable. In a broad sense, then, interlingual selection in the poetry of exile involves translation as a metaphoric textual journey and, vice versa, geographical migration as template for, and a form of, cross-cultural translation.[17]

However, in interlingual poetry, not everything is translation — the quest for commutable words and values. There are also combinatory developments laid down along what Jakobson calls the syntagmatic axis. While scrutinizing languages for shared or opposed meanings, the poet also undertakes a radical differentiation among them: through intentional code-switching, lexical and syntactic units of different languages are combined and adhere to one another within the concrete chain of the poetic discourse. Consider, for example, the coda of T. S. Eliot's *The Waste Land* with its embedded quotations from texts written in multiple codes (Dante's *Purgatorio*, the anonymous *Pervigilium Veneris*, and de Nerval's *El Desdichado*): 'London Bridge is falling down falling down falling down | *Poi s'ascose nel foco che gli affina* | *Quando fiam uti chelidon*—O swallow swallow | *Le Prince d'Aquitaine à la tour abolie*.'[18] The division of this string of verses into sequences written in Italian, Latin, French, and English superimposes a series of boundaries on the verse delimitation, leading to a marked alternation of rhythm and melody as well as unexpected caesural effects. Thus, while paradigmatic self-translation highlights the continual aspects of the journey metaphor, syntagmatic code switching frames the journey as discontinuous boundary crossing.[19]

Finally, there is in interlingual poetry an analogy to Jakobson's famous assertion that the poetic function of language '*projects the principle of equivalence from the axis of selection into the axis of combination*'.[20] There is in each poem that features more than one linguistic code an overarching set of interactions that equalizes and antagonizes the different parts of the text. In her hauntingly probing poem 'Новогоднее' [New Year's Greetings], for example, Marina Tsvetaeva switches from Russian to German to invoke the memory of the recently deceased Rilke: 'Уж не спрашиваешь, как по-русски | Nest? Единственная, и все гнезда | покрывающая рифма: звезды' [Why do you no longer ask what's the Russian for | "Nest"? There's one rhyme for all havens: | Heaven].[21] Here, the transfer is observable on both metrical and semantic levels: as a rhyme, the star rounds off the etymological identification of the German 'Nest' and the Russian 'гнездо'; as a symbol, the stars are said to cover with their poetic light all lexical nests in every language.

To sum up my argument to this point: although Shklovsky's model opens up the possibility of analysing the properly poetic dimension of interlinguality, it also rules out consideration of the context-specific sociohistorical situations (including exile) that generate interlinguality; Bakhtin's philosophy of language enables us to analyse interlinguality in terms of its being conditioned by, and conditioning in its turn, socio-historical contexts (including exile), but excludes poetry, which Bakhtin views only as an expression of monolingual consciousness; and Jakobson's model enables some degree of the analytic discrimination neglected by Shklovsky and vaguely metaphorized by Bakhtin. If my application of Jakobson's argument seems to push it beyond what it can strictly yield — that is, beyond a structural inquiry into the functions of language — it is important to grasp his concepts of selection and combination in their broad heuristic potential — as mental operations that organize experience — in the same way Jakobson himself does in 'Two Aspects of Language and Two Types of Aphasic Disturbances'. In this essay, as we have already seen, Jakobson attaches a foundational value to the principles of selection and combination, seeing them simultaneously at the core of two aphasic disorders, two key rhetorical figures, and two opposite stylistic tendencies in literary history. In a similar vein, selection and combination are of importance for understanding linguistic identities in exile: translation engages a mnemonic chain to mediate what is present and what is absent and code-switching creates a chain of speech out of differential units of meaning.[22]

However, Jakobson's model presents its own difficulties for the analysis of interlingual poems. On the one hand, Jakobson strictly limits the realm of selection and combination to the signs of the same code (a given language). On the other hand, he equally explicitly places the relations of similarity and contiguity at the very core of any poetic text. Does this suggest that under the principles of Jakobson's theory interlingual poems are to be considered as anomalous and even as non-poetry? If an interlingual poetic text is understood as a case of *parole*, then it is obvious that the model is premised on the assumption of a pervasive *langue*, the rules of which would provide the systemic context for the relations of similarity and contiguity. In the case of interlingual poems such a metalinguistic system cannot be associated with any of the living spoken languages. If there were such a metalinguistic system, it would be akin to Tsvetaeva's 'angelic' language, which transcends and reconciles her Russian and Rilke's German;[23] Remizov's splendid illuminations that arise above his ever-diminishing paragraphs in Russian and French;[24] or perhaps Benjamin's 'pure' language, 'a tensionless and even silent depository of the ultimate secrets for which all thought strives'.[25] However, it is precisely because of its being beyond the grasp of conceptual cognition that such a possibility was never envisaged by Jakobson. In 'On Linguistic Aspects of Translation' he argues that each language, as a system *sui generis*, implies a metalingual function that surveys and redefines that language *from within* and that excludes a metalanguage that would complement it *from outside*.[26] Of course, one may respond by claiming that it was not important for Jakobson to incorporate interlinguality since that was not, after all, his goal. Nevertheless, once we have granted interlingual poems poetic quality under Jakobsonian terms, we commit ourselves to the corollary claim that such poems involve certain constituents that create metalingual paradigmatic symmetries and anti-symmetries at least as a *tentative*, if not as an underlying function.

Another difficulty in applying Jakobson's model to interlingual poems consists in the fact that the working field of the principle of equivalence is circumscribed mainly by rhythmical factors (intonation, syllabic form, rhyme) and grammatical categories (phonology, morphology, syntax). However, such repetitions have very different implications in monolingual and interlingual poems. Not only have many interlingual poems proven to be modernist verbal constructs committed to free verse but also, on a more fundamental level, the principle of equivalence cannot connect the poetic units from different languages either by similarity or by contrast because each of these languages commands its own range of prosodic and syntactic templates. In macaronic passages of pre-modernist poetry, the disjunctive effect of foreign words and phrases may have been concealed by metrical patterns and rhymes. In modernist poetry, however, their differential quality looms large. Consider the following lines of Czeslaw Milosz's *Gdzie wschodzi słońce i kiedy zapada* [*Where the Sun Rises and where It Sets*]:

> Alpejska gwiazda spadająca, Alpine Shootingstar
> (*Dodecatheon Alpinum*)[27]

Although there are some *intralingual* phonological and rhythmical repetitions, there is no corresponding *interlingual* link between Polish, English and Latin designations of the flower. Moreover, even when two languages share the same system of versification, the actual metres may be entirely different in their effect. Likewise, in most cases the systems of grammatical categories do not fully overlap for any two languages: some languages have definite and indefinite articles, others have perfective and imperfective verbal forms; some have declination, and some do not; some have two grammatical genders and some have three or more, etc. Therefore, if Jakobson's theory is to have any validity for the analysis of interlingual poems, the principle of equivalence has to have its field of projection expanded to include non-rhythmical and non-syntactic — that is, *semantic* — units.

These tentative semantic categories may only be found in the realm of rhetorical figures. Poetic metaphors are a supreme example of Jakobson's projection principle working in reverse. We do not derive metaphors from a pre-existing system of resemblances; we begin with a primary equivalence established on the syntagmatic level: the sequence falls into two parts, a focal word (metaphor) and a frame in which it must be embedded. We then proceed by projecting the equivalence onto the paradigmatic axis in order to know more about the underlying poetic vision in which the two concepts can be pulled together. For instance, when we read the following distich from Pasternak's poem 'Гроза, моментальная навек' [Storm, Instantaneous Forever]:

Сто слепящих фотографий
Ночью снял на память гром

[The storm at night for souvenir
Took snap after dazzling snap.][28]

we first grasp the idea of lightning strikes that take snapshots of the surrounding landscape as an instance of metaphoric speech and *then* ask what kind of deeper metaphysical affinity grounds the equivalence of thunder and photography.

A similar transfer occurs in interlingual poems, but with the adjacent interlingual sequences, rather than image-concepts, representing the focus and the frame. We begin with the assumption that the word or syntactic unit in another language has both a denotative meaning and an additive, metaphoric value. It is only at the following stage that we draw paradigmatic implications and establish the metalingual vision that grounds such a metaphor. Tsvetaeva's image in 'New Year's Greetings' does not simply suggest that the lexical units of 'Nest' and 'гнездо' are semantically equivalent; their equivalence also suggests something more comprehensive, an underlying metaphoric link between the two language systems that is best seen from the exotopic perspective of nest–star. While on the one hand projecting a metalingual paradigm that links the constituent codes of the interlingual poem, the metaphor of the nest also bears an imprint of the coercions that give rise to interlinguality, on the other. For besides being an elevated, the nest is also a protective place, a haven.

It is obvious that expanding Jakobson's model along these lines takes us a step beyond his poetry of grammar. However, in his theory of parallelisms — at least in its stated form — there is nothing to exclude the possibility that the principle of equivalence can work in the reverse direction, from the syntagmatic into the paradigmatic. Quite to the contrary, he envisages that possibility when he compares equivalences in poetry with those in utterances such as '*Mare is the female of horse*': 'Poetry and metalanguage, however, are in diametrical opposition to each other: in metalanguage the sequence is used to build an equation, whereas in poetry the equation is used to build a sequence'.[29] Since the equivalences can work the other way round, my only point of disagreement with Jakobson is his double claim: a) that the metalingual function necessarily operates within the coordinate system of one language (even in translation); and b) that metalingual and the poetic function cannot overlap. The key difference that distinguishes interlingual and monolingual poetry is that in the former the metalanguage is constructed not as a firm coordinate system rooted in a single code, but as an interstitial metaphoric space evolving around textual boundaries between codes. In other words, in interlingual poetry the positional equivalences and oppositions established by the syntagmatic sequence build a metaphoric projection of metalanguage. Insights obtained by this paradigmatic projection are no less poetic than those obtained by applying the standard Jakobsonian model to monolingual poetry.

The Polyglot Monsters: Code Switching in Crnjanski's 'Lament over Belgrade'

To claim that interlingual poetry involves metaphors which create (rather than reflect) paradigmatic relations between languages may seem a natural thing to say. To argue that these tropes present imagery of outsideness is a step forward but one that opens a new question. In interlingual poems arising from exile, are these tropes in any respect connected to the duress of their context?

The core text I will use to address this question will be 'Lament nad Beogradom' [Lament over Belgrade, 1956], an interlingual poem by Serbian poet Miloš Crnjanski (1893–1977). The case is particularly apposite in the context of this study because Crnjanski was an implied exile: his residence outside Yugoslavia was never ordained but inferred retroactively. A passionate traveller in his youth, Crnjanski later became a political émigré at a time when his reputation, as well as his literary idiom, had already been established. Soon after the German occupation of Yugoslavia in April 1941, Crnjanski moved from Rome, where he previously had been employed as a press attaché in the Yugoslav Consulate, to London, where he spent the next twenty-four years. While residing in London, he initially worked for the Yugoslav Government in Exile, but after the Communist ascension to power in Yugoslavia in 1945 the royalist administration was dissolved and Crnjanski was left with only two options: to accept the humble and marginal status of a displaced person in London or to return to Belgrade and face possible recriminatory measures from the newly installed regime. The stakes were too high to risk returning, and Crnjanski stayed in London for the next nineteen years. Crnjanski's bilingual performance was determined by his peculiarly strenuous acculturation in England. On the one hand, for fear of becoming a victim of political conspiracy, Crnjanski tended to avoid contact with the Yugoslav émigré community and thereby foreclosed the possibility of using his native language in everyday speech situations. On the other hand, he developed a peculiar aversion towards the values and norms which he considered 'English', and this repulsion hampered his half-hearted attempts to improve his knowledge of the English language. It should come as no surprise, then, that he composed 'Lament over Belgrade' in a state of utter dejection.

Although a striking example of exilic interlinguality, 'Lament over Belgrade' has received little attention from critics in Europe and North America, and it deserves to be quoted in entirety before any analysis. I quote the original version in Serbian followed by my own tentative translation in which I attempt to balance the rhythmical and phonic richness of the poem against the demands of semantic correspondence:[30]

Lament nad Beogradom

JAN MAJEN i moj Srem,
Paris, moji mrtvi drugovi, trešnje u Kini,
priviđaju mi se još, dok ovde ćutim, bdim, i mrem,
i ležim, hladan, kao na pepelu klada.
Samo, to više i nismo mi, život, a ni zvezde
nego neka čudovišta, polipi, delfini,
što se tumbaju preko nas i plove, i jezde,
i urliču: 'Prah, pepeo, smrt je to.'
A viču i rusko 'ničevo'—
i špansko 'nada'.

Ti, međutim, rasteš, uz zornjaču jasnu,
sa Avalom plavom, u daljini, kao breg.
Ti treperiš, i kad ovde zvezde gasnu,
i topiš, ko Sunce, i led suza, i lanjski sneg.
U Tebi nema besmisla, ni smrti.
Ti sjajiš kao iskopan stari mač.
U Tebi sve vaskrsne, i zaigra, pa se vrti,
i ponavlja, kao dan i detinji plač.
A kad mi se glas, i oči, i dah, upokoje,
Ti ćeš me, znam, uzeti na krilo svoje.

ESPANJA i naš Hvar,
Dobrović mrtvi, šejk što se u Sahari beli,
priviđaju mi se još, kao utvare, vatre, var.
Moj Sibe poludeli, zinuo kao peš.
Samo to više nismo mi, u mladosti i moći,
već neki papagaji, čimpanzi, neveseli,
što mi se smeju i vrište u mojoj samoći.
Jedan se 'Leiche! Leiche! Leiche!' dere.
Drugi mi šapće: 'Cadavere!'
Treći: 'Leš, leš, leš'.

Ti, međutim, širiš, kao labud krila,
zaborav, na Dunav i Savu, dok spavaju.
Ti budiš veselost, što je nekad bila,
kikot, tu, i u mom kriku, vrisku, i vapaju.
U Tebi nema crva, ni sa groba.
Ti blistaš, kao kroz suze ljudski smeh.
U Tebi jedan orač peva, i u zimsko doba,
prelivši krv, kao vino, u novi meh.
A kad mi klone glava i budu stali sati,
Ti ćeš me, znam, poljubiti kao mati.

TI, PROŠLOST, i moj svet,
mladost, ljubavi, gondole, i, na nebu, Mljeci,
priviđate mi se još, kao san, talas, lepi cvet,
u društvu maski, koje je po mene došlo.
Samo, to nisam ja, ni Venecija što se plavi,
nego neke ruševine, aveti, i stećci,
što ostaju za nama na zemlji, i, u travi.

Pa kažu: 'Tu leži paša!—Prosjak!—Pas!'
A viču i francusko 'tout passe'.
I naše 'prošlo'.

Ti, međutim, stojiš nad širokom rekom,
nad ravnicom plodnom, tvrd, uzdignut kao štit.
Ti pevaš vedro, sa grmljavom dalekom,
i tkaš u stoleća, sa munjama, i svoju nit.
U Tebi nema moje ljudske tuge.
Ti imaš streljača pogled prav i nem.
Ti i plač pretvaraš kao dažd u šarene duge,
a hladiš, ko dalek bor, kad te udahnem.
A kad dođe čas, da mi se srce staro stiša,
Tvoj će bagrem pasti na me kao kiša.

LIŽBUA i moj put,
u svet, kule u vazduhu i na morskoj peni,
priviđaju mi se još, dok mi žižak drhće ko prut
i prenosim i zemlju, u sne, u sne, u sne.
Samo, to više nisu, ni žene, ni ljudi živi,
nego neke nemoćne, slabe, i setne, seni,
što mi kažu, da nisu zveri, da nisu krivi,
da im život baš ništa nije dao,
pa šapću 'não, não, não'
i naše 'ne, ne'.

Ti, međutim, dišeš, u noćnoj tišini,
do zvezda, što kazuju put Suncu u Tvoj san.
Ti slušaš svog srca lupu, u dubini,
što udara, ko stenom, u mračni Kalemegdan.
Tebi su naši boli sitni mravi.
Ti biser suza naših bacaš u prah.
Ali se nad njima, posle, Tvoja zora zaplavi,
u koju se mlad i veseo zagledah.
A kad umorno srce moje ućuti, da spi,
uzglavlje meko ćeš mi, u snu, biti, Ti.

FINISTÈRE i njen stas,
brak, poljupci, bura što je tako silna bila,
priviđaju mi se još, po neki leptir, bulke, klas,
dok, iz prošlosti, slušam, njen korak, tako lak.
Samo, to više nije ona, ni njen glas nasmejan,
nego neki kormoran, divljih i crnih krila,
što viče: zrak svake sreće tone u Okean.
Pa mi mrmlja reči 'tombe' i 'sombre'.
Pa krešti njino 'ombre, ombre'—
i naš 'grob' i 'mrak'.

Ti, međutim, krećeš, ko naš labud večni,
iz smrti, i krvi, prema Suncu, na svoj put.
Dok meni dan tone u tvoj ponor rečni,
Ti se dižeš, iz jutra, sav zracima obasut.
Ja ću negde, sam, u Sahari, stati,

u onoj gde su karavani seni,
ali, ko što uz mrtvog Tuarega čuči mati,
Ti ćeš, do smrti, biti uteha meni.
A kad mi slome dušu, koplje, ruku i nogu,
Tebe, Tebe, znam da ne mogu, ne mogu.

ŽIVOT ljudski, i hrt,
sveo list, galeb, srna, i Mesec na pučini,
priviđaju mi se, na kraju, ko san, kao i smrt
jednog po jednog glumca našeg pozorišta.
Samo, sve to, i ja, nismo nikad ni bili više,
nego neka pena, trenuci, šapat u Kini,
što šapće, kao i srce, sve hladnije i tiše:
da ne ostaju, ni Ming, ni yang, ni yin,
ni Tao, trešnje, ni mandarin.
Niko i ništa.

Ti, međutim, sjaš, i sad, kroz san moj tavni,
kroz bezbroj suza naših, večan, u mrak, i prah.
Krv tvoja ko rosa pala je na ravni,
ko nekad, da hladi tolikih samrtnički dah.
Grlim još jednom na Tvoj kamen strmi,
i Tebe, i Savu, i Tvoj Dunav trom.
Sunce se rađa u mom snu. Sini! Sevni! Zagrmi!
Ime Tvoje, kao iz vedrog neba grom.
A kad i meni odbije čas stari sahat Tvoj,
to ime će biti poslednji šapat moj.

Cooden Beach 1956

Lament over Belgrade

JAN MAYEN and my Srem,
Paris, my dead comrades, cherries in China,
still haunt me, here, as I keep quiet, wakeful, in demise,
and lie, cold, like a log in ash.
Yet, it's no longer us, life, nor stars
but some monsters, polyps, dolphins,
which roll over us, sail by, and speed,
and howl: 'Dust, ashes, death is what it is.'
And they also scream the Russian 'nichevo'—
and the Spanish 'nada'.

Thou, however, grow'st, under the fair star of morn,
with the blue Avala, in the distance, like a hill.
Even here Thou glitter'st, when the stars die out,
and meltest the ice of tears, like the Sun last snow.
In Thee there is no inanity, and no death.
Thou shinest like an old unearthed sword.
In Thee everything is risen, bounds and revolves,
and recurs, like day and like an infant's cry.
And when my voice, eyes, and breath find their rest
I know Thou wilt take me to Thy lap.

ESPAÑA and our Hvar
Dead Dobrović, a sheik in the Sahara glaring white,
still haunt me, like phantoms, fires, farce.
My Sibe, insane, gaping like a bass.
Yet, it's no longer us, in youth and force,
but some despondent parrots and chimpanzees,
laughing at me and yelling in my solitude.
One is shrieking 'Leiche! Leiche! Leiche!'
To me the other's whispering: 'cadavere!'
The third: 'Corpse, corpse, corpse'.

Thou, however, spreadst, like swanly wings,
oblivion, over the Danube and Sava, as they sleep.
Thou rousest merriment, which once used to be,
giggle, here, even in my scream, shriek, and moan.
In Thee there is no worm, not even from the grave.
Thou gleamest, like a human laugh through tears.
A ploughman singeth in Thee, even in wintertime,
having poured blood, into a new skin, like wine.
And when my head droops and my hours cease,
I know Thou wilt, like a mother, give me a kiss.

THOU, THE PAST, and my world,
youth, passions, gondolas, and Venetians in the sky,
you still haunt me, like a dream, a wave, a lovely bloom,
in the company of masks, that have come for me.
Yet, it's not me, nor Venice in the blue,
but some spectres, relics and sepulchres,
that remain on earth, and in the grass, after us.
So they say: 'Here rests a pasha!—A beggar!—A dog!'
And shout the French 'tout passe'.
And our 'gone'.

Thou, however, risest upon the wide river
and fertile plain, solid, upright as a shield.
Thou sing'st brightly, with a distant thunder,
and weavest into centuries lightning and Thy yarn.
In Thee there is no human grief of mine.
Unbowed and still is Thy gaze, as of an archer.
Thou turn'st tears, like rain, into iridal bright,
and soothest my breath, like a distant pine.
And when the hour cometh, my old heart to appease,
Thy black locust will fall, like rain, upon me.

LISBOA and my voyage,
into the world, spires in the air, and on sea foam,
still haunt me, whilst my candle quivers as a birch,
and this land I carry into dreams, into dreams, into dreams.
Yet, it's not women, nor living men, anymore,
but some shades, helpless, feeble and distressed,
saying they are not beasts, and not debased,
and that life had nothing on them to bestow,
so they whisper 'não, não, não'
and our 'no, no'.

Thou, however, breathest, in the silence of the night,
to the stars, leading the Sun right into Thy dream.
Thou listenest to Thy heart's beat, deep down,
pounding as a stone against the dark Kalemegdan.
For Thee, the pangs of ours are but small ants.
The tears we pearled Thou tossest into the dust.
But, soon after, bluing above, cometh out Thy dawn,
which had taken in my gaze, youthful and jocund.
And when my weary heart falls silent, to sleep,
the soft pillow in my slumber Thou wilt be.

FINISTÈRE, and her figure,
nuptial kisses, the storm so forceful in its pass,
still haunt me, a chance butterfly, poppies, and a spike,
as I listen to her pace, so light, from the past.
Yet, it's no longer her, with that beaming voice,
but some ferocious, black-winged cormorant
screams: the ray of every glee sinks into the Ocean.
And murmurs the words 'tombe' and 'sombre'.
And cries their 'ombre, ombre'—
and our 'grave' and 'dusk'.

Thou, however, soarst, timelessly, like our swan,
from death, and blood, on Thy flight, to the Sun.
As my daylight plunges into Thy fluvial abyss,
Thou risest, from the morn, bathed in beams.
Alone, I will halt, somewhere in the Sahara,
thither, whither caravans are just shades,
but, as a dead Tuareg's mother crouching by,
Thou wilt remain my comfort until I die.
When my soul, spear, arm and leg they break,
Thee, Thee, I know, they cannot, nay, unmake.

HUMAN LIFE, and a greyhound,
a dry leaf, a seagull, a doe, the moon on the open sea,
haunt me finally, as a dream, as passing away,
in succession, of the actors from our stage.
Yet, all that, and me, have never been more
than foam, fleeting bits, a whisper in China,
murmuring, like the heart, colder and softer,
that there remains no Ming, nor yang and yin,
no Tao and cherries, no mandarin.
No one and nothing.

Thou, however, shinest, in that gloomy dream of mine,
through our countless tears, eternal, into dusk and grime.
Like dew, Thy blood has fallen down on plains,
to cool many a moribund gasp, as in the old days.
Over again I embrace on Thy precipitous rock
Thee, and the Sava, and Thy lazy Danube.
The Sun is risen in my dream. Gleam! Rumble! Light!
Thy name, like thunder from a clear sky.
And when Thy old clock sounds the knell for me,
with my last whisper I will be calling Thee.

Cooden Beach 1956

Despite its focus on exilic disintegration, 'Lament over Belgrade' presents us with compositional and grammatical/phonic structures of extraordinary regularity. The poem has twelve stanzas, each containing ten lines, and the graphic layout creates six consecutive stanzaic pairs. In the original text, almost all the odd stanzas have the same rhyme and syllabic pattern: $a(6)$-$b(14)$-$a(15)$-$c(13)$-$d(15)$-$b(14)$-$d(14)$-$e(11)$-$e(9)$-$c(5)$;[31] even-numbered stanzas also have a rhyme and syllabic pattern that both links them together and differentiates them from the odd-numbered stanzas: $a(12)$-$b(13)$-$a(12)$-$b(14)$-$c(11)$-$d(11)$-$c(15)$-$d(12)$-$e(14)$-$e(12)$. The linear distribution of syntactic subjects and objects conveys the change from the image of the poet as metonymically attached to the home city (anterior stanzaic pairs 1–2, 3–4, and 5–6), to the image of that city as a metonymical extension of the poet's being after his anticipated death (posterior stanzaic pairs 7–8, 9–10, and 11–12). Furthermore, the differentiation between the anterior and the posterior sections of the poem is also rigorously carried out within the stanzas. Thus, in the odd-numbered stanzas, the syntactic cut separating the delusory images of a bygone youth from the monsters of the present is set in the fifth and sixth line with the antithetic form 'samo, to više i nismo mi [...] nego' [Yet, it's no longer us [...] but].[32] These and other equivalences and oppositions are precisely what Jakobson would highlight and there can be no doubt that their semantic value can be inferred by the application of his principle of equivalence.[33]

In addition to these standard rhythmic and grammatical equivalences, there are in 'Lament over Belgrade' dramatic code switches that impose their own intratextual boundaries. This alternative subdivision transforms the whole poem into a running commentary on the poet's struggle for the preservation of his linguistic identity in exile. Namely, the odd-numbered stanzas introduce random, fragmentary scenes of the exilic life marked by various monstrous creatures which emerge from all sides to shriek out disturbing foreign words in a number of languages: Russian, Spanish, German, French, Italian and Mandarin Chinese. The interlingual counterparts of Poe's ironic raven, these lurid creatures seem to take particular pleasure in transience and negation. The even-number stanzas, by contrast, are thematically focused on hospitable, intimate aspects of Belgrade; they present syntactically integrated, idyllic images that counteract the scenes of desolation in exile. The poem, thus, proceeds through several cycles in which the exiled poet's helpless, tormented consciousness returns time and again to the safe-haven of the language of home. The contrast with the odd-numbered stanzas is especially remarkable if one considers the selection of words that suggest the stately tranquillity of the city. There is no code-switching to foreign lexical units, and, with few exceptions, there are no loan-words either. Crnjanski conspicuously tunes his lexical range to Serbian words of ancient Slavonic lineage: 'breg' [hill], 'orač' [ploughman], 'stoleća' [centuries], 'štit' [shield], 'dažd' [rain], and so on.

Just as there is a clear opposition between the languages present in the text of poem, there is one between present and absent codes. In the Babylonish medley of the poem's odd-numbered stanzas there is a conspicuous lack of English — the official endogenous linguistic code of Crnjanski's place of exile. Extant manuscripts indicate that Crnjanski's verbal performance in England was determined by seclusion and a dearth of genuine communicative situations.[34] The result was a 'fossilized interlanguage', a formulaic buffer code that enabled basic communication but impeded any affective and poetic appropriation.[35] The absence of English in 'Lament' thus suggests a double banishment: because Crnjanski perceives that he has been foreclosed from mastering English for poetic purposes, he in turn exiles this language from his own poem. Still, English finds an oblique way into the poem through a curious calque: the English phrase 'Chinese whispers', signifying a game, becomes the mysterious 'šapat u Kini' [a whisper in China].[36]

Extending Jakobson's principle of equivalence from intralingual to interlingual relations takes one to a slippery terrain of intuitive interpretations. To be sure, one cannot quarrel with the claim that in interlingual poems, just as in any other poem, one looks for a criterion of compositional coherence and that this is most likely to be found in symmetries and anti-symmetries. But why does it seem so peculiarly out of place to argue that in the fifth stanza the Turkish word 'pasha', the French expression '(tout) passe' and the Serbian word 'pas' [dog] project the principle of equivalence from the axis of selection onto the axis of combination? Before becoming a part of the actual poetic sequence, these lexical units have not been connected by any abstract systemic framework, and it would be very awkward indeed to argue for pre-existing paradigmatic relations between them solely on the grounds of paronomasia. In other words, there is no link between these words prior to the one created by syntagmatic disposition. Would it make any more sense to claim that in the seventh stanza the Portuguese 'não' and the Serbian 'ne', two words occupying the same end position in a line, form a phonic coupling that highlights their semantic equivalence? One cannot help but be struck by how little relevance this statement has despite its methodological consistency: in fact, since both words derive from the same Indo-European root (*ne*) it would be equally pertinent to claim that the difference in their vowels conveys a putative opposition in their way of denial. Otherwise, we would be forced to commit ourselves to positing as paradigms grammatical categories of Proto-Indo-European — a highly precarious avenue since that language has not been entirely reconstructed.

Unless we are willing to take these and similar cases as mock illustrations of Jakobson's principle of equivalence — which they are not — we have to work on a different rationale, one that takes into account the metaphoric potential of code switching and then establishes the paradigmatic implications of that metaphoricity. Thus, while in the ninth stanza of 'Lament over Belgrade' Crnjanski uses the French words 'sombre' [sombre] and 'ombre' [shadow], it is obvious that these words summon possible auditive substitutes in other languages, such as the Spanish 'hombre' [man]. Furthermore, the 'ombre' is preceded by the possessive pronoun 'njino'[37] [their] and the Serbian words 'grob' [grave] and 'mrak' [dark] are said to be 'naše' [our]. These possessive determinants are not merely grammatical categories induced upon syntagmatic sequence. They indicate a wider paradigmatic trope that juxtaposes languages on an axiological scale. In 'Lament over Belgrade' we — whoever 'we' may be — belong to the sepulchral void of our language to no less extent than it belongs to us. However, the empty space of this verbal tomb is delineated by the rough surfaces of foreign tongues as they are perceived in exile.

Meanwhile, the gloomy crypt is not the only matrix of interlingual sequences in 'Lament over Belgrade'. On several occasions, the sinister code switching comes from an elevated point, a promontory or a celestial body, and descends upon the dazed subject. Yet, in the first stanza the stars do not come across as the radiating nests which Tsvetaeva so movingly conjures in her poem on Rilke. To the contrary, Crnjanski's stars appear as monstrous polyps and dolphins that sail over the firmament and shriek the words of despair in Serbian as well as in Spanish and Russian. Here, too, the interlingual paradigmatic network produces an ironic point no less uncanny than the one that unites 'ombre' and 'hombre' in the sepulchre. Namely, the Spanish 'nada' (nothing) is the auditive equivalent of Serbian 'nada' (hope): this homonymy promptly creates metaphoric synonymy in that the two are seen as equally futile emanations of an exilic heaven.

We may, thus, argue that in 'Lament over Belgrade' both tomb-like nadirs and celestial zeniths fulfil a twofold role. They both contrast the spatial setting for code switching and at the same time appear as poignant metaphors of that verbal strategy. But do these metaphors present similar visions of interlinguality? In order to comprehend paradigmatic implications of the two polarized images in more detail, we need to compare them with some other metaphors that capture exilic interlinguality in a more explicit way.

Capsule, Mountain Top, Nest and Abyss: Four Metaphors of Interlingual Outsideness

While it is true that Crnjanski left us no definite extraliterary pronouncement on linguistic pressures in exile, the relationship between language variety and geographic dislocation has been observed and evaluated from various pragmatic standpoints by other poets. Although these poets dwell on issues as different as the relative importance and sustainability of the mother tongue and the cultural template of the host community's tongue, in each case languages are considered as paradigms, and exile becomes, in various visual and auditory guises, a metaphor that assesses the very possibility and value of interlingual mediation. Let us now consider a few elaborate and well-differentiated instances of this metaphoric creation of the paradigmatic axis.

In his address to the audience of the Vienna Conference on literature in exile (1987), Joseph Brodsky argued that the specificity of the position of the writer in exile consists in his capacity to bracket all corollary and superfluous elements of his cultural identity and focus on that single quality that in his view constitutes the stuff of literature — the native language:

> For one in our profession the condition we call exile is, first of all, a linguistic event: he is thrust from, he retreats into his mother tongue. From being his, so to speak, sword, it turns into his shield, into his capsule. What started as a private, intimate affair with the language, in exile becomes fate — even before it becomes an obsession or a duty.[38]

This well-known parable need not strike one as typical of Brodsky,[39] but it is highly representative of a peculiar centripetal tendency that incites many displaced writers, including Crnjanski, to ascribe a supra-individual value to their exile. Indeed, Brodsky's capsule retains some of the cryptic quality of Crnjanski's tomb, but he gives it a more optimistic, ascendant spin. Before exile, the mother tongue is a repository for the poet's private idiom; in exile, the poet as a whole is assigned to that mother tongue. Its uteral shape shields him by encapsulating him, but it also enables his creativity to go through a period of gestation. The wider implications of Brodsky's capsule metaphor can only be apprehended if it is considered within the theoretical and historical context of the long-running quarrel concerning the relationship between a culture and its language. The Romantic philosophers of language, especially Herder, argued that language is a quintessential vehicle of the national spirit (*Volksgeist*), a privileged symbolic system which epitomizes everything for which its respective culture stands.[40] A corollary ideologem claimed that this spirit of culture is not embodied to an equal degree in all utterances pronounced within a language community. It is literary artefacts, especially the genres of poetry, that stand out among other arts as being entirely verbal and, for that reason, capable of encapsulating *via* language the specific ethos of a nation. By the same token, Brodsky's exilic capsule provides the writer, and more specifically the poet, with an unparalleled opportunity to bring this inherent potential to a successful fruition.

There is, however, another metaphoric construal of exilic interlinguality that, contrary to linguistic essentialism, stresses the cognitive and aesthetic advantages of language contact, however forcefully it may occur. Exile provides the writer with what Christine Brook-Rose aptly defines as '*the distance needed* for the transcending of regional/national themes into those of the human condition anywhere'.[41] Ironically, it is again Brodsky who proposes that a writer's linguistic consciousness in exile

> is, if you like, a remarkable situation psychically, because you're sitting on top of a mountain and looking down both slopes. I don't know if that's so or not in my case, but at least when I do something, my vantage is good. [...] It's always your own spot, right? But still, you see both slopes, and this is an absolutely special sensation. Were a miracle to occur and I were to return to Russia permanently, I would be extremely nervous at not having the option of using more than one language.[42]

For one thing, Brodsky's mountaineering metaphor provides a remarkable contrast to the imagery of 'Lament'. The even-numbered stanzas of Crnjanski's poem abound in various natural promontories and hills that form the landscape of Belgrade, but these elevations are never climbed: their shapes are admired from below, and so from only one side. Brodsky, however, insists on the elevated vantage point which brings two possible perspectives. His second metaphor thus presents an excellent illustration of a complementary strand of the Romantic philosophy of language, the one that emphasizes, with Humboldt, that acquiring another language means acquiring another world for one's mind and, indeed, another mind itself.[43] In this view, because each language imposes a specific conceptual grid upon reality, examining as many such grids as possible enables one to get as close as one can to a comprehensive cognizance of that reality.

Still, there is also semiotic consistency in Brodsky's competing metaphors: the capsule and the mountaintop substitute the political arbitrariness of the horizontal movement in exile for the axiological certitude of the vertical ascent. The two metaphors, opposed though they are, share one implicit assumption: that the perception of the primary and adoptive language is thoroughly segregated on a number of levels of the paradigmatic axis. First, they are differentiated spatially in that both capsule and the opposing slopes stand for the post-Babel dispersal of tongues and their distribution along seemingly arbitrary geographic lines. Second, they are also separated psychologically, since the writer is supposed mentally to be able to distinguish between two linguistic codes, each of which refers to its own conceptual network. Third, the languages are divorced aesthetically, in that each one commands its own static values.

However, such a segregative model, in its two versions, is not the only trope that has been articulated to represent the condition and processes of the writer's linguistic consciousness in exile. As we have already seen, Tsvetaeva created a metalingual effect through the metaphor of the nest, the elevated place laboriously built from many twigs taken from different trees. When in his memoir *Speak, Memory*, Nabokov recollects how his father, a passionate cyclist, used to 'take one's "bike by the horns" (*bïka za roga*)', he creates a supreme interlingual pun based on the scriptural homology and phonetic similitude of the English word 'bike' and the Russian word 'бык' [bull, ox].[44] Since in Russian taking the bull by the horns implies someone taking control of a situation, Nabokov consciously mistranslates *бык* as 'bike' and has his authoritative father taking the bike by its metaphorical horns (the handlebars). This is a superb example of what can be called the 'nesting' strategy. Just as in Picasso's *Tête de taureau* (1942) the animal's head is conjured by a metal bike-seat and its horns by the handlebars, so Nabokov uses an interlingual transfer to convey a point that would not be accessible without such interaction. Like the capsule, the interlingual nest is an insulated place of incubation for a fledgling; like the mountain top, it is an elevated point which gives a panoramic view. Unlike both the capsule and the mountain top, however, the nest does not keep languages separate one from the other; rather, it brings them together in a stereoscopic view made possible by the nest's composite construction.

Some other poets in exile have adhered to an interactive rather than segregative view but have evaluated that interaction in a negative way. For them, the authorial subject is not a controlling centre of discourse formation: exile affects one's linguistic faculty in all its formative aspects and pragmatic functions, including the poetic one. In his *Tristia* Ovid formulates a memorable autobiographic account of this process in what is the earliest case of a writer presenting a running commentary on his own poetic demise in exile:

> Saepe aliquod quaero verbum nomenque locumque,
> nec quisquam est a quo certior esse queam.
> Dicere saepe aliquid conanti — turpe fateri! —
> verba mihi desunt dedidicique loqui.
> Threïcio Scythicoque fere circumsonor ore,
> et videor Geticis scribere posse modis.
> Crede mihi, timeo ne Sintia mixta Latinis
> inque meis scriptis Pontica verba legas.

> [Often I am at a loss for a word, a name, a place, and there is none who can inform me. Oft when I attempt some utterance — shameful confession! — words fail me: I have unlearned my power of speech. Thracian and Scythian tongues chatter on almost every side, and I think I could write in Getic measure.][45]

This description is strikingly similar to the monster-words of Crnjanski's odd stanzas and contains a hint of a rather elaborate model of the irreversible breakdown of native idiom. The stages of this breakdown are interconnected: it is impossible to distinguish between the disturbance caused by Ovid's lack of verbal communication in Latin and the one that is caused by his contact with vernaculars spoken in Tomis on the Black Sea, his designated place of exile. First, the loss of verbal memory that arises from the isolation in exile is paralleled by a veritable auditory invasion of foreign words that progressively take possession of the poet's lexical store. Second, through the same auditory channel, the rhythmic regularities of the foreign syntax penetrate and take control over the poet's power of versification.

Some more recent examples of verbal disorientation in exile are remarkably consistent with the image of linguistic death presented by the Roman poet. In her memoir *Lost in Translation*, Eva Hoffman recollects her experience of the loss of the precious capacity verbally to apprehend the world in a manner both distinctly her own and distinctly poetic:

> Polish, in a short time, has atrophied, shrivelled from sheer uselessness. Its words don't apply to my new experiences; they're not coeval with any of the objects, or faces, or the very air I breathe in the daytime. In English, words have not penetrated to those layers of my psyche from which a private conversation could proceed. [...] I'm not filled with language anymore, and I have only a memory of fullness to anguish me with the knowledge that, in this dark and empty state, I don't really exist.[46]

Hoffman provides Ovid's insight with a linguistic rationale: the loss of verbal memory can be explained by a disconnection between signified (exilic experience) and signifier (the Latin or the Polish language). As in Ovid, the vigorous, sparkling words of the foreign language act upon the mind, 'penetrating' into a vacuous entity. But, in contrast to Ovid's account, it is precisely the incompleteness of this penetration that initiates in Hoffman the fear that the linguistic vacuum will bring the end of her spiritual life, the end of her world. In a way that contrasts completely with the upward movement of Brodsky's space capsule, the loss an inner language of 'private conversation' is compared to 'some black hole'[47] that is completely unlike the 'fathomless abyss' over which Humboldt's vision of the sovereign mind 'hovers' and 'from which [...] it can always create the more, the more it has been already replenished from that source'.[48] Instead of levitation over the abyss of language, Hoffman suggests that exile brings a fall into something akin to the 'tomb' and 'dusk' so compellingly represented by Crnjanski's black cormorant.

The overarching compatibility of the images developed by Tsvetaeva, Ovid and Hoffman makes the temporal and generic distance that separates their texts lose its differentiating force. It is this analogy that suggests the possibility of a different conception of exilic interlinguality not envisaged by Brodsky. In physics, interferences are defined as the conjuncture of two or more waves at a single point of an axial system, whereby these waves either strengthen or cancel each other. Analogously, in Tsvetaeva and Nabokov languages add to one another through a series of complex interactions between different language codes thereby enhancing our intellectual grasp of the world. By contrast, in the metaphors suggested by Ovid and Hoffman, the languages subtract from one another. The author in exile is not a sovereign consciousness that contemplates immutable linguistic essences and draws freely from them to build his or her poetic universe. On the contrary, the author emerges as a derivative instance in which a vacuum asserts its presence surreptitiously, through disturbing firstly the affective and then the creative part of the self.

Furthermore, while these poets in exile consider their interlingual experience in terms of either the segregation or the interference of codes, they use different visual templates to conjure up these two types of relations. In Brodsky's capsule and Hoffman's abyss, on the one hand, interlinguality is grasped as an enclosed space in which the poet surrenders to the exotopic situation and is determined by it. Enveloped by a protective shell of 'native' language or thrown into a black hole, the poet remains in a self-reflexive mode: interlinguality prompts one to reassess goals and the sustainability of a poetic vocation in exile. The metaphors of the mountain top and the nest, on the other hand, rely on open vistas rather than enclosures. Interlinguality is seen not as a peculiar condition but as an opportune vantage point from which to observe reality and achieve insights that could not be attained in a monolingual environment.

A Jakobsonian critic would likely be tempted to represent the exiled poets' paradigmatic construals of their interlingual experience in a table:

exotopic template \ relation	segregative	interferential
enclosed space	capsule	abyss
vantage point	mountain slopes	nest

Yet, this would be a mistake: just as particular languages are not connected by a super-language, so their metaphoric correlates do not form a self-regulating system. For one thing, the four metaphors are not pre-textual archetypes but retroactive projections of archetypes based on the poets' actual interlingual experience. Instead of informing interlingual sequence, each of these tropes is formed post factum — by the poet's interlingual performance and attitude toward it. All of them frame spaces defined by outsideness, but the images used to conjure up such spaces are entirely different in semantic bearing. In the case of the capsule, the external is a place of isolation and concentration; in the metaphor of the mountain top, it is a commanding position in which different codes unlock different aspects of the world; in the metaphor of the nest, it is a place of a harmonious synthesis; in the metaphor of the abyss, it becomes a place that is defined by conflict and the risk of annihilation.

However, it is important to note that semiotic mappings of an imagined metalanguage in the four authors testify to another aspect of their creativity. Namely, while creating exotopic spaces on the internal boundaries of interlingual poems, the four metaphors also bear the imprint of exile as an event that sets the scene for the interlingual experience. It is hardly surprising, for, after all, they represent the response of verbal imagination to one of the most severe human situations. The metaphors we use are not impervious monadic wholes, and the paradigmatic relations based on them cannot but be imbued with social and political values.

Exilic Eschatology: Metaphors as a Metalanguage of Code Switching Poetry

How, then, do these metalingual metaphors relate to the code-switching sections of Crnjanski's 'Lament over Belgrade'? Let us recall: Jakobson begins with the assumption that paradigmatic relations are locked in a monolingual system when he considers their distributional arrangement in poetic texts. In interlingual poetry, however, there are no pre-existing paradigmatic relations between languages which constitute the sequence. The only way to process any such equivalences is to begin with their distributional arrangement in the text and then determine their paradigmatic implications. This inversion of Jakobson's model is all the more important in that it also applies to the metaphoric nature of such equivalences. Since there are no ready-made templates to generate poetic metaphors, it is only when we identify them in an actual poetic sequence that we can explore their semiotic foundations. As the last section of this argument will show, Crnjanski's interlingual code switching in 'Lament over Belgrade' elicits tropes that converge towards some of the four exotopic metaphors. This convergence is not simply an effect of our interpretative procedures; it is also a function of the author's verbal performance and desire within an interlingual environment.

To begin with, in most of the odd-numbered stanzas there is a specific image employed to represent the abyss and vacuity. While the former is conjured by visions of empty and threatening holes, the latter is suggested by images that create outlandish catachreses and hiatuses. Thus, in the third stanza, the hole is configured by the fishlike mouth of his late friend Sibe Miličić: 'Moj Sibe poludeli, zinuo kao peš' [My Sibe, insane, gaping like a bass];[49] in the penultimate stanza the same hole is revealed in the peremptory emptiness that absorbs both yin and yang.[50] The hole becomes a grave in the fifth stanza with the epitaph 'Tu leži paša!' [Here rests a pasha!][51] and in the ninth stanza it appears as the Ocean where 'zrak svake sreće tone' [the ray of every glee sinks into the Ocean] and as the dark 'tombe'/'grob'.[52] The first stanza brings a peculiar catachresis: 'nego neka čudovišta, polipi, delfini | što se tumbaju preko nas i plove, i jezde' [but some monsters, polyps, dolphins, | which roll over us, sail past and speed].[53] Here, the monsters tumble, sail and glide over an unidentified and utterly void 'us'. Finally, the seventh stanza brings an equally incongruous image: 'kule u vazduhu i na morskoj peni' [spires in the air and on sea foam].[54] What we can deduce from all these examples is that both the abyss and vacuum appear in two main forms. On the one hand, they are exotopic spaces in the bosom of nature (ocean, grave, towers built on the sea-foam); on the other, they gape in the centre of the tormented subject (a dead friend with mouth open like a fish, the monsters tumbling above 'us'). As in Hoffman's metaphor, where the subject experiences, inside, a loss of fullness and then falls, outside, into a black hole, so Crnjanski sees abysses all around because he feels his own self as a deep void.

The most terrifying aspect of the void is that it is open to the intrusion suggested by the code switching at the end of the odd-numbered stanzas. 'Lament over Belgrade' is not only a grotesque vision of monsters that cry out the ominous foreign words 'ничего', 'nada', 'Leiche', 'cadavere', 'tout passe', 'ombre'. It is also an extended metaphor about the foreign words which acquire monstrous shapes as they become a part of the poem's language.[55] Here it is useful to draw a comparison with Ovid's description of the invasion of the *barbara lingua* in exile. Whereas Ovid does not go further than expressing the fear that the Thracian and Scythian tongues will infiltrate his verse, Crnjanski's 'Lament' deepens this anxiety as the perceived barbarisms take control of his auditory imagination and step into the actual poem. What for the Roman poet had to remain beyond the pale, in 'Lament' becomes the very fabric of the poem. The intrusion of foreign words, accompanied by the images of chasm and by catachreses, produces metaphoric equivalences tied together by the metaphor of the abyss.

The central metaphor of the odd-numbered stanzas is replicated in the tenth stanza, in which the Ocean is replaced by the river flowing beneath the fortress of Belgrade: 'Dok meni dan tone u tvoj ponor rečni' [As my daylight plunges into thy fluvial abyss].[56] However, this remains an exceptional case of parallelism between the odd- and even-numbered stanzas of the poem: on the whole, the even-numbered stanzas deploy a very different imagery and do so in a compositionally different way as well. Thus, the line I have just quoted is followed by a line in which the city is identified with the rising sun: 'Ti se dižeš, iz jutra, sav zracima obasut' [Thou risest from the morn, bathed in beams].[57] In addition to this image of levitation, the fourth and tenth stanzas suggest the security of enfoldment. Both stanzas begin with the stately image of the swan spreading its wings: 'Ti, međutim, širiš, kao labud krila, | zaborav' [Thou, however, spreadst, like swanly wings, | oblivion][58] and 'Ti, međutim, krećeš, ko naš labud večni' [Thou, however, soarst, timelessly, like our swan].[59] Both end with the image of the *mater dolorosa* embracing her dead son: 'A kad mi klone glava i budu stali sati, | Ti ćeš me, znam, poljubiti kao mati' [And when my head droops and my hours cease, | I know Thou wilt, like a mother, give me a kiss];[60] and 'ko što uz mrtvog Tuarega čuči mati' [as a dead Tuareg's mother crouching by].[61] The imagined spatial enfoldment is reflected in the correspondence of positions (beginning and end of stanzas, second and penultimate stanzaic pairs). It is also important to note that the sixth stanza begins with a distich in which the city is explicitly compared to a shield, the word Brodsky will use to describe the protective effect of the capsule: 'Ti, međutim, stojiš [...] | tvrd, uzdignut kao štit' [Thou, however, risest [...] solid, upright as a shield].[62] In Crnjanski's capsular vision, then, Belgrade is more than a spatial point marking the centre of the poet's exilic longing. It is also the visual, symbolic expression of the 'native' language which forms the poet in exile and is formed by him in its turn.

Is, however, this cultivated idiom still his *mother* tongue or his *personal* tongue? These even-numbered stanzas remind us of Brodsky's capsule image, and they are not free from their own ideological tension. Crnjanski's painstaking rhymes and assonances warn us against any referential fallacy: the monolingual poetic idiom cultivated in segregation is not the tribe's Ur-language but the product of artifice, no less cunningly wrought than its corresponding image of maternal embrace.

'Lament over Belgrade' remains an excellent example of how two tropes of metalingual relations, the interferential abyss and the segregative capsule, emerge from the linear arrangement of words from different languages. Moreover, the poem reveals that these tropes only make sense when considered in their mutual alternation. After exposure to the abysmal visions of the odd-numbered stanzas, in every even-numbered stanza Crnjanski retreats to the capsular space of his mother tongue for protection and the gestation of a monolithic poetic idiom. In these stanzas, the exotopy remains a distant position from which the poet can determine interlingual context and gain aesthetic benefit from his situation. In the odd-numbered stanzas, however, he is in dangerous proximity to language rivalry, in which verbal consciousness is determined by forces external to it.

This interpretation of metalingual tropes in 'Lament over Belgrade' still does not of course explain *why* they are arranged in such a way and with such semiotic elements. To be sure, 'Lament' does introduce a few nest-like images featuring a mixture of parts suspended at an elevated point in the air. In the sixth stanza Belgrade is seen as a celestial weaver who with lightning interlaces centuries into his yarn and then as a maker of a rainbow who transforms tears into bright-coloured stripes. Likewise, in the eleventh stanza the desolate exilic landscape is said to contain no yin or yang. We can safely assume that Crnjanski, the editor of an important anthology of Chinese lyric in the early 1920s, knew that this oppositional pair signified, among other contraries, north slope (yin) and south slope (yang). Yet, these scattered images, closely akin to the nest and the mountain, are not activated as metaphors of exilic interlinguality. While the yarn and rainbow do not refer to code-switching sequences at all, because the loanwords *yin* and *yang* are non-existent for the poet, their dualism does not bring light to interlinguality or, for that matter, to exile. It seems as if Crnjanski saw only two avenues for verbal consciousness in exile: it either falls back on its pre-exilic code or risks being erased in an open conflict of codes.

Although light and fire do not figure as semiotic elements in Brodsky's and Hoffman's metaphors, their distribution in 'Lament over Belgrade' neatly points to metalingual relations defined by capsule and abyss. In each even stanza, Crnjanski associates Belgrade with one or another luminous form of heaven: like a distant star, the city shines into his slumber, and, like sudden lightning, it illumines his landscape. However, Crnjanski's luminosity remains substantially different from Tsvetaeva's radiating nest. 'Lament's' light is ignited not through the mutual friction of words from multiple languages but through the crepuscular combustion of a single idiom. It is this capsular idiom that sets on fire other segregated codes while at the same time making them as spurious as carnivalesque effigies, 'utvare, vatre, var' [phantoms, fires, farce].[63] Yet this capsular idiom is still part of a metalanguage:

it communicates a metaphor that connects interlingual sequences into a meaningful, if ambiguous, whole.

What is it that moves Crnjanski's interlingual switches towards an alternation of abyss and capsule rather than towards nest and/or mountain top? In exile, the poet's primary concern is not to relate to a static linguistic system (there is none at hand), but to bridge the divide between, on the one hand, previously acquired and, on the other hand, developmental features of verbal activity. The ultimate touchstone for the success of this process is the ability to form a sequence — conversational or poetic — from whatever linguistic elements exist in one's mnemonic store and in the dynamics of everyday discourse. As we have already seen, this process may result in the juxtaposition of codes within isolated sequences or in the interaction of codes within a single sequence. Furthermore, these possibilities may be assessed optimistically, as a boost to creativity, or pessimistically, as a demise of poetic speech. 'Lament over Belgrade' indicates that Crnjanski's stance was a peculiar mixture of probing approaches and defensive strategies. If he was trying to master the English language and make it a part of his idiom, he was also not ready to relinquish the precarious status of Serbian as the primary and self-referential code. The failure he soon faced in the first task meant that even more emphasis would be given to the second one. In other words, incomplete integration of codes was followed by their increased segregation on compositional, syntactic, and metaphoric levels.

What can one positively say about metalingual interplay of the four metaphors? Or, alternatively, what can one say by using this metalanguage? Not much — apart from re-enforcing the postulate that it is elsewhere. The metalingual instance that arises in the interlingual poetry of exile is not an economic and impersonal vehicle of communication, or, for that matter, a socially endorsed system of language universals; rather, it is the author's personal mirage of a poetic metalanguage. The textual code switching relies on the trauma of enforced interlinguality to draw individual semiotic templates of exotopy. Since language codes fall into paradigmatic order only after the event, according to the extent to which the poet succeeds in making them a part of the poetic sequence, the metalanguage can only communicate a record of the individual poet's struggle to do so.

In conclusion, I would like to discuss briefly how the model applied here relates to the earlier criticisms of Jakobson's theory of equivalences. For example, Michael Riffaterre has questioned the relevance of equivalences in aesthetic perception of the poem: 'How are we to pass from description to judgment — that is, from a study of the text to a study of its effect upon the reader?'[64] The same argument is replicated by Jonathan Culler who matter-of-factly remarks: 'To say that there is a great deal of parallelism and repetition in literary texts is of little interest in itself and of less explanatory value. The crucial question is what effects patterning can have.'[65] In both comments, the somewhat awkward word 'effect' conceals a highly pertinent question: how is the reader supposed to perceive, discriminate and semantically activate grammatical parallelisms? And with the advent of various deconstructive approaches in literary theory — approaches that addressed precisely this pragmatic side of the reading experience — Jakobson's theory was consigned to a marginal position and engaged with scepticism. The interpretative model applied here retrieves some elements of Jakobson's theory while at the same time having the advantage of eliminating this criticism. To say that in the interlingual poetry of exile the relations between codes are transferred from the syntagmatic axis onto the paradigmatic axis means that at least some paradigms are the effects rather than driving force of a poetic text. They are not already given in an immutable linguistic system but shaped by a sustained poetic effort in a specific historical situation. In other words, the emergence of metalingual metaphors that transcend and illuminate the code-switching sequences is at the same time a projection of the author's desire for a comprehensive poetic language *and* a reflection of the linguistic duress of his or her exile. These aspects are, furthermore, inseparable: every projection is a reflection. The nowhere of exile projects an imaginary nowhere that emerges especially clearly in some lines by Milosz:

> Kto mnie potępi jeżeli ojczyzny
> I tu i nigdzie szukałem,
> Myląc dialekty, prowincjonalizmy
> Z oceanowym chorałem?
>
> [Who can blame me for seeking a native land
> Here or perhaps nowhere,
> Mixing dialects and provincial idioms
> With an oceanic choir?][66]

Therefore, this modified version of Jakobson's model does not merely describe the interlingual poems of exile but also tells us something about how they achieve their poetic effect. Moreover, it is precisely interlingual poems of exile such as 'Lament over Belgrade' that prompt us critically to re-examine his theory and reclaim some of its tenets for insight into the rhetorical tropes that negotiate textual and socio-political fields of experience. Thus, 'Lament over Belgrade' shows how symmetries and anti-symmetries remain crucial to our activating the semantic potential of such poems not only in poetic but also in metalingual aspects of the text. For if we allow that in code-switching poems the metalingual function can also be the field in which the poetic function asserts itself, and that such a metalingual function may work from outside rather than from within particular languages, we open an important pathway: the exploration of the intrinsic pragmatism of paradigms — the ways in which they are posited, evaluated, and interpreted in a manner that reflects both our historical position and our innermost desires.

Notes to Chapter 5

1. Conrad Aiken, 'An Anatomy of Melancholy', in Allen Tate (ed.), *T. S. Eliot: The Man and his Work* (Harmondsworth: Penguin, 1971), p. 202.
2. Ibid, p. 201.
3. Julia Kristeva, 'A New Type of Intellectual: The Dissident', in *The Kristeva Reader*, ed. by Toril Moi (Oxford and Cambridge, MA: Blackwell, 1986), p. 298.
4. James Joyce, *A Portrait of the Artist as a Young Man* (London: Jonathan Cape, 1930), pp. 231, 281.
5. For other modernist articulations of this trope, see Bertolt Brecht's poem 'Die Auswanderung der Dichter', in *Gedichte*, vol. v (Frankfurt am Main: Suhrkamp Verlag, 1964)), p. 14, and Danilo Kiš's essay 'Variations on Central European Themes', in *Homo Poeticus: Essays and Interviews* (Manchester: Carcanet, 1996), pp. 112–13.

6. Rainer Maria Rilke, *Duino Elegies* (London: The Hogarth Press, 1963), pp. 24–25.

7. It would be hasty to jump to etymological conclusions about a word which, in Shklovsky's usage, works as a poetic neologism to no less extent than as a theoretical concept. Yet, while most scholars have pointed out the importance (and even dominance) of the link with the adjective *странное*, the spatial connotations of *страна* are not entirely out of place. From the Formalist vantage point, these two words would appear as the two sides of the same coin minted by the poetic language. Namely, Shklovsky's concept of the resurrection of the word is not only about creating new words in the way Khlebnikov and Kruchenikh did in their Futurist poetry. It is also about discovering an unfamiliar and noetically rough side of old words by making surprising and discrepant links between them. The whole point of *остранение* can be captured by this semantic turn: what we think is known to us (*страна*, our habitual realm) suddenly becomes unfamiliar (*странное*, odd). Beyond the Russian etymology, it is interesting to note that some other Slavic languages preserve the same homonymy. It will suffice to recall the elusive and yet more than simply coincidental link between the Serbian words *strana* (a defined territorial/spatial realm, as in the four sides of the world) and *strano* (unfamiliar and foreign). In the latter language, there are words and idioms which fuse the two and where one could hardly tell which component is preponderant. Thus, *stranstvovati* means experiencing the strangeness of travelling through foreign lands and *na strani* (literally 'on a foreign side') is a prepositional construction designating a foreign land. Finally, such a connection is not without a parallel in other, non-Slavic languages. The one widely known example, exploited by Freud in his essay 'Das Unheimliche', is the curious ambivalence of the adjective *heimlich* in the German language: it means something that is intimate and at the same time hidden, secret and unknown. It belongs to our habitual home (*Heim*) — and perhaps land (*strana*) — and still at certain dramatic moments strikes us as disturbing (*unheimlich*) and disruptive in its oddness. Of course, this digression is in no way meant to disregard the many examples from other languages where a clear distinction between the territorial unit and estrangement is upheld on the lexical level. *Land* and *outlandish* in the English language, as well as *pays* and *dépaysement* in French, secure the difference between the certitude of space and the perplexity of cognitive apparatus through the use of negational prefixes.

8. Viktor Shklovsky, 'Art as Technique', in L. T. Lemon and M. J. Reis, eds, *Russian Formalist Criticism: Four Essays* (Lincoln and London: University of Nebraska Press, 1965), p. 22.

9. George Steiner, *After Babel* (London: Oxford University Press, 1975), pp. 178, 188–92. For the aesthetic background to Shklovsky's and Steiner's argument within the Formalist theories of poetic language, see Tzvetan Todorov's 'Three Conceptions of Poetic Language', in R. L. Jackson and S. Rudy, eds, *Russian Formalism: A Retrospective Glance (A Festschrift in Honor of Victor Erlich)* (New Haven, CT: Yale Center for International and Area Studies, 1985) pp. 130–37 (pp. 130–35).

10. Mikhail Bakhtin, 'Response to a Question from the *Novy Mir* Editorial Staff', in *Speech Genres and Other Late Essays* (Austin: University of Texas Press, 1986), p. 7.

11. Mikhail Bakhtin, 'From the Prehistory of Novelistic Discourse', in Bakhtin, *The Dialogic Imagination* (Austin: University of Texas Press, 1981), p. 68.

12. Mikhail Bakhtin, 'Discourse in the Novel', in *The Dialogic Imagination*, pp. 286–87.

13. See Ferdinand De Saussure, *Course in General Linguistics* (London: Peter Owen, 1960), pp. 122–27 and Roman Jakobson, 'Two Aspects of Language and Two Types of Aphasic Disturbances', in Jakobson, *Language in Literature* (Cambridge, MA, and London: The Belknap Press of Harvard University Press, 1987), pp. 95–114.

14. 'Теории безусловного соответствия стиха духу языка, непротивления формы материалу, мы противопоставляем теорию организованного насилия поэтической формы над языком' [To the theory of unconditional correspondence of the verse to spirit of the language we counterpropose a theory of the organised violence of poetic form over language] (my translation). See Roman Jakobson, *O cheshkom stikhe*, in Jakobson, *Selected Writings*, vol. v (The Hague: Mouton Publishers, 1979), p. 15.

15. In his text 'What Is Poetry?', Jakobson insists that 'both the domain of art and its relationship to the other constituents of the social structure are in constant dialectical flux'. Roman Jakobson, 'What Is Poetry?', in *Selected Writings*, vol. III (The Hague: Mouton Publishers, 1981), pp. 749–50.

16. John Keats, 'La Belle Dame Sans Merci', in *Poetical Works* (Oxford and New York: Oxford University Press, 1970), p. 351.

17. On the history of this metaphor, see Susan Bassnett's *Translation Studies* (London and New York: Routledge, 1988), pp. 1–6.

18. T. S. Eliot, 'The Waste Land', in *Selected Poems* (London: Faber and Faber, 1961), p. 67.

19. Tzvetan Todorov's rendition of Bakhtin's вненаходимость as 'exotopie' is a highly revealing example of interlingual equations in scholarly discourse. It establishes the semantic equivalence through translation (the concept of geographic and symbolic outsideness) and at the same time involves a linguistic displacement (the Russian neologism rendered into a Greek coinage and then appended by a French suffix). When using this concept in the present essay, I thus refer both to its underlying metaphoric value and to its performative interlingual effect. See: Tzvetan Todorov, *Mikhaïl Bakhtine: le principe dialogique* (Paris: Éditions du Seuil, 1981), pp. 155–56.

20. Roman Jakobson, 'Linguistics and Poetics', in *Selected Writings*, vol. III (The Hague: Mouton Publishers, 1981), p. 27. Italics in the original.

21. Marina Tsvetaeva, 'Novogodnee', in Tsvetaeva, *Poem of the End: Selected Narrative and Lyrical Poems with Facing Russian Text* (Woodstock and New York: Ardis Publishers, 2004), pp. 110–11. In this quotation, the pair 'haven/Heaven' is the translator's inventive though not entirely accurate rendition of the Russian 'гнезда/звезды' [nests/stars].

22. That metaphor and metonymy may be of importance for understanding of exile is suggested by Maria Louise Ascher in her essay 'The Exile as Autobiographer: Nabokov's Homecoming', pp. 67–86, in Domnica Radulescu (ed.), *Realms of Exile: Nomadism, Diasporas, and Eastern European Voices* (Lanham, MD: Lexington Books, 2002), pp. 67–86.

23. Tsvetaeva, 'Novogodnee', pp. 110–11.

24. Julia Friedman, 'Blok's "Gift of Hearing" through Remizov's "Audible Colours"', *Slavic and East European Journal*, 47.3 (2003), pp. 367–92.

25. Walter Benjamin, 'The Task of the Translator', in *Selected Writings (Volume I, 1913–1926)* (Cambridge, MA, and London: The Belknap Press of Harvard University Press, 1996), p. 259.

26. Roman Jakobson, 'On Linguistic Aspects of Translation', in *Selected Writings*, vol. II (The Hague and Paris: Mouton Publishers, 1971), pp. 262–63 and 'Le métalangage d'Aragon', in *Selected Writings*, vol. III (The Hague: Mouton Publishers, 1981), pp. 148–54.

27. Czeslaw Milosz, *Gdzie wschodzi słońce i kiedy zapada* (Kraków: Znak, 1980), p. 99.

28. Boris Pasternak, 'Groza, momental'naya navek', in *Izbrannoe v dvukh tomakh*, vol. I (Moscow: Hudozhestvennaya literatura, 1985), p. 109. Translation in Boris Pasternak 'Storm, Instantaneous Forever', in *Selected Poems* (London: Allen Lane, 1983), p. 72.

29. Jakobson, 'Linguistics and Poetics', p. 27.

30. The original text and my translation of 'Lament over Belgrade' are presented here by courtesy of the Miloš Crnjanski Foundation, Belgrade, which holds the copyright to Crnjanski's works. The original text is quoted from Miloš Crnjanski, *Pesme* (Beograd: Nolit 1983), pp. 263–69. For an earlier translation of 'Lament over Belgrade' by Borislava Šašić, who follows only semantic correspondence, see Crnjanski, 'Lament over Belgrade', in *Serbian Literary Quarterly*, I (Spring 1988), 33–38.

31. The only exceptions are the eight line of the fifth odd stanza (11 syllables) and the seventh line of the sixth odd stanza (15 syllables).

32. Crnjanski, 'Lament nad Beogradom', p. 265.

33. For a list of correspondences between the odd and even stanzas of 'Lament over Belgrade', see Aleksandar Petrov, *Poezija Crnjanskog i srpsko pesništvo* (Beograd: Vuk Karadžić, 1971), pp. 121–38. The list is not complete as the divides of the internal vs. external stanzas and of anterior vs. posterior stanzas have not been explored in this, or indeed, any study.

34. Crnjanski, *A Novel about London*, manuscript No. P702/I/П/16. *Legat Miloša Crnjanskog* (Courtesy of the National Library of Serbia).

35. Josiane F. Hamers and Michel H. A. Blanc, *Bilinguality and Bilingualism* (Cambridge: Cambridge University Press, 1989), pp. 225–28; Svetozar Koljević, 'Linguistic Aspects of the International Theme in *Roman o Londonu*', in David Norris (ed.), *Miloš Crnjanski and Modern Serbian Literature* (Nottingham: Astra Press, 1988), p. 76.

36. Crnjanski, 'Lament nad Beogradom', p. 268.

37. 'Njino' is a dialectal form of 'njihovo' with a distinctly exclusivist, distancing undertone.

38. Joseph Brodsky, 'The Condition We Call Exile', in John Glad (ed.), *Literature in Exile* (Durham, NC: Duke University Press, 1990), p. 108.

39. For instance, in his poem 'Колыбел'ная трескового мыса' [Lullaby of Cape Cod], he declares that 'Перемена империи связана с гулом слов | с выделеньем слюны в результате речи' [The change of Empires is intimately tied | to the hum of words, the soft, fricative spray | of spittle in the act of speech] and in 'Строфы' [Strophes] that 'Знаешь, все, кто далече | по ком голосит тоска — | жертвы законов речи, | запятых, языка' [You know, dear, all whom anguish | pleads for, those out of reach | are prey of the laws of language — | periods, commas, speech]. See Joseph Brodsky, *Peremena imperii* (Moscow: Nezavisimaya gazeta, 2001), pp. 284, 318. English translation in: Joseph Brodsky, *A Part of Speech* (Oxford: Oxford University Press, 1980), pp. 110, 140.

40. J. G. Herder, *Philosophical Writings* (Cambridge: Cambridge University Press, 2002), pp. 147–54. For a discussion of the broader intellectual context from which Herder's theory emerges, see Richard Bauman and Charles L. Briggs, *Voices of Modernity: Language Ideologies and the Politics of Inequality* (Cambridge and New York: Cambridge University Press, 2003), pp. 163–96.

41. Christine Brook-Rose, 'Exsul', in Susan Rubin Suleiman (ed.), *Exile and Creativity: Signposts, Outsiders, Travelers, Backward Glances* (Durham, NC: Duke University Press, 1998), p. 15 (my emphasis).

42. Solomon Volkov, *Conversations with Joseph Brodsky: A Poet's Journey through the Twentieth Century* (New York: The Free Press, 1998), pp. 185–86.

43. Wilhelm von Humboldt, *On Language: The Diversity of Human Language-Structure and its Influence on the Mental Development of Mankind* (Cambridge: Cambridge University Press, 1988), p. 167.

44. Vladimir Nabokov, *Speak, Memory: An Autobiography Revisited* (London: Weidenfeld and Nicolson, 1967), p. 40.

45. *Tristia* III. 14. 43–50 in Ovid, *Tristia, Ex Ponto* (London and Cambridge, MA: Harvard University Press, 2002), pp. 154–57. A very similar statement is found in *Tristia* V. 7. 51–64 (pp. 238–39).

46. Eva Hoffman, *Lost in Translation* (London: Vintage, 1998), pp. 107–08.

47. Ibid, p. 108.

48. von Humboldt, *On Language*, pp. 146–47.

49. Crnjanski, 'Lament nad Beogradom', p. 266.

50. Ibid, p. 268.

51. Ibid, p. 266.

52. Ibid, p. 268.

53. Ibid, p. 265.

54. Ibid, p. 267.

55. The Archive department of Radio Belgrade preserves a precious audio record of Crnjanski reciting 'Lament over Belgrade' in 1975 (track no. 3889). Although this reading was recorded many years after the poem's composition, the poet's perception of exile as interlingual inferno had remained unchanged. The record shows how at the end of the odd stanzas, Crnjanski thoroughly modified his voice to make the foreign words resemble the actual shrieks of animals.

56. Crnjanski, 'Lament nad Beogradom', p. 268.

57. Ibid., p. 268.

58. Ibid., p. 266.

59. Ibid., p. 268.

60. Ibid., p. 266.

61. Ibid., p. 268.

62. Ibid., p. 267.

63. Ibid., p. 266.

64. Michael Riffaterre, 'Describing Poetic Structures: Two Approaches to Baudelaire's *Les Chats*', *Yale French Studies*, 36/37 (October 1966), 200–42 (p. 202).

65. Jonathan Culler, 'Jakobson's Poetic Analyses', in Culler, *The Structuralist Poetics* (Ithaca, NY: Cornell University Press, 1975), p. 71.

66. Czeslaw Milosz, *Gdzie słońce wschodzi i kiedy zapada*, p. 114. Translation in Czeslaw Milosz, *The Collected Poems* (London: Viking, 1988), p. 279.

AFTERWORD

Exiles will know that at the end of a journey it is good to remind oneself of its starting point. This study opened with the disquieted and nostalgic claim of Paul von Wartenburg that the spirit of modernity had uprooted exile, that epitome of uprootedness — even if it befalls us, which is increasingly rare, we are no longer capable to feel the fundamental sadness of it. However, everything that has been presented in this book suggests that exile is very much alive, that it is intrinsically lively, and that it can enliven other practices and discourses.

In a nutshell, this book has identified ethico-political contradictions of direct banishment and proposed the term 'implied exile' to describe all those alternative patterns of eviction from a country where force was not communicated directly but by detour. This indirect exile has subsequently been followed up by the exile's reconstruction of that force. This elicitation should not be connected with the proverbial sullen pain of exile exposed to the sword of the sovereign power. For the implied exile, who is banished with no force, a part of the peculiar pleasure accorded by his or her condition consists in the opportunity to recreate force by their own imaginative resources. The paradoxical sense of empowerment and creativity in capturing the sovereign force is something that connects the implied exiles from Cicero to Brodsky.

The argument on implied exile took as the theoretical background three different strands of modernist and postmodernist thought: the literary criticism of exile, Carl Schmitt's and Giorgio Agamben's theories of sovereignty and exception, and the linguistic study of metaphor and metonymy. By providing numerous case studies from antiquity to the twentieth century, I have sought to demonstrate how each of these fields can benefit from the notion of implied exile and its rhetoric of force. My principal aim was, therefore, not to criticize them but to bring them together and sensitize them to their own liminal cases and possibilities for further development.

Literary criticism, as we have seen, has been bent on exile as the finished semiotic product: an archetypal human condition, a distinct literary theme (and mythos) and an extraterritorial and transhistorical community of exiled writers. Its principal binary has been that between the hard-earned creative freedom of exile and the servitude at the hands of the unimaginative state. The case studies in this book suggest that far from being dull the sovereign power can be very imaginative and resourceful in finding ever new ways to communicate force to people who are about to leave or have left. Furthermore, it has also become clear that these methods of encoding duress do not disappear but inform the literary imagination of the exiles. The overall picture has not been a disassociation of the political power and literary imagination but rather the dialogue between two forms of imagination, the political and the literary one, about whether departure was forceful or voluntary.

The ever stimulating research of Carl Schmitt and Giorgio Agamben has shed light on the metaphysical premises of the sovereign power and on its political pitfalls, best seen in the formal and informal states of exception. Yet, there is in their analyses an empty chair which I believe is reserved for the implied exile as an exception from the sovereign exception. In largely the same way, the implied exile eludes the conceptual frame of both the domestic *hostis* (Schmitt) and of *homo sacer* (Agamben). The state cannot articulate the stance of existential hostility against an exile nor for that matter capture his or her bare life. By the implied consensus, the exile has been surrendered to another sovereign power and capture happens only in imagination: on the side of the sovereign, as the threat of death penalty if he or she returns; on the side of the exile, as paranoid imagination. The sovereign capture in imagination and the imaginative capture of the sovereign power are intrinsically connected.

The cross-field research into metaphor and metonymy has pointed to the rhetorical pivots of the individual psychic life (Freud) and of language, as a system (Jakobson) and as a chain of signification (Lacan). In the pragmatic turn of the conceptual linguists (Lakoff and Johnson), it has also been instrumental in articulating the interaction between cognitive universals and cultural frames. This study has tried to show that these frameworks have a broader field of application, not only in the everyday language and the political discourse, but also in the insidious articulation of force. That force is not included in discourse and is often meant to remain so. To suggest that in implied exile force is metonymically displaced to various proxies in space and in time and that it is reconstructed as metaphor means to reverse the heuristic hierarchy: one starts from the political field as the realm of metonymy and follows it up to its metaphoric implications.

Therefore, the theoretical frameworks as different as literary criticism, tropology of law, and conceptual linguistics have something to gain from the study of implied exile which in itself is an indicator of the relevance of this phenomenon in the present time. Now, von Wartenburg suggested another point with which this study largely disagrees, namely that exile had been experienced in very different ways in antiquity and in the modern period. As a matter of fact, direct banishment has largely disappeared from the law as its metaphysical anchorage has been dissolved. However, the sundry methods of the rhetorical displacement of force — evasion from the legal process, foreclosure from entrance, informal duress — have lived from the Roman Republic right unto the present period. And so have the modes of its imaginative elicitation, which spread from politics to law and literature and even to legendry.

However, what these case studies have shown is not merely the general forcefulness of literary imagination and its predilection for metaphors. The displaced force of exile informs literary texts at different levels and in different ways. These patterns are multifaceted and often very elusive: the metaphors differ depending on the time, the author, and the technology of power, and they will not always be easily traceable to their metonymic templates. However, the pragmatic link has emerged in the critical number of cases to justify the claim that the sovereign power tends to displace force whereas the writer tends to condense it at the strategic loci of the text. The force of implied exile can be elicited as an isolated forceful image in the poetic text, for example as fire that can connect and burn both the state and the exile. Force can also appear in the text's underlying political outlook, as a persecutory society that perversely chases the exile away and then chases him or her up. Force can also appear as the uncanny paternal metaphor of textual cohesion, in which the father(land) holds together the memory and the text. Finally, force can also be elicited at the level of language, as a polyglot monster that traverses the different linguistic–political territories of the text.

One needs to bear in mind that the force elicited in the texts of the implied exiles is not an abstract force but one with a clearly defined political vector. This force establishes a very specific connection between the exile and the sovereign power and it is precisely this feature that separates it from traditional *topoi*. Duress can be self-inflicted, as if the writer wanted to consummate in exile a death penalty which may have been hinted at home (or which he or she insinuates). It can also be directed against the state, as if he or she were involved in an imaginative drive for restitution. Finally, force can undergo a visionary transformation and turn into a myth or a transcendental image that goes beyond its immediate rhetorical contest. Literary texts, thus, emerge as amphibian structures, capable of playing out and outplaying the sovereign power: on the one hand, they absorb political impulses but, on the other hand, they also transform them by mechanisms of modification and subversion.

WORKS CITED

AESCHYLUS. *Agamemnon, Libation Bearers, Eumenides, Fragments*, translated by Herbert Weir Smyth (Cambridge, MA: Harvard University Press; London: William Heinemann, 1971)

AGAMBEN, GIORGIO. *State of Exception* (Chicago, IL, and London: Chicago University Press, 2005)

——*Homo Sacer: Sovereign Power and Bare Life* (Stanford, CA: Stanford University Press, 1998)

AGASSI, JOSEPH, and YEHUDA FRIED. *Paranoia: A Study in Diagnosis*, Boston Studies in Philosophy of Science, 50 (Dodrecht: D. Reidel, 1976)

AIKEN, CONRAD. 'An Anatomy of Melancholy', in *T. S. Eliot: The Man and His Work*, ed. by Allen Tate (Harmondsworth: Penguin, 1971), pp. 196–202

ALIGHIERI, DANTE. *The Divine Comedy*, 6 vols, translated by Charles Singleton (London: Routledge and Princeton NJ: Princeton University Press, 1971–75)

——*The Odes of Dante*, translated by H. S. Vere-Hodge (Oxford: Clarendon Press, 1963)

——*La vita nuova e il Canzoniere* (Milan: Ulrico Hoepli, 1921)

——*Epistolae: The Letters of Dante*, translated by Paget Toynbee (Oxford: Clarendon Press, 1920)

AMBROSE, BISHOP OF MILAN. *De officiis* (Oxford: Oxford University Press, 2004 [electronic edition])

AMÉRY, JEAN. 'On the Necessity and Impossibility of Being a Jew', in Michael L. Morgan (ed.), *A Holocaust Reader: Responses to the Nazi Extermination* (Oxford and New York: Oxford University Press, 2001), pp. 27–42

ANDERSON, GEORGE K. *The Legend of the Wandering Jew* (Providence, RI: Brown University Press, 1965)

ANDERSON, WILLIAM. *Dante the Maker* (London, Boston, MA, and Henley: Routledge & Kegan Paul, 1980)

ANONYMOUS. *Kurtze Beschreibung und Erzehlung von einem Juden mit Namen Ahasuerus*, Volksbuch, 1602

AQUINAS, ST THOMAS *Summa theologiae*, 61 vols (London: Blackfriars and Eyre & Spottiswoode London, 1963)

ARISTOTLE. *Poetics* / Longinus, *On the Sublime* / Demetrius, *On Style*, edited and translated by Stephen Halliwell (London and Cambridge, MA: Harvard University Press, 1995)

——*Treatise on Rhetoric*, translated by Theodore Buckley (London: Bell & Daldy, 1872)

ASCHER, MARIA LOUISE. 'The Exile as Autobiographer: Nabokov's Homecoming', in Domnica Radulescu (ed.), *Realms of Exile: Nomadism, Diasporas, and Eastern European Voices* (Lanham, MD: Lexington Books, 2002), pp. 67–86

AUGUSTINE. *The City of God/Against the Pagans* (Cambridge: Cambridge University Press, 1998)

AUSTIN, JOHN. *The Province of Jurisprudence Determined*, translated by Alan C. M. Ross (Cambridge: Cambridge University Press, 2001)

BACHELARD, GASTON. *The Psychoanalysis of Fire* (London: Routledge & Kegan Paul, 1964)

BACON, FRANCIS. *Essays* (London: J. M. Dent & Sons, 1972)

BAKHTIN, MIKHAIL. 'Response to a Question from the *Novy Mir* Editorial Staff', in *Speech Genres and Other Late Essays*, translated by Vern W. McGee (Austin: University of Texas Press, 1986), pp. 1–7

—— *The Dialogic Imagination*, translated by Caryl Emerson and Michael Holquist (Austin: University of Texas Press, 1981)

BAMMER, ANGELIKA. 'Introduction', in Angelika Bammer, *Displacements: Cultural Identities in Question* (Bloomington and Indianapolis: Indiana University Press 1994), pp. xi–xx

—— 'Mother Tongues and Other Strangers: Writing "Family" Across Cultural Divides', in *Displacements: Cultural Identities in Question*, ed. by Angelika Bammer (Bloomington and Indianapolis: Indiana University Press, 1994), pp. 90–109

BARÈRE, BERTRAND. 'Éloge de J. J. Rousseau, Citoyen de Genève', in Barère, *Éloges académiques* (Paris: Renouard, 1806), pp. 223–81

BANHAM, REYNER. *The Architecture of the Well-Tempered Environment* (London: The Architectural Press, 1969)

BARTHES, ROLAND. 'The Death of the Author', in *Image, Music, Text*, translated by Stephen Heath (London: Fontana Press, 1977), pp. 142–48

BASSNETT, SUSAN. *Translation Studies* (London and New York: Routledge, 1988)

BAUMAN, RICHARD (with Charles L. Briggs). *Voices of Modernity: Language Ideologies and the Politics of Inequality* (Cambridge and New York: Cambridge University Press, 2003)

BAUMAN, RICHARD A. *Human Rights in Ancient Rome* (London: Routledge, 2000)

—— *Crime and Punishment in Ancient Rome* (London and New York: Routledge, 1996)

BENJAMIN, WALTER. 'Critique of Violence', in *Selected Writings (Volume 1: 1913–1926)* (Cambridge, MA, and London: The Belknap Press of Harvard University Press, 1996), pp. 236–52

—— 'The Task of the Translator', in *Selected Writings (Volume 1: 1913–1926)* (Cambridge, MA, and London: The Belknap Press of Harvard University Press, 1996), pp. 253–63

BENTHAM, JEREMY. *The Principles of Morals and Legislation* (New York: Prometheus Books, 1988)

BERKE, JOSEPH H. (et al.). *Even Paranoids Have Enemies: New Perspectives on Paranoia and Persecution* (London and New York: Routledge, 2001)

BETHEA, DAVID M. *Joseph Brodsky and the Creation of Exile* (Princeton, NJ: Princeton University Press, 1994)

Bible: New International Version (London: Hodder & Stoughton 2000)

BODIN, JEAN. *Les six livres de la république* (Lyons: Imprimerie de Jean de Tournes, 1579)

BOOTH, WAYNE. *The Rhetoric of Fiction* (Chicago, IL and London: Chicago University Press, 1961)

BOYD, BRIAN. *Nabokov's Pale Fire: the Magic of Artistic Discovery* (Princeton, NJ: Princeton University Press, 1999)

BOYD WHITE, JAMES. *Heracles' Bow: Essays on the Rhetoric and Poetics of the Law* (London and Madison: University of Wisconsin Press, 1985)

BOYM, SVETLANA. *The Future of Nostalgia* (New York: Basic Books, 2001)

—— 'Conspiracy Theories and Literary Ethics: Umberto Eco, Danilo Kiš and *The Protocols of the Zion*', *Comparative Literature*, 51.2 (Spring 1999), 97–122

—— 'Estrangement as a Lifestyle: Shklovsky and Brodsky', in Susan Rubin Suleiman (ed.), *Exile and Creativity: Signposts, Travelers, Outsiders, Backward Glances* (Durham, NC, and London: Duke University Press, 1998), pp. 241–62

BRAHAM, RANDOLPH. *The Politics of Genocide* (New York: Columbia University Press, 1981)

BRECHT, BERTOLT. *Gedichte*, 8 vols (Frankfurt am Main: Suhrkamp Verlag, 1960–76)

—— *Selected Poems*, translated by H. R. Hays (New York: Grove Press; London: Evergreen Books, 1959)

BREMOND, CLAUDE. *Logique du récit* (Paris: Éditions du Seuil, 1973)

BRODSKY, JOSEPH. *Peremena imperii* (Moskva: Izdatel'stvo Nezavisimaya gazeta, 2001)

—— 'The Condition We Call "Exile"', in John Glad (ed.), *Literature in Exile* (Durham, NC, and London: Duke University Press 1990), pp. 100–30

——— *To Urania: Selected Poems, 1965–1985* (London: Penguin Books, 1988)

——— 'In the Shadow of Dante', in Brodsky, *Less than One: Selected Essays* (Harmondsworth: Viking, 1986), pp. 95–112

——— *A Part of Speech* (Oxford: Oxford University Press, 1980)

BROOK-ROSE, CHRISTINE. 'Exsul', in Susan Rubin Suleiman (ed.), *Exile and Creativity: Signposts, Travelers, Outsiders, Backward Glances* (Durham, NC: Duke University Press 1998), pp. 9–24

BRUNO, GIORDANO. *The Ash Wednesday Supper*, translated by E. A. Gosselin and L. S. Lerner (Hamden, CT: Archon Books, 1977)

BURKE, EDMUND. *Reflections on the Revolution in France* (London: Everyman's Library, 1964)

CASSIUS DIO, *Dio's Roman History*, vol. III (Cambridge, MA: Harvard University Press, 1993)

CIELENS, ISABELLE. *Trois fonctions de l'exil dans les œuvres de fiction d'Albert Camus: initiation, révolte, conflit d'identité* (Uppsala: Almqvist & Wiksell, 1985)

CICERO. *Pro lege Manilia, Pro Caecina, Pro Cluentio, Pro Rabirio perduellionis*, translated by H. Grose Hodge (Cambridge, MA, and London: Harvard University Press, 2000)

——— *Rhetorica ad Herennium*, translated by Harry Caplan (Cambridge, MA: Harvard University Press; London: William Heinemann, 1995)

——— *De re publica / De legibus*, translated by Clinton Walker Keyes (Cambridge, MA, and London: Harvard University Press, 1994)

——— *Pro Archia, Post reditum in Senatu, Post reditum ad quirites, De domo sua, De haruspicum responsis, Pro Plancio*, translated by N. H. Watts (Cambridge, MA, and London: Harvard University Press, 1993)

——— *In Catilinam I–IV, Pro Murena, Pro Sulla, Pro Flacco* (Cambridge, MA: Harvard University Press; London: William Heinemann, 1989)

——— *Pro Sestio*, translated by R. Gardner (Cambridge, MA: Harvard University Press; London: William Heinemann, 1984)

——— *Pro T. Annio Milone Oratio* and 'Appendix to the Speech on Behalf of Titus Annius Milo', in *Pro Milone*, translated by N. H. Watts (Cambridge, MA: Harvard University Press; London: William Heinemann, 1972), pp. 1–136

——— *Letters to Atticus*, 3 vols, translated by D. R. Shackleton Bailey (Cambridge, MA: Harvard University Press; London: William Heinemann, 1956)

——— *De Oratore*, translated by E. W. Sutton (Cambridge, MA: Harvard University Press; London: William Heinemann, 1942)

CLAASSEN, JO-MARIE. *Displaced Persons: The Literature of Exile from Cicero to Boethius* (London: Duckworth, 1999)

CONTINI (ed.), Gianfranco. *Poeti del Duecento*, vol. II (Milan and Naples: Riccardo Ricciardi, 1960)

COVER, ROBERT. 'Violence and the Word', *Yale Law Journal*, 95.8 (1986), 1601–29

CRANSTON, MAURICE. *The Solitary Self: Jean-Jacques Rousseau in Exile and Diversity* (London: Penguin and Chicago, IL: Chicago University Press, 1997)

CRESSY, DAVID. *Bonfires and Bells* (Stroud: Sutton Publishing, 2004)

CRNJANSKI, MILOŠ. 'Lament over Belgrade' (translation by Borislava Šašić), *Serbian Literary Quarterly*, 1 (Spring 1988), 33–38

——— 'Lament nad Beogradom', in Crnjanski, *Pesme* (Beograd: Nolit, 1983), pp. 263–69

——— *A Novel about London*, manuscript No. P702/I/П/16. *Legat Miloša Crnjanskog* (Courtesy of the National Library of Serbia)

——— 'Lament nad Beogradom', Audio recording of the author (1975), Audio Archive of Radio Belgrade, track. No. 3889

CULLER, JONATHAN. 'Jakobson's Poetic Analyses', in *The Structuralist Poetics* (Ithaca, NY: Cornell University Press, 1975), pp. 55–74

Dällenbach, Lucien. *Le Récit spéculaire* (Paris: Seuil, 1977)

Damrosch, Leo. *Jean-Jacques Rousseau: Restless Genius* (Boston, MA: Houghton Mifflin, 2005)

Davis, Douglas. *Death, Ritual and Belief: The Rhetoric of Funerary Rites* (London and New York: Continuum, 2002)

Deleuze, Gilles, and Félix Guattari. *A Thousand Plateaus: Capitalism and Schizophrenia*, translated by Brian Massumi (London: The Athlone Press, 1988)

Derrida, Jacques. 'Force de loi: le "fondement mystique de l'autorité"', *Cardozo Law Review*, 11.5–6 (1990), 920–1044

De Saussure, Ferdinand. *Course in General Linguistics*, translated by Wade Baskin (London: Peter Owen, 1960)

Diderot, Denis (ed). *Encyclopédie ou dictionnaire raisonné des sciences, des arts et des métiers*, facsimile edition, 35 vols (Stuttgart: Friedrich Frommann Verlag [Günther Holzboog], 1967)

Dodds, E. R. *The Greeks and the Irrational* (Berkeley and Los Angeles: University of California Press, 1956)

Dokumenty venshneĭ politiki SSSR, vol. iv (Moskva: Gosudarstvennoe izdatel'stvo politicheskoĭ literatury, 1960)

Dworkin, Ronald. *Law's Empire* (Oxford: Hart Publishing, 1998)

——'Law as Interpretation', *Critical Inquiry*, 9 (1982), 179–200.

Eliot, Thomas Stearns. *To Criticize the Critic and Other Writings* (New York: Farrar, Straus & Giroux, 1965)

——'The Waste Land', in *Selected Poems* (London: Faber and Faber, 1961), pp. 49–74

Erasmus, Desiderius, *Adages* in *Collected Works of Erasmus* vols. 31–36 (Toronto: University of Toronto Press, 1982)

Esslin, Martin. *Brecht: A Choice of Evils* (London: Methuen Ltd, 1980)

Etkind, Alexander. *Eros of the Impossible: The History of Psychoanalysis in Russia*, trans. by Noah and Maria Rubens (Boulder, CO: Westview Press, 1997)

Euripides, *Orestes*, in *Euripides in Four Volumes*, vol. ii, translated by Arthur S. Way (Cambridge, MA: Harvard University Press; London: William Heinemann, 1988), pp. 121–277

Farrell, John. *Paranoia and Modernity: Cervantes to Rousseau* (Ithaca, NY, and London: Cornell University Press, 2006)

Fernández-Galiano, Luis. *Fire and Memory: On Architecture and Energy*, translated by Gina Cariño (Cambridge, MA, and London: The MIT Press, 2000)

Field, Andrew. *VN. The Life and Art of Vladimir Nabokov* (London: Queen Anne Press, 1987)

Fish, Stanley. *Doing What Comes Naturally: Change, Rhetoric, and the Practice of Theory in Literary and Legal Studies* (Oxford: Clarendon Press, 1989)

Flaubert, Gustave. *Madame Bovary*, translated by Eleanor Marx Aveling and Paul de Man (New York and London: W. W. Norton, 2005)

——*Madame Bovary* (Paris: Garnier Frères, 1971)

Forsdyke, Sara. *Exile, Ostracism and Democracy: The Politics of Expulsion in Ancient Greece* (Princeton, NJ, and Oxford: Princeton University Press, 2005)

Frazer, James George. *Myths of the Origin of Fire: An Essay* (London: Macmillan, 1930)

Freud, Sigmund. 'Der Familienroman der Neurotiker', in Freud, *Gesammelte Werke*, vol. vii (Frankfurt am Main: Fischer Taschenbuch Verlag 1999), pp. 225–31

——'Das Unheimliche', in Freud, *Gesammelte Werke*, vol. xii (Frankfurt am Main: Fischer Taschenbuch Verlag, 1999), pp. 227–68

——'Die Verdrängung', in Freud, *Gesammelte Werke*, vol. x (Frankfurt am Main: Fischer Taschenbuch Verlag, 1999), pp. 247–61

——*Totem und Tabu* in Freud, *Gesammelte Werke*, vol. ix (Frankfurt am Main: Fischer Taschenbuch Verlag 1999)

——*Die Traumdeutung, Über den Traum* in Freud, *Gesammelte Werke*, vol. II–III (Frankfurt am Main: Fischer Taschenbuch Verlag, 1999)

——'Family Romances', in *The Standard Edition of the Complete Psychological Works of Sigmund Freud*, vol. IX (London: The Hogarth Press and the Institute of Psychoanalysis, 1959), pp. 235–41

——'Psychoanalytic notes upon an autobiographical account of a case of paranoia (dementia paranoides)', in *The Standard Edition of the Complete Psychological Works of Sigmund Freud*, ed. by James Strachey, vol. XII (London: The Hogarth Press and the Institute for Psychoanalysis, 1958), pp. 1–82

—— *The Interpretation of Dreams*, in *The Standard Edition of the Complete Psychological Works of Sigmund Freud*, ed. by James Strachey, vol. IV (London: The Hogarth Press and the Institute of Psychoanalysis, 1958)

——'The "Uncanny"', in *The Standard Edition of the Complete Psychological Works of Sigmund Freud*, ed. by James Strachey, vol. XVII (London: The Hogarth Press and the Institute of Psychoanalysis, 1957), pp. 217–56

——'Repression', in *The Standard Edition of the Complete Psychological Works of Sigmund Freud*, ed. by James Strachey, vol. XIV (London: The Hogarth Press and the Institute for Psychoanalysis, 1957), pp. 141–58

—— *Totem and Taboo*, in *The Standard Edition of the Complete Psychological Works of Sigmund Freud*, ed. by James Strachey, vol. XIII (London: The Hogarth Press and the Institute for Psychoanalysis, 1957)

FRIEDMAN, JULIA. 'Blok's "Gift of Hearing" through Remizov's "Audible Colours"', *Slavic and East European Journal*, 47.3 (2003), 367–92

FRYE, NORTHROP. *Fearful Symmetry: A Study of William Blake* (Princeton, NJ: Princeton University Press, 1969)

——*Anatomy of Criticism: Four Essays* (Princeton, NJ: Princeton University Press, 1957)

GIBBS, RAYMOND W. *The Poetics of Mind: Figurative Thought, Language and Understanding* (Cambridge: Cambridge University Press, 1994)

GIESEY, RALPH E. *The Royal Funeral Ceremony in Renaissance France* (Geneva: E. Droz, 1960)

GRASMÜCK, ERNST LUDWIG. *Exilium: Untersuchungen zur Verbannung in der Antike* (Paderborn: Ferdinand Schöningh, 1978)

GREENIDGE, A. H. J. *The Legal Procedure of Cicero's Time* (Oxford: Clarendon Press, 1901)

GREIMAS, ALGIRDAS JULIEN. *Sémantique structurale: recherche de méthode* (Paris: Librairie Larousse, 1966)

GRINBERG, LEÓN, and GRINBERG, REBECA. *Psychoanalytic Perspectives on Migration and Exile* (New Haven, CT. and London: Yale University Press, 1989)

GUÉHENNO, JEAN. *Jean Jacques Rousseau*, 2 vols, translated by John and Doreen Weightman (London: Routledge and Kegan Paul and New York: Columbia University Press, 1966)

GUILLEMIN, HENRI. *Cette affaire infernale* (Paris: Librairie Plon, 1942)

GUILLÉN, CLAUDIO. 'On the Literature of Exile and Counter-Exile', *Books Abroad*, 50 (Spring 1976), 271–80

GUIRAUD, JEAN. *Histoire de l'inquisition au Moyen Âge*, 2 vols (Paris: Éditions Auguste Picard, 1938)

HALPERT ZAMIR, LILY. *Danilo Kiš: jedna bolna, mračna odiseja* (Beograd: Ateneum, 2000)

HAMERS, JOSIANE F. and MICHEL H. A. BLANC. *Bilinguality and Bilingualism* (Cambridge: Cambridge University Press, 1989)

HAMILTON, BERNARD. *The Medieval Inquisition* (London: Edward Arnold, 1981)

HART, H. L. A. *The Concept of Law* (Oxford: Oxford University Press, 1997)

HARVEY, ROBERT. *Search for a Father: Sartre, Paternity, and the Question of Ethics* (Ann Arbor: University of Michigan Press, 1991)

HEGEL, GEORG WILHELM FRIEDRICH. *Outlines of the Philosophy of Right*, translated by T. M. Knok (Oxford: Oxford University Press, 2008)

—— *The Philosophy of History*, translated by J. Sibree, ebook (Kitchener: Batoche, 2001)

HEINE, HEINRICH. *Almansor*, in *Historisch-kritische Gesamtausgabe*, vol. V (Hamburg: Hoffmann und Campe, 1994), pp. 7–68

HERACLITUS. *The Art and Thought of Heraclitus*, translated by Charles H. Kahn (Cambridge: Cambridge University Press, 1979)

HERDER, J. G. *Philosophical Writings*, translated by Michael N. Forster (Cambridge: Cambridge University Press, 2002)

HERZEN, ALEXANDER. *My Past and Thoughts*, translated by Constance Garnett (Berkeley, Los Angeles and London: University of California Press, 1982)

HEYM, STEFAN. *Ahasver* (München: btb Verlag, 2005)

—— *The Wandering Jew*, translated by Stefan Heym (Evanston, IL: Northwestern University Press, 1999)

—— *Nachruf* (Munich: C. Bertelsmann, 1988)

HOBBES, THOMAS. *Leviathan* (Oxford: Oxford University Press 1998)

HOFFMAN, EVA. *Lost in Translation* (London: Vintage, 1998)

HOFSTADTER, RICHARD. *The Paranoid Style in American Politics and Other Essays* (London: Jonathan Cape, 1966)

HOLTON, MILNE, and VASA D. MIHAILOVICH (eds.), *Serbian Poetry from the Beginnings to the Present* (New Haven, CT: Yale Center for International and Area Studies, 1988)

HOMER, *The Iliad*, 2 vols, translated by A. T. Murray (Cambridge, MA, and London: Harvard University Press, 1993)

HOMERING, WOLFGANG (ed.), *Stefan Heym: Im Gespräch mit Dirk Sager* (Berlin: Ullstein, 1999))

VON HUMBOLDT, WILHELM. *On Language: The Diversity of Human Language-Structure and its Influence on the Mental Development of Mankind*, translated by Peter Heath (Cambridge: Cambridge University Press, 1988)

HUTCHINSON, PETER. *Stefan Heym: The Perpetual Dissident* (Cambridge: Cambridge University Press, 1992)

ILIE, PAUL. *Literature and Inner Exile: Authoritarian Spain, 1939–1975* (Baltimore, MD, and London: Johns Hopkins University Press, 1980)

JAKOBSON, ROMAN. 'Two Aspects of Language and Two Types of Aphasic Disturbances', in Jakobson, *Language in Literature* (Cambridge, MA, and London: The Belknap Press of Harvard University Press, 1987), pp. 95–114

—— 'Linguistics and Poetics', in *Selected Writings*, vol. III (The Hague: Mouton Publishers, 1981), pp. 18–51

—— 'Le métalangage d'Aragon', in *Selected Writings*, vol. III (The Hague: Mouton Publishers, 1981), pp. 148–54

—— 'What Is Poetry?', in *Selected Writings* vol. III (The Hague: Mouton Publishers, 1981), pp. 740–50

—— 'O cheshkom stikhe', *Selected Writings*, vol. II (The Hague: Mouton Publishers, 1979), pp. 3–130

—— 'The Dominant', in Ladislav Matejka and Krystyna Pomorska (eds), *Readings in Russian Poetics: Formalist and Structuralist Views* (Ann Arbor, MI: Michigan Slavic Publications 1978), pp. 82–87

—— 'On Linguistic Aspects of Translation', in *Selected Writings*, vol. II (The Hague and Paris: Mouton Publishers, 1971), pp. 260–66

JASPERS, KARL. *Heimweh und Verbrechen* (Munich: Belleville Verlag, 1996)

JONES, ERNEST. *The Life and Work of Sigmund Freud* (Harmondsworth: Penguin, 1964)

JOSEPHSON, MATTHEW. *Jean-Jacques Rousseau* (London: Victor Gollancz Ltd, 1932)

JOYCE, JAMES. *A Portrait of the Artist as a Young Man* (London: Jonathan Cape, 1930)

KANTOROWICZ, ERNST H. *The King's Two Bodies: A Study in Medieval Political Theology* (Princeton, NJ: Princeton University Press, 1997)

KAPLAN, CAREN. *Questions of Travel: Postmodernist Discourses of Displacement* (Durham, NC, and London: Duke University Press, 1996)

KEATS, JOHN. *Poetical Works* (Oxford and New York: Oxford University Press, 1970)

KELLY, GORDON P. *A History of Exile in the Roman Republic* (Cambridge: Cambridge University Press, 2006)

KENNER, HUGH (ed.). *The Translations of Ezra Pound* (London: Faber and Faber, 1953)

KINGSLEY-SMITH, JANE. *Shakespeare's Drama of Exile*, ebook (Basingstoke: Palgrave Macmillan, 2003)

KIŠ, DANILO. *Early Sorrows* (New York: New Directions, 1998)

——'Variations on Central European Themes', in *Homo Poeticus: Essays and Interviews* (Manchester: Carcanet, 1996), pp. 95–114

——'Life, Literature', in Susan Sontag (ed.), *Homo Poeticus: Essays and Interviews* (Manchester: Carcanet, 1996), pp. 231–50

——'Nabokov, or Nostalgia', in Kiš, *Homo Poeticus: Essays and Interviews* (Manchester: Carcanet, 1996), pp. 149–55

——*Porodični cirkus* (Beograd: Srpska književna zadruga, 1993)

——*Hourglass*, translated by Ralph Mannheim (London: Faber and Faber, 1990)

——'Nabokov ili: Nostalgija,' in Kiš, *Život, Literatura* (Sarajevo: Svjetlost, 1990), pp. 59–66

——*Garden, Ashes*, translated by William J. Hannaher (London: Faber & Faber, 1985)

KOLJEVIĆ, SVETOZAR. 'Linguistic Aspects of the International Theme in *Roman o Londonu*', in David Norris (ed.), *Miloš Crnjanski and Modern Serbian Literature* (Nottingham: Astra Press, 1988), pp. 75–87

KÖVECSES, ZOLTÁN. 'The Scope of Metaphor', in Antonio Barcelona (ed.), *Metaphor and Metonymy at the Crossroads: A Cognitive Perspective* (Berlin: De Gruyter Mouton, 2003), pp. 79–92

KRAEPELIN, EMIL. *Psychiatrie: Ein Lehrbuch für Studierende und Ärzte*, vol. IV (Leipzig: Barth, 1915)

KRISTEVA, JULIA. 'A New Type of Intellectual: The Dissident', translated by Seán Hand, in Toril Moi (ed.), *The Kristeva Reader* (Oxford and Cambridge, MA: Blackwell, 1986), pp. 292–300

KUHN, TOM. '"Visit to a Banished Poet": Brecht's *Svendborg Poems* and the Voices of Exile', in Ronald Speirs (ed.), *Brecht's Poetry of Political Exile* (Cambridge: Cambridge University Press, 2000), pp. 47–65

LACAN, JACQUES. *The Seminar of Jacques Lacan (Book 3: Psychoses, 1955–1956)*, translated by Russell Grigg (London: Routledge, 1993)

——*De la psychose paranoïaque dans ses rapports avec la personnalité* (Paris: Éditions du Seuil, 1975)

——*Le séminaire III (Les Psychoses)* (Paris: Éditions du Seuil, 1981)

——*Écrits* (Paris: Éditions du Seuil, 1966)

LAKOFF, GEORGE, WITH MARK JOHNSON. *Metaphors We Live By* (Chicago, IL, and London: The Chicago University Press, 2003)

——*Women, Fire, and Dangerous Things: What Categories Reveal about Mind* (Chicago, IL: Chicago University Press, 1990)

LEA, HENRY CHARLES. *A History of the Inquisition in Spain*, 4 vols (London and New York: Macmillan, 1922)

——*A History of the Inquisition of the Middle Ages*, 3 vols (New York: Harper & Brothers, 1888)

LEVIN, HARRY. 'Literature and Exile', in Levin, *Refractions: Essays in Comparative Literature* (New York: Oxford University Press, 1966), pp. 62–81

LEWIS, AUBREY, 'Paranoia and Paranoid: A Historical Perspective', *Psychological Medicine*, I.I (1970), 2–12

MACARTNEY, CARLILE A. *October Fifteenth: A History of Modern Hungary, 1929–1945* (Edinburgh: Edinburgh University Press, 1961)

MACHIAVELLI, NICCOLÒ. *The Chief Works and Others*, 3 vols (Durham, NC: Duke University Press, 1965.

MARTZ, LOUIS L. *Milton: Poet of Exile* (New Haven, CT, and London: Yale University Press, 1986)

MCCARTHY, MARY. 'Exiles, Expatriates and Internal Émigrés', *The Listener*, Thursday 25 November 1971, vol. 86, No. 2226, pp. 705–08

MCCLENNEN, SOPHIA. *The Dialectics of Exile: Nation, Time, Language, and Space in Hispanic Literatures* (West Lafayette, IN: Purdue University Press, 2004)

MEIGE, HENRY. *Le Juif-errant à la Salpêtrière* (Paris : [n. pub.], 1893)

MENDELSOHN, EZRA. *The Jews of East Central Europe between the World Wars* (Bloomington: Indiana University Press, 1987)

MILOSZ, CZESLAW. *The Collected Poems 1931–1987*, translated by Czeslaw Milosz (London: Viking, 1988)

—— *Gdzie wschodzi słońce i kiedy zapada* (Kraków: Znak, 1980)

MILTON, JOHN. *Poetical Works* (Oxford and New York: Oxford University Press, 1988)

MOMMSEN, THEODOR (ed.). *The Digest of Justinian*, 4 vols (Philadelphia: University of Pennsylvania Press, 1985)

—— *Römisches Strafrecht* (Graz: Akademische Druck- U. Verlagsanstalt, 1955)

MONTESQUIEU, CHARLES DE SECONDAT. *The Spirit of the Laws*, translated by Thomas Nugent (New York: Hafner, 1962)

NADLER, STEVEN. *Spinoza: A Life* (Cambridge: Cambridge University Press, 1999)

NABOKOV, VLADIMIR. *Strong Opinions* (London: Weidenfeld and Nicolson, 1974)

—— *Speak, Memory: An Autobiography Revisited* (London: Weidenfeld and Nicolson, 1967)

—— *Pale Fire* (London: Weidenfeld and Nicolson, 1962)

—— *Drugie berega* (Ann Arbor, MI: Ardis, 1954).

—— *Conclusive Evidence* (New York: Harper & Brothers Publishers, 1951)

—— 'Mademoiselle O.', *Mesures*, 2.2 (April 1936), 145–72

NICOL, CHARLES. 'Politics', in Vladimir E. Alexandrov (ed.), *The Garland Companion to Vladimir Nabokov* (New York and London: Garland Publishing Inc. 1995), pp. 625–28

OVID. *Tristia, Ex Ponto*, trans. by A. L. Wheeler (London and Cambridge, MA: Harvard University Press, 2002)

PARACELSUS, *Schriften Theophrasts von Hohenheim genannt Paracelsus*, ed. by Hans Kayser (Leipzig: Im Insel Verlag, 1921)

PASTERNAK, BORIS. 'Groza momental'naya navek', in *Izbrannoe v dvukh tomakh*, vol. I (Moscow: Khudozhestvennaya literatura, 1985), p. 109

—— 'Storm, Instantaneous Forever', in Pasternak, *Selected Poems*, trans. by. J. Stallworthy and P. France (London: Allen Lane, 1983), pp. 72–73

PEPYS, SAMUEL. *The Diary of Samuel Pepys*, 11 vols, ed. by Robert Latham and William Matthews (London: G. Bell and Sons Ltd, 1970–83)

PETROV, ALEKSANDAR. *Poezija Crnjanskog i srpsko pesništvo* (Beograd: Vuk Karadžić, 1971)

PLATO. *Complete Works*, ed. by J. M Cooper and D. S. Hutchinson (Indianapolis, IN: Hackett, 1977)

PLUTARCH. *The Life of Cicero*, translated by J. L. Moles (Warminster: Aris & Philips, 1988)

'A Poet's Second Exile', *Time*, 19 June 1972

POLIAKOV, LÉON. *The History of Anti-Semitism, Volume I: From the Time of Christ to the Court Jews* (London: Elek Books, 1967)

POLYBIUS. *The Histories*, 6 vols, trans. by W. R. Paton (London and Cambridge, MA: Harvard University Press, 1972)

PORTER, JOHN R. 'Madness and ΣΥΝΕΣΙΣ in *Orestes*', in John R. Porter, *Studies in Euripides' Orestes* (Leiden, New York, and Köln: E. J. Brill, 1994), pp. 298–313

PROPP, VLADIMIR. *Morphology of the Folktale*, translated by Laurence Scott (Austin: University of Texas Press, 1968)

PYNE, STEPHEN. *Vestal Fire: An Environmental History, Told Through Fire, of Europe and Europe's Encounter with the World*, ebook (Seattle, WA: University of Washington School of Law, 2012)

QUINTILIAN. *Institutio oratoria*, translated by Donald Russell (Cambridge, MA, and London: Harvard University Press, 2001)

RAPPORT, NIGEL and ANDREW DAWSON (eds). 'Home and Movement: A Polemic', in *Migrants of Identity: Perception of Home in a World of Movement* (Oxford and New York: Berg, 1998), pp. 19–38

READ, ANTHONY, and FISHER, DAVID. *Kristallnacht: The Unleashing of the Holocaust* (New York: Peter Bedrick Books, 1989)

RICOEUR, PAUL. *The Rule of Metaphor: The Creation of Meaning in Language*, translated by Robert Czerny with Kathleen McLaughlin and John Costello (London and Henley: Routledge, 1978)

RIFFATERRE, MICHAEL. 'Describing Poetic Structures: Two Approaches to Baudelaire's *Les Chats*', *Yale French Studies*, 36/37 (October 1966), 200–42

RILKE, RAINER MARIA. *Duino Elegies*, trans. by J. B. Leishman and S. Spender (London: The Hogarth Press, 1963)

ROBINS, ROBERT S. and POST, JERROLD M. *Political Paranoia: The Psychopolitics of Hatred* (New Haven, CT, and London: Yale University Press, 1997)

ROBINSON, MARC. *Altogether Elsewhere* (Boston, MA, and London: Faber and Faber, 1994)

ROSE, PAUL LAWRENCE. *Revolutionary Antisemitism in Germany from Kant to Wagner* (Princeton, NJ: Princeton University Press, 1990)

ROSS, DANIEL 'The Text You Read (and Write) May Be Your Own: The Family Romance in Danilo Kiš' *Garden, Ashes*' *The Review of Contemporary Fiction*, 14.1 (1994), 136–43

ROUSSEAU, JEAN-JACQUES. *Discourse on Political Economy and Social Contract*, translated by Christopher Betts (Oxford: Oxford University Press, 1999)

——*Rousseau Judge of Jean-Jacques: Dialogues*, translated by Judith R. Bush, in Roger D. Masters and Christopher Kelly (eds.), *The Collected Writings of Rousseau*, vol. 1 (Hanover, NH, and London: University Press of New England, 1990)

——*Emile; or, On Education*, translated by Allan Bloom ([New York]: Basic Books, 1979)

——*The Confessions*, translated by J. M. Cohen (London: Penguin Books 1978)

——*Correspondance complète de Jean Jacques Rousseau*, 52 vols (Oxford: The Voltaire Foundation, 1965–98)

——*Œuvres completes I (Les Confessions, autres textes autobiographiques)* (Paris: Gallimard, 1959)

RUBIN SULEIMAN, SUSAN. 'Introduction' in Susan Rubin Suleiman (ed.), *Exile and Creativity: Signposts, Travelers, Outsiders, Backward Glances* (Durham, NC, and London: Duke University Press, 1998), pp. 1–6

RUEBEL, JAMES S. 'The Trial of Milo in 52 B.C.: A Chronological Study', *Transactions of the American Philological Association*, 109 (1979), pp. 231–49

SAID, EDWARD W. 'Reflections on Exile', *Granta*, Winter 1984–85, pp. 157–72

SALLUST. *The Jugurthine War / The Conspiracy of Catiline*, translated by S. A. Handford (London: Penguin, 1963)

SARTRE, JEAN-PAUL. *Words*, translated by Irene Clephane (Harmondsworth: Penguin Books, 1971)

——*Les Mots* (Paris: Gallimard, 1964)

SAVONAROLA, GIROLAMO. *Selected Writings of Girolamo Savonarola*, ebook (New Haven and London: Yale University Press, 2006).

SCHLEINER, WINFRIED. 'Aeneas's flight from Troy', *Comparative Literature*, 27.2 (Spring 1975), 97–112

SCHMITT, CARL. *The Concept of the Political*, translated by Matthias Konzen and John P. McCormick (Chicago, IL, and London: The University of Chicago Press, 2007)

——*Political Theology: Four Chapters on the Concept of Sovereignty*, translated by George Schwab (Chicago, IL, and London: The University of Chicago Press, 2005)

—— *The* Nomos *of the Earth*, translated by G. L. Ulmen (New York: Telos Press, 2003)

SCRIBNER, ROBERT W. *Popular Culture and Popular Movements in Reformation Germany* (London: The Hambledon Press, 1987)

SHAKESPEARE, WILLIAM, *The Library Shakespeare* (Quarry Bay: Midpoint Press, 2005)

SHAW, CHRISTINE. *The Politics of Exile in Renaissance Italy* (Cambridge: Cambridge University Press, 2000)

SHKLOVSKY, VIKTOR. 'Art as Technique', translated and edited by L. T. Lemon and M. J. Reis, in *Russian Formalist Criticism: Four Essays* (Lincoln, NE, and London: University of Nebraska Press, 1965), pp. 3–24

SLOBIN, GRETA. 'Why the First-Wave Russian Literary Diaspora Embraced Shklovskian Estrangement', *Poetics Today*, 26.4 (Winter 2005), 697–718

SMITH, CLEMENT LAWRENCE. 'Cicero's Journey into Exile', *Harvard Studies in Classical Philology*, 7 (1896), 65–84

SOPHOCLES, *Antigone, The Women of Trachis, Philoctetes, Oedipus at Colonus*, translated by Hugh Lloyd-Jones (Cambridge MA, London: Harvard University Press, 1994)

STAROBINSKI, JEAN. *Jean-Jacques Rousseau: la transparence et l'obstacle suivi de Sept essais sur Rousseau* (Paris: Gallimard, 1971)

STELZIG, EUGENE L. *The Romantic Subject in Autobiography: Rousseau and Goethe* (Charlottesville, VA and London: University Press of Virginia, 2000)

STEINER, GEORGE. *After Babel* (London: Oxford University Press, 1975)

STRACHAN-DAVIDSON, JAMES LEIGH. *Problems of the Roman Criminal Law*, 2 vols (Oxford: Clarendon Press, 1912)

TABORI, PAUL. *The Anatomy of Exile* (London: Harrap, 1972)

TERESA OF AVILA, SAINT. *The Life of St. Teresa*, translated and edited by E. Allison Peers, in *The Complete Works of Saint Teresa of Jesus*, vol. 1 (London and New York: Sheed and Ward, 1944), pp. 1–300

THOMPSON, MARK. *Birth Certificate: The Story of Danilo Kiš* (Ithaca, NY, and London: Cornell University Press, 2013)

TODOROV, TZVETAN. 'Three Conceptions of Poetic Language', in *Russian Formalism: A Retrospective Glance (A Festschrift in Honor of Victor Erlich)*, ed. by R. L. Jackson and S. Rudy (New Haven, CT: Yale Center for International and Area Studies, 1985), pp. 130–37

——*Mikhaïl Bakhtine: le principe dialogique* (Paris: Éditions du Seuil, 1981)

TOMASHEVSKY, BORIS. 'Literature and Biography', in Ladislav Matejka and Krystyna Pomorska (eds), *Readings in Russian Poetics: Formalist and Structuralist Views* (Ann Arbor, MI: The University of Michigan Press 1978), pp. 47–55

TOYNBEE, JOCELYN M. C. *Death and Burial in the Roman World* (London: Thames and Hudson, 1971)

TROTSKY, LEON. *My Life* (New York: Grosset & Dunlap, 1960)

TSVETAEVA, MARINA. 'Novogodnee', in Tsvetaeva, *Poem of the End: Selected Narrative and Lyrical Poems with Facing Russian Text*, trans. by Nina Kossman with Andrew Newcomb (Woodstock and New York: Ardis Publishers, 2004), pp. 108–17

TYNJANOV, YURI. 'On Literary Evolution', in Ladislav Matejka and Krystyna Pomorska (eds.), *Readings in Russian Poetics: Formalist and Structuralist Views* (Ann Arbor: Michigan Slavic Publications 1978), pp. 66–78

UGREŠIĆ, DUBRAVKA. 'A Question of Perspective', in Ugrešić, *Karaoke Culture*, translated by David Williams and Ellen Elias-Bursac (Rochester, NY: Open Letter, 2011), pp. 203–46

——'The Writer in Exile', in Ugrešić, *Thank You for Not Reading*, translated by Celia Hawkesworth (London: Dalkey Archive Press, 2003), pp. 127–48

VELLEIUS PATERCULUS. *Compendium of Roman History and Res Gestae Divi Augusti*, translated by Frederick W. Shipley (New York: G. P. Putnam's Sons, 1924)

VERVAET, STIJN. 'Pisati subjekat nakon Holokausta: Konstantinovićev *Ahasver, ili traktat o pivskoj flaši*', *Sarajevske sveske* 41–42 (June 2013), [special issue on Radomir Konstantinović edited by Davor Beganović and Branislav Jakovljević], pp. 94–104

VICO, GIAMBATTISTA, *The New Science*, translated by Thomas Goddard Bergin and Max Harold Fisch (Ithaca, NY, and London: Cornell University Press, 1984)

VIRGIL. *Virgil in Two Volumes: Eclogues, Georgics, Aeneid I–VI*, translated by H. Rushton Fairclough (Cambridge, MA: Harvard University Press; London: William Heinemann, 1978)

VOLKOV, SOLOMON. *Conversations with Joseph Brodsky: A Poet's Journey through the Twentieth Century* (New York: The Free Press, 1998)

Völkischer Beobachter, issues of 1 March 1933 and 9 May 1937

VULETIĆ, IVANA. *The Prose Fiction of Danilo Kiš, Serbian Jewish Writer: Childhood and the Holocaust* (Lewiston, NY: Edwin Mellen Press, 2003)

WALBERER ULRICH (ed.). *10. Mai 1933: Bücherverbrennung in Deutschland und die Folgen* (Frankfurt am Main: Fischer Taschenbuch Verlag, 1983)

WALL, THOMAS CARL. 'Au hasard', in Andrew Norris (ed.), *Politics, Metaphysics and Death: Essays on Giorgio Agamben's 'Homo Sacer'* (Durham, NC, and London: Duke University Press, 2005), pp. 31–48

WARD, REGINALD SOMERSET. *Maximilien Robespierre: A Study in Deterioration* (London: Macmillan, 1934)

WARREN, JAMES. *Presocratics* (London: Routledge 2014)

VON WARTENBURG, PAUL GRAF YORCK. *Die Katharsis des Aristoteles und der 'Oedipus Coloneus' des Sophokles* (Berlin: Verlag von Wilhelm Hertz, 1866)

WEINREICH, OTTO. *Menekrates, Zeus und Salmoneus* (Stuttgart: Kohlhammer, 1933)

WHITE, KENNETH. *L'Esprit nomade* (Paris: Bernard Grasset, 1987)

WIESEL, ELIE. *Night*, translated by Stella Rodway (London: Penguin, 1981)

WITTLIN, JOSEPH. 'Sorrow and Grandeur of Exile', *Polish Review*, 2 (Spring/Summer 1957), 99–111

YEATS, WILLIAM BUTLER. *The Collected Poems of W. B. Yeats*, ed. by Richard J. Finneran (New York: Macmillan, 1993)

ZOJA, LUIGI. *The Father: Historical, Psychological and Cultural Perspectives*, ebook, translated by Henry Martin (London: Routledge, 2003)

INDEX

9 781781 883488